Mind and Body

East meets West

Seymour Kleinman, PhD, Editor
The Ohio State University

Big Ten Body of Knowledge Symposium Series,
Volume 15

Human Kinetics Publishers, Inc.
Champaign, Illinois

87-552

Library of Congress Cataloging-in-Publication Data
Main entry under title:

Mind and Body.

    (Big ten body of knowledge symposium series ; v. 15)
    Bibliography: p.
    1. Mind and body—Congresses.   2. Philosophy, Compara-
tive—Congresses.   3. East and West—Congresses.
I. Kleinman, Seymour.   II. Series.
BF150.M55 1986   796'.01   85-19710
ISBN 0-931250-79-X

Developmental Editor: Gwen Steigelman, PhD
Production Director: Sara Chilton
Copy Editor: Olga Murphy
Typesetters: Aurora Garcia and Sandra Meier
Text Layout: Gail Irwin
Cover Design: Jack W. Davis

ISBN: 0-931250-79-X
Copyright © 1986 by Human Kinetics Publishers, Inc.

Printed in the United States of America
10   9   8   7   6   5   4   3   2   1

Human Kinetics Publishers, Inc.
Box 5076, Champaign, IL 61820

Contents

Preface

Minds and bodies—East and West: What concepts and cultures could be more disparate? Historically, philosophically, and culturally these areas reflect a separation of people and place that only recently show signs of coming together.

Although only a written record of a "coming together of East and West" is offered in this volume, it should be noted that more than just a "meeting of minds" occurred when scholars addressed these issues at a symposium held at The Ohio State University in the fall of 1983. For the first time, an entire conference was devoted to addressing the mind-body problem from both Eastern and Western perspectives. These meetings, however, did not take place in a philosophical vacuum, for it was evident at the outset that the vast majority of participants were not only theorists, but practitioners as well. In a sense they were a reflection of a culture in transformation: a culture actively engaged in transcending mind-body, subject-object dichotomies.

During the planning stages of this symposium, it was clear that if meaningful dialogue were to take place, participants (presenters and audience) must become more than verbally involved. Opportunities for practice and technique instruction were scheduled during awareness sessions which proved to be extremely valuable in enhancing explanations of theories. These kinds of lived experiences (to use the phenomenological phrase) help give credence and justification to the intellectual axiom of the "whole person" doctrine.

Although educators have espoused this principle for years, it has yet to become a reality in practice. Learning and training continue to be treated synonomously in our schools which always seem to be last in recognizing and instituting change in this society. Because of this, teaching and learning continue to be fractionated.

However, it was heartening to see more than 100 "theoretical practitioners" come together to consider themes and issues dealing with Eastern and Western conceptions of consciousness and the person, Eastern and Western movement forms, and emerging views of movement as art. What resulted was a realization and awareness of the connections and relationships which exist in all of these areas. Perhaps what was started at this meeting of minds and bodies will provide impetus to a whole person doctrine of education which will become manifest in practice as well as in thought.

Seymour Kleinman,
Editor

SECTION I

The other side
of the paradigm

In his paper which appears at the end of this volume, Thomas Hanna states, ''The past 20 years has witnessed the solution of the mind-body problem, not by philosophical debate but by cultural transformation.'' I think that the reader will see evidence of this transformation in the pages which follow.

Willis Harman's keynote address sets the stage by pointing to signs which are appearing: signs challenging us to begin to regard the world and ourselves in a new way. Harman identifies ideas and events which signify what has been termed a *paradigm shift*. The knowledge, understanding, and rules of the game of life are shifting inexorably, and we must come to grips with their relevance and implications. This dictum holds true for the educator of today and tomorrow, specifically, as well as for the citizenry at large.

The challenge to teachers, and, for that matter, the challenge to all of us, is to reject this bifurcation of mind and body, not only intellectually, but in our teaching, communicating, and living. It is a task which is long overdue, but by continuing to ignore it, we invite our own demise. Each of the authors in this volume calls our attention to it in one way or another, and the reader is invited and encouraged to address what must be regarded as a fundamental issue of our time.

In 1975, Adam Smith's *Power of Mind* appeared. The first section in this book is entitled ''This Side of the Paradigm.'' He defines *paradigm* as ''a shared set of assumptions...When we are in the middle of the paradigm, it is hard to imagine any other paradigm.'' Changes in the last few years indicate that we are no longer in the middle of the paradigm. We are much closer to the edge, and we are beginning to get a glimpse of what may be around the corner. It is hoped that this book will provide some impetus in that direction and will enable us to see more clearly ''the other side of the paradigm.''

The changing image of man/woman: Signs of a second Copernican revolution

Willis W. Harman
SRI International

The changing view of physical education is part of a larger movement with profound implications for the future industrial society. In physical education we see a new appreciation of the Eastern martial arts, yoga, t'ai chi, and other non-Western disciplines. In the health area an appreciation of acupuncture, native herbal medicines, faith healing, and a wide assortment of traditional and holistic approaches not too long ago dismissed as "prescientific" has emerged. In the culture at large, we find fascination with psychic phenomena, reincarnation, astrology, pyramid power, extraterrestrial beings, and a host of topics that had been presumably laid to rest as superstitious ideas not fit for a scientific age. Does all of this represent a passing fad, an anxiety response to the rapid change of our times, or a fundamental belief shift and societal transformation? Probably all of the above.

In this chapter I would like to (a) examine the history of the mind/body split and some pertinent aspects of science, (b) explore the nature of an emerging paradigm, and (c) discuss some implications for the future of our society.

THE MIND-BODY SPLIT

The tendency in the Western world to consider the body separately from the mind and spirit goes back at least as far as 12th-century Cordoba. One of the classical debates of history took place there between the philosopher Ibn Arabi and the Islamic scholar Averroes. The former argued that the empirical study of the physical world should not be separated from religion; Averroes' arguments carried the day.

Five centuries later, Descartes made a formal distinction between mind and matter which influenced European thought for the next several hundred years—namely, that matter may be ultimately described in quantifiable terms. This tendency to dichotomize mind and matter (body) was but an extension of the secularization of values that took place in Western Europe at the end of the Middle Ages. The basis of the values guiding individual lives and societal institutions was shifting away from the traditional religious base toward a more pragmatic, utilitarian base. By the 19th century, these tendencies had become so strong that a positivistic philosophy permeated science: Only what could be physically measured could be studied by science, and only what was studied by science was real.

Thus, about half a century ago, a "great debunking" took place—the debunking of religion by science. Whatever was to be known about the human mind would be learned through studying the brain and behavior; whatever was of value in religious understanding would be reexplained by the methods and findings of science. It would not be until the 1980s that a scientist of the stature of Nobel laureate Roger Sperry (1981) would claim:

> Current concepts of the mind-brain relation involve a direct break with the long-established materialist and behaviorist doctrine that has dominated neuroscience for many decades. Instead of renouncing or ignoring consciousness, the new interpretation gives full recognition to the primacy of inner conscious awareness as a causal reality....Once science modifies its traditional materialist-behaviorist stance and begins to accept in theory and to encompass in principle within its causal domain the whole world of inner, conscious, subjective experience (the world of the humanities), then the very nature of science itself is changed. (pp. 1-15)

THE NATURE OF THE EMERGING PARADIGM

One of the central findings characterizing the emerging understanding of the mind is that a major portion of mental activity goes on in the unconscious mind, outside of conscious awareness. We have *beliefs* that are easily accessible to the conscious mind and others that are held unconsciously (e.g., the notorious inferiority complex). We *choose* unconsciously as well as consciously. For example, in the phenomenon of repression there is an unconscious decision to hide memories, feelings, and such from conscious awareness. The Freudian superego, or internalized parent, chooses certain behaviors and goals and punishes deviations with guilt feelings. We also *know* unconsciously; with biofeedback training, we find that we know unconsciously how to relax muscle tensions, change brain waves, alter heartbeat or blood pressure, and change blood flow and skin temperature; however, we do not know until a biofeedback signal is provided to instruct us.

Among unconscious beliefs are beliefs about potentialities and limitations. These tend to be true in experience because they are believed, rather than the reverse. A ready example is provided by the phenomena of hypnosis. Acceptance that a person cannot lift a chair weighing a few pounds produces a complete inability to raise the chair off the floor. On the other hand, a more positive suggestion may lead to the body being able to perform feats it could not otherwise do, such as form a rigid bridge between two chairs or lift a heavy object.

One of the ways of changing these limiting beliefs is to make use of the unconscious mind's characteristic which registers what is vividly imagined to be true much the same as it registers actual experience. Thus, an athlete training for the high jump improves performance by repetitiously imagining sailing over the bar, higher than he or she has ever jumped it before. Imagining and affirming as true that which is not yet true reprograms the unconscious mind to make it true in the perceptions and ultimately in the reality.

What are the ultimate limits of the mind-body system? Exploration of a wide variety of types of extraordinary capabilities—from peak athletic performance, to creative problem solving, to the paranormal—leads to serious questioning whether there are any limits at all that are not in the end present because of individual and collective unconscious beliefs.

Timothy Gallway teaches "the inner game of tennis." As he explains it, the unconscious mind already knows how to play tennis. It is mainly necessary for the ego-mind to get out of the way. Similarly, imagining the body's immune system successfully combating cancer cells has had positive results in the treatment of cancer. The role of the mind in healing and in the functioning of the body's immune system is only recently being explored in the emerging science of psychoneuroimmunology; we only fail to notice because it functions so well. We have only begun to tap the potentialities.

In the tradition of our ancestors, man was possessed of a conscience, an inner and valid sense of morals and values. This, in the course of scientific progress tended to be explained away as conditioning, the Freudian superego—an internalized authoritarian parent figure. More recently, through studies of creativity and psychotherapy, the potentiality of the creative/intuitive mind has been recognized again. The creative problem-solving capability of the mind functions more effectively the more it is trusted and called upon. In a similar manner, our capacity for intuitive judgment is realized. Whether or not the time-honored term *conscience* is employed, there does seem to be a deep part of our mind that knows what is most satisfying, what we most truly want to be and do.

The same techniques of imagery and affirmation used in training athletes are also useful in enhancing access to this deep intuitive mind. We are fragmented in our typical enculturated state. The conscious ego-mind wants one thing; the internalized authoritarian parent sends guilt signals indicating it wants something else; the deep intuition gently guides in still another direction. The old-fashioned descriptor, a "person of integrity," refers to a state of being integrated, wherein the mind is so aligned with deep intuition that inner conflict is removed and all fragments are aligned, wanting the same thing. This integration can be achieved through repeated affirmation (that is, "talking" to the unconscious) to the effect that such alignment becomes the person's sole desire (a classical form of prayer).

IMPLICATIONS FOR THE FUTURE

Throughout the history of science, new discoveries have had two major effects on society: There have been *applications* of the knowledge in technology and management as well as *implications* that affected all aspects of society from its values and goals to its institutions and traditions. For example, the discoveries of Copernicus and Galileo had direct applications in the field of astronomy, but these were overshadowed in their effect by the implications which followed, that is, the displacement of the earth as the center of the universe. Similarly, it was the implications, far more than the applications, that decided the importance of paleontological discoveries challenging Biblical interpretations of the age of the earth, Darwin's evolutionary hypothesis, and Freud's discoveries about the unconscious.

As science comes to recognize and correct its past "blind spot" and neglect of the world of inner experience, there no doubt will be direct applications in such fields as psychotherapy, physical education, counseling, health care, and executive development. In the long run, however, the implications will be the most important.

The developments presently seen in physical education involving new appreciations of the integral nature of the mind-body system are but a fragment of a larger movement in the culture that includes new placings of the boundaries of science and new understandings of our magnificent potentialities. That movement is centrally concerned with values, meanings, and goals.

Modern society has been confused about values, especially since the great debunking of religion by science. A sign of this confusion has been the substitution of pseudo-values such as economic indicators to guide our societal decision making. It would not be an exaggeration to claim that the fundamental problem of modern society is a crisis in meaning. Technologically speaking, we are increasingly capable of doing almost anything we can imagine doing. As that capability increases, we seem less and less able to agree on what is worth doing. Emerging now is a basis for a new consensus on goals. A rough transition time probably lies ahead: Chaos may reign and we may be more confused than ever. For whenever there is fundamental evolutionary advance as seems to lie ahead, there has to be a breakdown of old structure in order to make way for the new.

In summary, to view current shifts in physical education as part of a far broader change of historic proportions seems possible. Indeed, today we get the feeling that history is in the making, and we are privileged to be a part of it.

SECTION II

The Western view: Answers and questions

The conception of the "whole person," generally regarded to be a modern phenomenon in the West, is called into question by Carmelo Bazzano. In his essay, "The Body's Role in the Philosophy of the Renaissance Man," he points out that the Renaissance period recognized the inadequacy of the dualistic position held by the Church and the aristocracy. For example, the view expressed by Vegio and Vergerio (early Renaissance philosophers) that ball playing was neither exclusively an activity of the mind nor of the body, but "a worthy and liberal activity" provides evidence that the "whole child" conception of education is not exclusively a 20th-century contribution. It is clear that both dualism and attempts to overcome the problems present in a dualistic framework have maintained a side-by-side relationship down through the centuries.

Saul Ross presents a clear and well-thought-out argument rejecting dualism as a viable approach to education in general and physical education in particular. He calls for focusing attention on education of the person and challenges philosophers of physical education "to render an account of physical action knowledge." Propositional knowledge does no service to physical education because it has little to do with it. Ross, in a sense, is asking for a phenomenological epistomology—something that may seem contradictory but, nevertheless, deserves investigation.

Susan Bandy, in "A Humanistic Interpretation of the Mind-Body Problem in Western Thought," offers an excellent review of the two humanistic schools of thought (rationalism and vitalism) and their implications for physical education and sport. Rejecting an objective and instrumental conception of the body, she argues for the development and expression of individual self-consciousness and for the experience and expression of "self."

In his essay, "Teleology and Fitness," Cliff Balkam focuses on a very contemporary concern—health and fitness; he uses Aristotle's attempt to identify "an intelligible distinction between health and fitness. Both states existentially demonstrate a resolution of the mind-body dichotomy. However, he contends that health and fitness are different in kind rather than degree. Also, in a teleological sense, health and fitness have different goals. Fitness is extrinsic and it results in establishing a level of performance. Health, on the other hand, consists of a congruence between human purposes and the purposes implicit in how our bodies are designed and function. Health is the happy state of enjoying bodily existence and, as such, is an end in itself.

Candace Norton's contribution, "Cultural Narcissism and the Resurrection of the Indecent Fitness Machine," affirms Balkam's view of health as intrinsic. External pressures have created an age and a generation which pursues fitness for the wrong reasons. As a result, the fragmentation of mind and body continues to exist. An environment which nurtures wellness and supports long-term involvement with positive health practices is a necessary condition for overcoming the cultural bias of dualism in consciousness as well as in practice.

All of the contributors to this section have drawn upon Western thought and behavior in pointing out the limits to self-understanding in a world which separates mind from body. In a sense, they take us to the edge of our traditional paradigm and set the stage for the exploration of alternatives.

The body's role in the philosophy of the Renaissance man

Carmelo Bazzano
University of Massachusetts at
Boston

The Italian Renaissance marked a period characterized by a new concern for man. There was a gradual rediscovering of man's possibilities; and, as fascinating new vistas opened, men of this age were compelled to climb still higher.

Petrarch, unanimously acclaimed as the first Renaissance man, reached these conclusions literally in his climb of Mount Ventoux. Each step upward opened new horizons. He observed that by willing and performing the actual conquest of the mountain, he could set for himself an arduous course which was tremendously rewarding for the effort expended. Petrarch (1336/1948, p. 38) wrote, "From the start we encountered a good deal of trouble, for the mountain is a steep and almost inaccessible pile of rocky material. However, what the Poet says is appropriate, 'Ruthless striving overcomes everything.' "

Still further, Petrarch noted that by turning his gaze from the outer world to the inner self, he was faced with a new and potentially more rewarding world to discover. The physical experience, therefore, opened the door for the intellectual experience.

Petrarch's adventure takes us to the heart of the issue being investigated, the body-mind relation during the Renaissance, a fundamental issue for the philosophers of the Middle Ages. Saint Thomas had decreed that the body was mortal, but the soul was eternal. Accepting this premise, it followed naturally that the mind was worthy of the utmost cultivation, whereas the body, because of its temporality, was to be ignored.

Some radical religious orders felt the body was to be mortified. They believed that its suffering would aid in the purification of the soul whose final aim was to free itself from the encumbrance of the body. As Jesus said,

> Love not the things that are in the world (John 2:15), my kingdom is not of this world (John 18:36), the wisdom of this world is foolishness with God (I Cor. 3:19), flesh and blood cannot inherit the kingdom of God (I Cor. 15:50).

These were the teachings of the Church that hung like the mythical sword of Damocles over the head of early Christians.

Of course, this kind of philosophy could only flourish in the static medieval society where life was pleasant for a small minority. The great majority of the people dwelled in a state of semiservitude. The Church philosophy served to give its stamp of approval to a societal order convenient to itself and the nobles. This class looked approvingly to the teaching of the Church because such teachings kept an exploited people concerned with the eternal life.

EMERGENCE OF A NEW CLASS

Unfortunately for the Church and the nobles, things were changing quickly, especially after the Crusades. These military adventures represented, ironically, the apex of power in medieval society and also marked the beginning of its end. Once the Crusades were over, the Italian maritime republics, which had transported the fighting men from west to east and vice versa, had established a flourishing commerce with the people of the East. Commerce provided opportunities for a new class of people to emerge and accumulate wealth. The people of the new class were mostly merchants who hardly fit in the scheme of medieval structure. Also, the merchants, who were making money by providing goods for the body, did not look favorably on the traditional philosophy of life expounded by the ruling classes.

But there was more. These merchants acquired not only riches, but also power. With it, they wrestled political decision making from the hands of the nobles and the Church. Newly acquired power made the merchants aware of themselves as men with possibilities, as men who could control their own destinies.

The merchants were also generous with their monies by supporting literati and artists who were caught up in the same ferment—namely, an awareness that they were living in a new and different time. These self-styled literati humanists studied the classics in their original form and in them discovered people like themselves who yearned to be free and able to govern their own lives. They saw the ancients as people who had dared and who, in fact, had achieved. The humanists could see plenty of examples of Roman grandeur in their own cities. In other words, the humanists discovered what the Greeks meant by *paideia* and the Romans by *humanitas*.

The result of all this study, reflection, and acting produced a new vision best expressed by Swiss historian Jacob Burckhardt (1891, p. 25):

> A changed attitude of mind towards man and his environment, substituting for the medieval conception of man as a miserable sinner striving against the world and the flesh, man as an interesting and beautiful creature, in a beautiful and interesting world.

MAN AS THE CENTRAL ACTOR

After the revolution had taken place, the philosophers started to speculate about the issues it had provoked. The Platonic Academy of Florence, for example, was sponsored by the enlightened merchant Lorenzo il Magnifico for exactly this purpose. Pico della Mirandola and Ficino, the major exponents of the Academy, worked out a philosophical theory of the dignity of man in the universe. Pico della Mirandola (1486/1948, p. 225) thus expressed the view that

> We have set thee at the world's center that thou mayest from thence more easily observe whatever is in the world. We have made thee neither of heaven nor of earth, neither mortal or immortal, so that with freedom of choice and with honor, as though the maker and molder of thyself, thou mayest fashion thyself in whatever shape thou shalt prefer.

Expressed here is an intriguing view of the fluidity of human nature: No more man split in body and mind, one aspect pulling away from the other, but one united man who was not prefabricated, known only by the quality of his actions. Bruni, the politician, Poggio, the writer, Piccolomini, the Pope—all echoed this thought: "We are not born nobles; nobility is acquired and demonstrated through one's actions."

Pomponazzi, the other major philosopher of the Renaissance, tackled the body-mind problem and concluded that the soul is also mortal. He (Pomponazzi, 1516/1948, p. 272) wrote,

> In all its operations the intellect needs the body and the corporeal sense images it furnishes. Aristotle is clear on this point, and he is confirmed by our own experience....Hence, the soul is a material form, a bodily function generated by the parents and not by special creation, the supreme and most perfect of material forms, but not capable of operating in any way or existing without the body.

The philosophy expressed by the Renaissance philosophers gave conscience to what was happening. Man was no longer limited by the social class in which he was born; neither had he to live according to the canons of the Church. In fact, he was free to make himself in a world in which he had considerable powers. The old Greek dictum "Man the measure of all things" was taken as the guiding light.

VISUAL EXPRESSION OF RENAISSANCE PHILOSOPHY

Philosophy and thought of this age in which man had center stage was perhaps best expressed with images in the visual arts. The first building which represented the new spirit was the Pazzi chapel. Compared to the architectural colossi of the Middle Ages, which by their enormity, complexity, and ornamentation, dwarfed man, the chapel was a song to the dignity of man. The building was simple and elegant and well proportioned. As Kenneth Clark (1963, p. 94) observed, "Everything is adjusted to the scale of reasonable human necessity. They are intended to make each individual more conscious of his powers as a complete and intellectual being."

But it is with Michelangelo's work that the tension between the human and the divine can most powerfully be seen. Michelangelo's supermen knew what they wanted, they knew where they were going, they were at one with their powerful bodies. They were hardly eager to admit God's primacy. Their world and themselves were the results of their makings.

The Renaissance men knew exactly how to forge themselves. They were familiar with the classical models and adopted the universal man as their beacon. Baldassare Castiglione (1910), in his long essay "The Courtier," delineated this figure. Castiglione's ideal individual was first and foremost a man of action. He was skilled in the arts of war and at home in all the manly exercises. He was also a master of the all-important art of speech, and in addition, he had the wit and intelligence of a scholar.

LIBERAL EDUCATION

The educated man of the Renaissance, as seen by Castiglione, was formed by a confluence of intellectual and physical experiences. No conflict existed between the body and the mind. Education had to proceed from all the avenues available of which the body was a notable one. The educators of the Renaissance were quick in appreciating and implementing this point.

Vergerio has been called the first educator of the Renaissance because his work *De Ingenuis Moribus* was the first educational effort of the new consciousness. He (Vergerio, 1402/1897, p. 75) recommended a liberal education thus defined:

> We call those studies liberal which are worthy of a free man: those studies by which we attain and practice virtue and wisdom: that education which calls forth, trains and develops those highest gifts of body and of mind which ennoble man, and which are rightly judged to rank next in dignity to virtue only.

The education proposed by Vergerio is intellectual and physical; the result proceeding from these two directions is the virtuous man who can function in any circumstance. The body, in Vergerio's views, is not the antithesis of the mind; rather, the two complement each other. In fact the two—body and mind—converge and become one in the character of the student. "A lazy life," he (Vergerio, 1402/1897, p. 100) wrote, "weakens the soul and the body; whereas by living laboriously one strengthens both."

CONVERGENCE OF MIND AND BODY IN PHYSICAL ACTIVITY

The belief that education had to be both physical and mental was echoed by all the major Renaissance educators echoed the belief that education had to be both physical and mental. For instance, Maffeo Vegio (1491/1953, pp. 13, 15) in his educational tractate, *De Educatione Liberorum*, stated,

> Let us now talk about gymnastics, which is very useful in resting and restoring from toil; furthermore it gives our youth the opportunity to be trained in the arts of war and most important it is a means for the community and the individual to preserve health....Ball playing is a worthy and liberal activity, besides being a healthful exercise.

Vergerio considered liberal education as education which sharpened both the body and the mind. Vegio saw ball playing as an activity which was essentially synonymous with liberal education because it strengthened both the body and the mind. Ball playing, therefore, was neither an activity of the mind or of the body; it was an integrated and total experience.

Vittorino de Feltre, the founder of la Giocosa, the most famous Renaissance school, left nothing in writing; yet, it has been ascertained that physical education was held daily in his school, regardless of weather conditions. Platina, a student at La Giocosa, wrote that his schoolmaster participated in jumping, running, and ball games because he felt that physical activities strengthened the mind and the body.

CONCLUSION

Many other Renaissance educators deserve to be mentioned: Gian Battista Alberti, the "universal man" par excellence is one. This author, artist, architect, athlete, and businessman was also concerned with education. In his tract *Della Famiglia*, Alberti (1496/1971) insisted upon making physical education an integral part of education. He (Alberti, 1496/1971, p. 71) wrote,

Cato, that good man of antiquity, was not ashamed, and it did not seem a burden to him, to teach his sons swimming, fencing and other civil and military skills in addition to letters, and he believed it was a father's duty to teach his children all the virtues worthy of free men. He did not think it just to call anyone free who lacked any of these virtues.

Here Alberti unequivocably pressed the view that a person lacking in physical skills could not be called liberally educated.

In this chapter I have endeavored to indicate the important role of the body in the philosophy of the Renaissance man, showing that the body during this age was thought of as an integral part of the persona. It was an aspect of man worthy of cultivation because, basically, man was of this world, and, consequently, his education was to be concerned with the here and now. Society needed a virtuous citizen both physically and mentally alert who could exercise his role in peace and in war.

The philosophy expressed by the Renaissance philosophers and educators insisted on the body being as one with the man and not as an entity distinctly separated from the mind.

Thus, as suggested, this new realization of the body's value helped free man of the medieval hostile mind-body imagination and moved toward the creation of the possibility of a total man, united.

REFERENCES

Alberti, G.B. (1971). *Della famiglia*, (Guarino, Trans.). Lewisburg, PA: Buckwell University Press.(Original work published 1496)

Burckhardt, J. (1891). *The civilization of the Renaissance in Italy*. New York: Oxford University Press.

Castiglione, B. (1910). *Il cartegiano* [The courtier]. Florence: G.C. Sansoni.

Clark, K. (1963). *Civilization*. New York: Harper and Row.

Della Mirandola, G.P. (1948). On the dignity of man. In Cassirer (Ed. and Trans.), *The Renaissance philosophy of man* (p. 225). Chicago: The University of Chicago Press. (Original work published 1486)

Holy Bible. Revised Standard Edition.

Petrarch, F. (1948). The ascent of Mount Ventoux. In Cassirer (Ed. and Trans.), *The Renaissance philosophy of man* (p. 38). Chicago: The University of Chicago Press. (Original work published 1336)

Pomponazzi, P. (1948). On immortality. In Cassirer (Ed. and Trans.), *The Renaissance philosophy of man* (p. 272). Chicago: The University of Chicago Press. (Original work published 1516)

Vegio, V. (1953). *De educatione liberorum*. (V. Horkan, Trans.). Washington, D.C. Catholic University Press. (Original work published 1491)

Vergerio, P.P. (1897). De ingenius moribus. In Harrison (Ed. and Trans.), *Vittorino de feltre and other humanist educators*. Cambridge: Cambridge University Press. (Original work published 1402)

Cartesian dualism and physical education: Epistemological incompatibility

Saul Ross
University of Ottawa

THE "NEW" PHYSICAL EDUCATION

Late in the 19th and early in the 20th centuries, major changes in thinking encompassing philosophy, politics, and education, amongst many others, pervaded the American social scene. Under the influence and urging of such seminal thinkers as G. Stanley Hall, Edward Thorndike, John Dewey, and William Heard Kilpatrick, the progressive movement emerged, advanced, and flourished, extending its ideas into many aspects of life. Their teachings and ideals also had an impact on the leaders in physical education—men such as Thomas Wood, Clark Hetherington, and Luther Halsey Gulick, who are generally credited with formulating the conceptual framework upon which "the new physical education" would be elaborated (Weston, 1962, p. 51).

These leaders shifted the focus of physical education away from the European (Swedish and German) formal schools of gymnastics with its medical and biological orientation by moving it squarely into the domain of education. Physical education's new educational orientation was championed in the 1920 to 1940 era by authors such as Jay B. Nash and J.F. Williams. They not only carried the banner of "the new physical education," but vigorously attacked the previous conception of physical education (which may be more accurately described as physical culture or as physical training) with its narrow concern for bodily development and physical health.

J.F. Williams, the man credited with coining the term *physical education* as education through the physical, fired the first salvo in what has become known in the physical education literature as "The Great Debate." He juxtaposed the two rival notions: "No one can examine earnestly the implications of physical education without facing two questions. These are: Is physical education an education *of* the physical? Is physical education an education *through* the physical?" (Williams, 1930b, p. 279). Some concomitant learning takes place in the education of the physical and, as well, an education through the physical would produce some distinct physical gains. However, it is important to realize that in these two questions there are (a) two distinct points of view, (b) two radically different ways of looking at physical education, (c) two different ways of understanding the meaning, scope, and aim of education, (d) two conceptions of man, and (e) two implicit epistemological theories.

Supporters of the education-of-the-physical school of thought identify strong muscles and firm ligaments as the main outcome, a position staunchly defended by McCloy (1936) in his "How About Some Muscle?" rebuttal to the original attack launched by Williams (1930a, b). Williams rejected the education-of-the-physical notion, which implies that the body can be educated as a thing apart from the mind, on a number of grounds. These are (a) its focus on the cult of muscles and motor or skill learning was too narrow and limited; (b) its general orientation was incompatible with the progressivist ideal of education for complete living; and (c) its dualistic conception of man where mind and body can be regarded as distinct and separate entities. Defending his own position by contrasting it with the notion implicit in the education-of-the-physical view, Williams (1930b) asserted that "modern physical education with its emphasis upon education through the physical is based upon the biologic unity of mind and body" (p. 279). Its goals extend to total education accomplished through the medium of physical activity. Basic to this concept is the belief that education of the *mind* may, indeed, does occur *through* the education of the body.

Williams gives no explanation for his notion of "the biologic unity of mind and body" save for a passing reference to the then emerging philosophy of behaviorism. No further consideration of the mind-body problem in relation to physical education in his writings is made beyond pointing out that a dualistic conception of man allows for the notion of a cult of muscles where the body can be "educated" as a thing apart from the mind and beyond asserting the unity of mind and body in his own conception of physical education. Neither is any such discussion found in McCloy's views in defending his position. Indeed, the entire corpus of literature devoted to the philosophy of physical education is marked by a paucity of attention to this important topic; it is a subject which has not attracted the attention of scholars in the field either from a metaphysical or an epistemological perspective.

I regard this lack of scholarly attention as a major omission because the very notion of physical education—be it as education *of* or as education *through* the physical—involves persons. Unless we clearly understand what a person is, we cannot be very effective as educators. In part to remedy this oversight, and in part to augment and develop what Williams barely started, there is a need to examine and analyze what most philosophers regard as the clearest articulation of the dualistic conception of man—the thesis posited by Descartes, the father of modern philosophy. An analysis of his position will show that there cannot be such a thing as physical education whether it is interpreted as education *of* the physical or as education *through* the physical. Furthermore, the analysis will also show that under the Cartesian thesis, the common notion of education as a process and as an institution generally understood to involve teachers and students cannot be.

DESCARTES' DUALISTIC CONCEPTION OF MAN

Descartes insisted that epistemology is the proper starting point of all philosophy. His basic philosophical question is, "What do I know?" He hopes to be able to answer that query by reflection on the beliefs he finds himself disposed to hold. Posing the question in this manner shifts the problem from a general approach to knowledge to an emphasis on the *individual* thinking man. Before attempting to answer questions about what *men* may know, Descartes saw the primary task as attempting to determine what *a man* may know. Changing the focus from the general to the individual carries with it a shift in the locus of the problem of knowledge from the external, communal world to the "internal" world of the mind. All replies now become individualistic.

In addition, such a shift in locus involves certain consequences that have been extremely detrimental to physical education in its quest to be recognized as an integral part of education. This will become clearer from the discussion in the succeeding sections. For now it is sufficient to note where knowledge is restricted to the individual's internal thought processes, human physical action, executed by the "body," cannot be regarded as a manifestation of knowledge. For Descartes, knowledge must be indubitable, but undubitability cannot be achieved through sense perception; thus, bodily activity cannot yield knowledge nor can human physical action be regarded as an expression of knowledge. Under this thesis, physical education is confronted with insurmountable obstacles in regard to its proper place in the educational spectrum.

Method of deducing knowledge

In common with many other philosophers who confront the problem of knowledge, Descartes deals with the issue of skepticism. However, unlike other philosophers who devote their efforts to the refutation of skepticism while elaborating their own epistemology, Descartes adopts what might best be described as a methodological skepticism. His procedure is quite simple and direct: He rejects as being absolutely false everything, all beliefs which he should have the slightest cause to doubt, and then sees if he can eventually find anything which is entirely indubitable (Descartes, 1637/1968, p.53; 1642/1951, p. 23). The tone and underlying optimism indicate confidence in finding some truth which is indubitable and certain to serve as the base upon which to build the edifice of knowledge. Such a system of knowledge—the ideal of knowledge—is a systematic, ordered body of propositions dependent one on the other.

Although Descartes is not a skeptic, his initial epistemological position does not include taking any instance of human knowledge for granted. His efforts are devoted to proving that there are examples of human knowledge; for Descartes, knowledge is restricted to what is certain and indubitable. To achieve this goal, his method is to prove to himself that he knows something with a certainty that is able to withstand any conceivable criticism. Success in this endeavor demands careful consideration of the manner in which the proof is obtained and presented should anyone doubt the validity of the claim. Influenced by his training in mathematics, particularly geometry, Descartes believed that if he could find a set of certain statements that could serve as axioms for a deductive system, both consistent and complete, the theorems which could be developed from them would build an irrefutable and uncontestable system of knowledge. The notion of a deductive system is very important, for it eliminates the possibility of error; rational, logical thinking is the only certain way to proceed.

Argument against empirical knowledge

Our senses often deceive us, and so they cannot be trusted as a source of knowledge nor as an avenue through which knowledge is discovered. Descartes' argument against empirical knowledge rests on two grounds. First, it is well known that we sometimes see things which do not exist and that, conversely, we sometimes overlook things which are right in front of us. Equally well known is the fact that our senses deceive us at times; a straight stick will appear bent when part of it is submerged in water. Secondly, we are unable to tell always with absolute certainty whether we are awake or dreaming. There is always room for doubt, and where there is doubt, there is also the possibility of confusion. Impressions from dreams are mixed with reality. If dreams and states of waking are at times confused, how can it ever be known by someone with certainty that he or she is awake, or dreaming, at any given moment? Because there is no way to tell, the result is that no sense experience can serve as the source of knowledge. We can always be wrong about sense experience, meaning that our senses cannot provide the conclusive, irrefutable evidence needed for knowledge.

Proof of existence

Everything based on sense perception can be doubted, even the existence of one's own body. Descartes is therefore compelled to turn away from sense perception in his search for certainty, but at the very same time, he must still deal with the problem of his existence, both bodily and nonbodily. Denial of the existence of his body is not necessarily the denial of his own existence. The body and the senses are not needed to confirm his own existence; it is confirmed whenever he thinks about the problem. For every time Descartes ponders his existence, he knows for certain that he exists. "I think, therefore I am" is a necessary truth every time the statement is uttered. Where the existence of material things is acknowledged, the existence of a thinking substance, mind, presents no problem. Even if Descartes is deceived into believing that all material things exist, *he* still must exist, for there must be some existent being which is deceived. He (Descartes, 1642/1951) states,

> There can be no slightest doubt that I exist, since he deceives me; and let him deceive me as much as he will, he can never make me be nothing as long as I think that I am something. Thus, after having thought well on this matter and after examining all things with care, I must finally conclude and maintain that this proposition: *I am, I exist*, is necessarily true every time that I pronounce it or conceive it in my mind. (p.23)

Under any and all circumstances, as long as Descartes thinks, he exists.

For Descartes, the act of doubting is part of the act of thinking, so every time he doubts, it is further confirmation of his existence. It is also, in a paradoxical way, further proof for the certain and indubitable status of his knowledge claim, "I think, therefore I am," which is the end product of his method of doubt. Certain knowledge of one's existence is the first principle, or axiom, but what Descartes then needs to decide is what precisely the "I" is that exists. "But I do not yet know sufficiently clearly what I am, I who am sure that I exist" (Descartes, 1642/1951, p. 24). In pondering this question, Descartes cannot deviate from his established principle of accepting only that which is entirely certain and indubitable; the only certain and indubitable thing he knows is that he is "a thing which thinks. And what more?...I am not this assemblage which is called a human body" (p. 26). The "I" that exists is not a bodily person but a thinking person who knows through pure "intellection" and not through sensation. To leave no doubt about what the "I" is, Descartes (p. 42) adds, "I understand perfectly that I am a being that thinks and that is not extended."

Differences between mind and body

Mind is defined by Descartes as an unextended substance, an immaterial, thinking thing which does not exist in space but does exist in time. In contrast, *body* is defined as a bounded figure which can be located in some place, occupying space in such a way that every other body is excluded from it; it can be perceived by the five senses. Body is a material, nonthinking, extended substance. Two additional differences distinguish mind from body: (a) Mind is known with certainty, for it is a necessary truth that it exists every time I think, but body, which is known through sense perception, is open to doubt—therefore, knowledge of the body cannot be a necessary truth; and (b) body is divisible while mind is indivisible.

Descartes is very clear about mind and body as separate and distinct entities: "And certainly my idea of the human mind, in so far as it is a thinking being, not extended in length, breadth, and depth, and participating in none of the qualities of body, is incomparably more distinct than my idea of anything corporeal" (p. 51). Conversely, it can be stated that the body, as an extended substance, cannot participate in any of the qualities of the mind because the major quality of mind is intellection. It should be noted that the last phrase in the quotation just cited further underscores Descartes' view that the only thing which cannot be doubted is the existence of his own mind.

Minds are characterized by predicates that do not apply to bodies, while bodies are characterized by predicates that do not apply to minds. The distinction is radical: Minds and bodies are ontologically different types which are mutually exclusive so much so that Ryle (1949, p. 11) describes a Cartesian person as living through two collateral histories—one consisting of what happens in and to his body, the other consisting of what happens in and to his mind. Events of the body are public because it is an extended, material substance, but events of the mind are private because it is an unextended, immaterial substance. A Cartesian person can be regarded as a composite of two essentially distinct substances, and when we refer in any way to such a person, we are actually referring to one, and sometimes to both, of the separate substances. Strictly speaking, under the Cartesian thesis, whenever I use the personal pronouns "I" or "you" to refer to a person, only one substance—mind—is indicated. But a strict interpretation is possible only on a very abstract level, for in reality, we cannot identify another mind, we can only identify another body. This "unique" situation yields two uses of the term *person*: One sees the person as mind only, and the other more commonly accepted usage sees the person as a combination of mind and body.

According to Descartes two things, mind and body, can be made to exist separately by God.

> From this very fact that I know with certainty that I exist, and I find that absolutely nothing else belongs (necessarily) to my nature or essence except that I am a thinking being, I readily conclude that my essence consists solely in being a body which thinks (or a substance whose whole essence or nature is only to think). And although perhaps, or rather certainly, as I will soon show, I have a body with which I am very closely united, nevertheless, since on the one hand I have a clear and distinct idea of myself in so far as *I am only a thinking and not an extended being, and since on the other hand I have a distinct idea of a body in so far as it is only an extended being which does not think, it is certain that this "I" (that is to say, my soul, by virtue of which I am what I am) is entirely (and truly) distinct from my body and that it can (be or) exist without it.* [italics added] (Descartes, 1642/1951, p. 74)

Virtually the same passage appears in the *Discourse on Method* (1637/1968, p. 54) leaving no doubt that for Descartes the "I" is confined exclusively to the thinking substance, mind, and that mind and body are separate and distinct entities. If mind can exist without the body, then it is only a contingent fact that I have the body I do have now.

One of the central doctrines of the *Meditations*, if not *the* most important, is the real distinction between mind and body. This is shown by the full title of the work: *Meditations on First Philosophy, in which the Existence of God and the Real Distinction between Mind and Body are Demonstrated.*

Such a radical division and separation of mind and body creates problems with regard to any account for ordinary, everyday bodily occurrences. Descartes (1642/1951, p. 76) feels compelled to modify his stance.

Nature also teaches me by these feelings of pain, hunger, thirst, and so on that I am not only residing in my body as a pilot in his ship, but further-more, that I am intimately connected with it, and that (the mixture is) so blended, as it were, that (something like) a single whole is produced.

Where Descartes had insisted that mind and body were separate and distinct en-tities, he now claims that they are intimately connected. At first, he maintains that he is a being whose sole essence is thinking and that the substance which thinks is ontologically different and exclusive from bodily substance. But now it appears that he is modifying his dualistic thesis when he argues that sensa-tions and images can only arise in the mind through its union with a material body. While it is reasonable to believe that sensations do arise in the body, serious, insurmountable problems still remain regarding how two such disparate substances, mind and body, which are irreducible to each other, can become in-timately connected.

Even on the assumption that answers to the problem just cited can be provided—and to date this has not happened—from the epistemological perspec-tive of physical education and education, nothing changes. According to Descartes, the pure intellect of the mind gains knowledge by reflection upon itself in the case of intellectual imagination to add to its store of knowledge. Descartes' epistemological position is that there is no conceptual connection between any thought, or mental occurrence, and *any* physical occurrence. Even if there was some conceptual connection, no knowledge would be produced because bodily sensations can always be doubted, and imagination can surely conjure up inexis-tent or false images. Only the intellect, reflecting upon itself in its close associa-tion with God, can produce knowledge. For Descartes, it is the business of the mind alone, and not of the mind and body, to decide the truth of all matters where there may be some doubt.

Three specific features of the Cartesian view are identified by Langford (1977, p. 66): (a) Mind and body are exclusive kinds of things; (b) being a mind or body is a yes/no kind of thing; and (c) the mind, as characterized by privacy, is thought of in highly individualistic, nonsocial terms. These features provide the specific context for the analysis which will show that holding a Cartesian view of man is inimical to both the notion of physical education as well as to the notion of education.

THE INCOMPATIBILITY OF PHYSICAL EDUCATION AND EDUCATION WITH CARTESIAN PHILOSOPHY

Education of the physical

Physical education, as education of the physical with its emphasis on the train-ing and development of the body, including the acquisition of motor skills, gives the impression that no thinking is needed, that there is no mental involvement. The very claim that there can be such a thing as education of the physical is open to the charge of being unintelligible when discussed within a Cartesian concep-tion of man. Under that thesis, physical is contrasted with mental to show the difference between the two and it is only the mental, the thinking component, which can be educated. Physical substances, by their very nature, are not the sorts of things which can think, and so it follows that a Cartesian body, a physical substance, cannot be educated. True, the muscles of the body can be strengthened to delay the onset of fatigue and enhance health and can be trained to perform a myriad of tasks more efficiently, such as the most complex motor skills; but that training cannot be construed as education because truths are not transmitted. Minds, thinking things, can be educated, but nonthinking things, such as bodies, cannot.

What may, at first sight, appear to be physical education turns out to be something which cannot be called education because that which is to be educated is an uneducable physical substance. Or, if one insists on calling it education, it would have to be under a special definition of that term, one devoid of epistemological connotation. Our ordinary understanding of the term *education* includes the transmission of knowledge; but that understanding is inappropriate when applied to a Cartesian body, for the body is a substance which cannot incorporate into itself such a thing as knowledge. The conception of physical education as education *of* the physical is, therefore, completely incompatible with a Cartesian conception of man because the very idea of knowledge is ruled out.

Education through the physical

Replacing the conception of physical education as education *of* the physical with its successor, physical education as education *through* the physical appears to eliminate the problems encountered by the former conception. Implicit in the latter view is the belief that physical education contributes to the social, psychological, physical, and intellectual development of the individual. In effect, it is the *mind* that is educated through the education of the body during vigorous physical activity. Claiming that it is the mind that is being educated appears to be perfectly compatible with Descartes' theory, but even this claim encounters a number of very serious difficulties.

In the Cartesian view, what is essential to the mind is its ability to reflect on its own activity in thinking; therefore, it needs no stimulation or input from external sources. Thus, it can be a mind and know that it is and what it is without knowing anything at all about the physical world or other minds. Knowledge is developed deductively from the first axioms or principles which were discovered without resorting to sensory experiences or information garnered from the external world. True knowledge comes about as a result of developing further theorems from the initial axioms. Consequently, external events in the form of instruction, whether in reference to physical activity or mental activity are both superfluous and redundant.

Difficulties in mentally educating the Cartesian mind

Another consequence arises from the notion that the Cartesian mind is essentially complete as a mind. Acquiring a new or improved body, improving various motor skills, gaining knowledge of the external world, or entering into social relationships makes no essential difference to the mind. These experiences may affect the modes of consciousness or perhaps even the content of the mind, but logically, they cannot alter the essence of the mind which is essentially complete at all times. One cannot even state that the mind was complete at birth because it could well have existed as a complete mind well before birth. A Cartesian mind can exist in the bodies of various and sundry other people, past and present. Wherever and whenever a Cartesian mind exists, it is essentially complete as a mind. Our concept of education, however, always implies changes of a fundamental or nontrivial kind. Education changes the kind of person one is, making one, in a sense, a different person. One is simply not the very same person about whom certain things happen to be true; the Cartesian view of mind is not amenable to change of this kind. It is not, therefore, possible to educate the person (here person is used in the strict Cartesian sense as referring only to the mind) because the person, in being a mind, is a complete whole from the start.

A further difficulty confounds the idea of educating a Cartesian mind which stems from the view that the concept of education is above all a social process involving teachers and students. No matter how narrowly or how broadly education is defined, one basic, essential element must be present: There must be a "meeting of minds." According to Descartes' description and definition of mind, mental happenings (which would be the process and products of education) occur in insulated fields known as minds. Ryle (1977) notes the consequences:

> There is, apart maybe from telepathy, no direct causal connection between what happens in one mind and what happens in another. Only through the medium of the public physical world can the mind of one person make a difference to the mind of another. The mind is its own place and in his inner life each of us lives the life of a ghostly Robinson Crusoe. People can see, hear and jolt one another's bodies, but they are irremediably blind and deaf to the workings of one another's mind and inoperative upon them. (p. 13)

By describing mind as an immaterial, unextended substance, Descartes created a situation where there is no way to identify mind. Intersubjectivity becomes impossible. We have no way of knowing that other minds exist, and so it follows that no "meeting of minds" is possible. Without this meeting, we must conclude that even the Cartesian mind cannot be educated.

From an epistemological perspective, one additional issue needs to be raised regarding the Cartesian mind and its source of knowledge. Epistemological analysis is not only concerned with analyzing the nature and validity of our present knowledge, but is also concerned with examining our sources of knowledge. Frequently, the analysis of our present knowledge cannot be undertaken without first exploring the source.

A Cartesian mind is complete in itself; it learns all it needs to know about itself from itself, or from God, and confirms its knowledge either on the basis of rational logic or on an appeal to the infallibility and honesty of God. While such knowledge may be valid, its source is forever hidden behind an impenetrable wall. By placing the source of our knowledge beyond the reach of ordinary mortal epistemological analysis, Descartes compels us to accept on the basis of pure faith. Acceptance on the basis of pure faith either precludes the need for epistemological analysis, or else limits the scope so severely that very few philosophers would be attracted to such an enterprise.

CONCLUSION

Our analysis has shown that a Cartesian person cannot be educated physically nor can such a person be educated mentally. A Cartesian mind, in being complete as a mind right from the start, does not require external stimuli for its intellectual development, nor can it trust bodily sensations as a source of knowledge because there always exists the possibility that our senses will deceive us. Knowledge cannot be gained through or from physical activity. Acceptance of a Cartesian conception of man renders the term *physical education* under both the education of and education through the physical interpretations, meaningless. Furthermore, acceptance of a Cartesian conception of man also precludes the possibility of elaborating an epistemology of human action, where such an epistemology would explicate the knowledge that an agent has in performing the action. Such knowledge cannot be transformed into propositional statements. We can point to the knowledge and tell many things about it, but the exact, specific knowledge is only demonstrated in the action itself. This form of knowledge is of direct interest to physical education, but to date, it has not commanded the attention of physical education philosophers who, almost totally, have neglected epistemology.

Neither has much effort been devoted in the physical education literature to the mind-body problem and the theory of persons. One interpretation of the Cartesian thesis sees a person as a composite of two distinct entities, a mind and a body. By positing the existence of these two distinct and different sorts of entities, Descartes provides the ingredients for the concept of a person, but this does not, by itself, provide an account of the concept of a person as such. The ingredients are there but the problem of the relationships between such disparate components still has not been solved. If we keep the components separate, we could then go on to say that a person consists of two parts, a mind and a body, and so education of the whole person would simply require educating both parts. Success in this educational venture would result in, as the familiar saying has it, a sound mind in a healthy body. But we have just seen that the Cartesian body is not the sort of thing which can be educated and, for various other reasons, neither can the Cartesian mind be educated. Because both components of the Cartesian conception of man do not appear to be educable, the concept of education of the whole man is inapplicable to a Cartesian conception of man.

For physical education to merit consideration as an educational endeavor, an alternate model of man is required. Within the theory of persons there are four possible options: (a) a combination of two separate entities, mind and body, such as described by Descartes; (b) mind only, such as described by Berkeley (Armstrong, 1710/1965); (c) body only, such as described by materialist and physicalist theories; and (d) an integrated, unified entity. We have seen that the first option is not viable for physical education (nor for education) from both an epistemological and educational perspective. The second option is a philosophical position no longer seriously considered, but if it were a viable option, the notion of physical education would obviously be unintelligible.

While the third option appears to be very attractive for physical education, it has great difficulties in accounting for the ''self,'' and without a self, we have no way of distinguishing mere bodily movement from action. Of greater consequence is the fact that without a self there can be no learning, hence no knowing and so, once again, the notion of education is destroyed. We are left with one final possibility—man as an integrated, unified entity, a model that is consonant with the notion that education is of the whole man. Enunciating and elaborating a theory of an integrated, unified person is a challenge that should rank as a very high priority with philosophers of physical education.

Under an integrated, unified model of man, physical education is not education *of* the physical nor is it education (of the mind) *through* the physical: It is education of the person. Whenever such a person engages in action, both decisions and judgments are involved. Decisions made and judgments rendered presupposes concepts; hence, a person's actions are always conceptual in nature, or thought-impregnated. This is the knowledge that is of concern to physical education, a wide-ranging, infinite variety of nonpropositional concepts, knowledge that is in the action. Because epistemologists have devoted almost all of their efforts to describing and analyzing propositional knowledge, it now becomes the task of philosophers of physical education to render an account of the knowledge that is pertinent to their domain—physical action knowledge.

REFERENCES

Armstrong, D.M. (1965). Introduction. In G. Berkeley (Ed.), *Berkeley's Philosophical Writings*. (pp. 7-34) New York, NY: Collier Books. (Original work published 1710)

Descartes, R. (1968). *Discourse on method and the meditations*. Translated with an introduction by F.E. Sutcliffe, Penguin Books. (Original work published 1637)

Descartes, R. (1951). *Meditations on first philosophy*. Translated with an introduction by L.J. Lafleur. Indianapolis, IN: Bobbs-Merrill. (Original work published 1642)

Langford, G. (1977). Education is of the whole man. *Journal of Philosophy of Education, 13*, 65-72.

McCloy, C.H. (1936). How about some muscle? *The Journal of Health and Physical Education, 7*(5), 302-303, 355.

Ryle, G. (1949). *The concept of mind*. New York: Barnes & Noble Books.

Weston, A. (1962). *The making of American physical education*. New York: Appleton-Century-Crofts.

Williams, J.F. (1930a). A fundamental point of view in physical education. *The Journal of Health and Physical Education, 1*(1), 10-11, 60.

Williams, J.F. (1930b). Education through the physical. *Journal of Higher Education, 1*(5), 279-282.

A humanistic interpretation of the mind-body problem in Western thought

Susan J. Bandy
San Diego State University

There has been a certain "disquieting ambiguity" about the relation of the mind and body, such that this relation has been one of the oldest and most fundamental problems of philosophy. The resolution of this problem is a critical one because a culture's regard and practice of sport are fashioned, in large measure, by the views it holds of the body and its relation to the mind.

Philosophic interpretations of the mind-body problem have either tended to a cosmological or material, a theological or spiritualistic, or an ontological or humanistic nature (Osterhoudt, 1981, p. 19). Both the materialistic and spiritualistic interpretations offer a dualistic resolution of the problem in which the mind and body are considered as distinct, independent substances which interact with or accompany one another. Within materialistic interpretations, the mental is reduced to or explained in terms of the physical; the material, unthinking body reigns over the immaterial, thinking mind. An objective notion of the body as a concrete thing which one possesses is advanced by this view. Within spiritualistic interpretations, the physical is reduced to and explained in terms of the mental; the mind reigns over the body. The body is seen as something to which one is temporarily attached and that which must be overcome for human fulfillment.

A humanistic interpretation, however, provides a monistic view of the mind-body problem, one that preserves the intrinsic character and identity of mind and body and reveals the harmonious, unified relation between them. According to this interpretation, a subjective notion of the body is advanced, one in which the body is seen as what one is rather than merely something one has.

Humanistic interpretations of the mind-body problem in Western thought have taken two main forms: *rationalism* and *vitalism*. Rationalism resolves the problem in the direction of the mind while vitalism tends toward an explanation of the problem in the direction of the body.

This chapter examines the rationalistic and vitalistic views of the mind-body problem within Western philosophic thought, in general, and philosophic inquiry within physical education and sport, in particular. Lastly, it suggests the implications of each view for sport and physical education.

RATIONALISTIC INTERPRETATIONS
OF THE MIND-BODY PROBLEM

Rationalistic interpretations of the mind-body problem in modern Western philosophy stem largely from Descartes' materialistic solution to the spiritualistic dualism of Plato. Spinoza was among the first to attempt to reconcile the dualistic view of Descartes. Like Descartes, Spinoza was a rationalist and maintained that knowledge was obtained by thought. Unlike Descartes, however, Spinoza claimed that thought/mind and extension/body are not separate substances but attributes of one single, independent substance—God—the one great reality. According to Spinoza, mind and body are independent attributes of one substance. There can be no interaction between these attributes. They are independent of one another and do not influence each other: "Mind cannot produce changes in body nor the body changes in mind" (Thilly & Wood, 1957, p. 323).

Spinoza's resolution of the mind-body problem left traces of dualism which Schelling and then Hegel attempted to overcome. Schelling claimed that mind/thought and body/being are not two parallel attributes of the absolute. They are progressive stages in the evolution of an absolute principle, the evolutionary process from the unconscious or subconscious stage to self-consciousness. Nature, according to Schelling, is not distinct from reason; it is a stage in the evolution of reason. It is through man, the highest product of nature, that the goal of self-consciousness is realized.

Schelling's view is completed by Hegel who, like Schelling, claimed that nature and mind or reason are one. Hegel posited that the absolute is a differentiated absolute and is a subject rather than a substance, as Schelling had claimed. Idea, reason, or consciousness constitutes ultimate reality and is the unifying principle of human experience (Singer, 1983; Osterhoudt, 1981). All of life is an unconscious thinking, developing toward self-consciousness.

According to this view, it is the progressive unfolding of Idea, reason, or self-consciousness that overcomes the duality and separation of subject/object, mind/body. Idea or consciousness actualizes itself as phenomena, which constitutes the first stage in the actualization of Idea. The development of knowledge assumes the form of idea; that is, knowledge develops in accord with Idea, the progressive unfolding of rational self-consciousness. It progresses through a series of succeeding stages: Starting from a primitive level of self-consciousness wherein knowledge is of a starkly objective sort in which all things appear unrelated, it progresses to less primitive levels wherein knowledge is of a consciously objective sort in which all things appear differentiated. At the most complex level, knowledge is of a self-conscious sort in which the unity of things is realized.

At the most primitive stage, mind and body appear unrelated. The mind perceives the body as separate and unrelated, an object one has. Progress in thought to the consciously objective level reveals the differentiation between mind and body. One is led to conclude that things cannot exist "in themselves," apart from consciousness; that is to say, whatever exists must exist within consciousness. With this, the identity and separation of mind and body are revealed. The realization that things are objects that can be known suggests the existence of a mind which knows objects. The progression of thought to the self-conscious level reveals the interdependence and relatedness of mind and body. Realized is that both mind and body derive their identity and meaning from the resolution of their opposition: One is meaningless without the other. It is at this level that the unity of self is revealed. The body is no longer viewed as object but is seen as what one is.

Rationalistic humanism asserts the independence as well as the interdependence and relatedness of the mind and body. While considered as independent and distinct aspects of the self, mind and body are not viewed as exclusively separate. They are viewed instead as parts of a developing and unified self. The identity of mind and body is revealed only as it is understood and experienced as it is "in and for itself" and as it relates to the other and to the whole, the self (Osterhoudt, 1981, p. 22).

According to rationalistic humanism, a dualistic view of the relationship of the mind and body as well as an objective regard for the body stems from a starkly objective and experiential level of knowledge, one that has not progressed to the conscious and self-conscious levels of thought, reason, or idea.

VITALISTIC INTERPRETATIONS OF THE MIND-BODY PROBLEM

After Hegel, there was an antirationalistic turn to subjectivity and experience in Western philosophic thought. Philosophic arguments were advanced for the experiential and subjective basis of knowledge with the development of phenomenology and existentialism, which constitute the vitalistic interpretations of the mind-body problem.

Bergson and Husserl provided the foundational insights for the vitalistic view which was later advanced by phenomenologist Merleau-Ponty and existentialists Heidegger, Jaspers, Sartre, and Marcel. Bergson's view of "my body" as the center of action for objects (later expressed in Marcel's "my body qua mine," Sartre's "body-for-itself," and Merleau-Ponty's "body proper") was a precursor to the notion of embodiment, central to the vitalistic resolution of the mind-body problem. Husserl (1965, p. 20) rejected an examination of the objective world, advocated a "return to things themselves," and favored a "reflective consideration of a thinking subject."[1] He maintained that the ultimate foundation and source of all knowledge is intuition. According to his view, everything presents itself originally at the intuitive level. His "return to things themselves" advocates an experientially based knowledge in which subject and object are not separate but present to each other at the intuitive level (Kockelmans, 1967, pp. 29-30).

It is through the work of French philosopher Merleau-Ponty, however, that the phenomenologic resolution of the mind-body problem is perhaps best explained. As in the case of Husserl, Merleau-Ponty maintained a preobjective and experiential understanding of the body. The world is "already there" prior to reflection (Zaner, 1964, p. 143). Mind and body are "inexorably inseparable" as consciousness is "primordially embodied." The self is perceived as embodied, body-subject, both mind and body simultaneously. The body can no longer be considered as an exclusively physical thing. "It is only by *experiencing* my body-proper that I can *apprehend it as experienced by me*" (Zaner, 1971, p. 138). The significance of the body is elevated by this view as man's "being-in-the-world" is made possible through the body. It is through the "lived body" that the world is meaningfully disclosed to man.

Not unlike phenomenology, existentialism turns away from objectivity and reflection toward subjectivity and experience. Existentialism asserts as well a preobjective understanding of the body; the body is experienced first, prior to reflection.

Heidegger, one of the earliest proponents of existentialism, in an attempt to explain the meaning of a distinctly human existence, maintained that human ex-

---

[1]According to Husserl's view, consciousness can become human and "worldly" only by being embodied, by its experiential relation to the animate organism. Consciousness takes on the character of being by means of its experiential relation to that corporeal body which embodies it (Zaner, 1971, p. vii).

istence cannot be understood as pure consciousness, but rather through an authentic and active "being-in-the-world." Accordingly, Being, or *Dasein* presupposes existence and is exemplified in experience (Mehta, 1971, p. 51). Heidegger's view transcends the subject/object, mind/body distinction as Being is a consciousness embodied in the world.

In a similar fashion, Jaspers argues against the objectification of human existence, maintaining that human existence is characterized by its free, human subjectivity or *Existenz*. Existenz cannot be understood objectively or rationally. It is experienced being, the "being-within-myself," that transcends the subject/object, mind/body distinction.

It is in the work of Sartre and Marcel that existentialism is provided with perhaps its most well-developed resolution of the mind-body problem. For Sartre, consciousness is an embodied consciousness initially. To know the body is to experience the body as "being-for-itself," as subject. A purely cognitive knowledge of the body reveals the body as object, never "my body" as subject, but as the "body-for-others" (Zaner, 1964, pp. 81-82).

Not unlike Sartre, Marcel suggests a preobjective, experiential understanding of and noninstrumental union of mind and body as evidenced by his claim "I am my body." An individual's experiences in the world presuppose his or her body: "What is *lived* by man concretely provides the access to the interpretation and comprehension of man's concrete condition" (Zaner, 1964, pp. 18-19). The body is subject as it is experienced and felt. This view transcends the opposition of the subject who asserts the existence of objects and object as asserted by the subject. According to Marcel, *primary* (objective) reflection destroys the link between a person and his or her body and thereby reduces the body to object. The unity of mind and body is recaptured only through *secondary* (subjective) reflection.

Vitalistic humanism maintains that the opposition and consequent separation of mind and body are transcended as the self is initially apprehended and experienced as a unified self. That is to say, the self is experientially known (as opposed to cognitively known) as an embodied consciousness without separation of mind and body. The body is viewed as the locus of man's existence in the world, as that which makes possible his or her authentic, active existence and participation in the world as subject: "The body is construed as the distinctly human mode of existence engaged in the world as subject" (Osterhoudt, 1981, p. 21).

According to vitalistic humanism, a dualistic view of the relationship of the mind and body and an objective regard for the body stems from a cognitive and detached attempt to explain and understand the relationship. Reflection as to the nature of this relationship destroys the unity of self and thereby reduces the body to object, as something one has. The unity of self and body as subject is initially and preobjectively "known," or apprehended as it is experienced.

HUMANISTIC INTERPRETATIONS OF THE MIND-BODY PROBLEM IN PHYSICAL EDUCATION

A dualistic view of the nature of mind-body relationships has provided the theoretical foundation for the development of American physical education since its inception. Acceptance of the rationalized movements of the German and Swedish systems of gymnastics in American physical education suggest "the reification of human movement" and an objective regard for the body (Broekhoff, 1972). With the development of an indigenous system of physical education in

America, a dualistic view of the nature of the relationship of mind and body characterized the philosophy of such notable leaders as Wood, Hetherington, Williams, and Gulick. According to these philosophies, the body, as well as physical education, was regarded as an instrument to achieve biological, sociological, psychological, and educational ends.

With the development of more sophisticated philosophic inquiry within sport and physical education, the mind-body problem has been equally as "disquieting and ambiguous" as it has been for philosophy in general. And not unlike philosophy in general, humanistic resolutions of the problem have advanced both rationalistic and vitalistic views of sport and physical education in general and the body in particular.[2]

The rationalistic interpretation of sport and physical education has been advanced largely through the work of Osterhoudt. According to his interpretations, sport and physical education emerge from man's "rational impulse to self-knowledge" (Osterhoudt, 1973, p. 339), should be fashioned "by a rational, self-conscious, and intellectual interest" (Osterhoudt, 1973, p. 350), and, in the end, should contribute to and be an expression of an individual's rational, self-consciousness. The body, according to this view, is seen as an integral aspect of an "organically unified and developing self," and with the mind as "distinct participants in the organic union of life" (Osterhoudt, 1981, p. 22).

Vitalistic interpretations of sport and physical education have been advanced in Slusher's (1967) existential-tending *Man, Sport and Existence* and in the phenomenologic-tending work of Kleinman (1979), Kaelin (1979), Meier (1979), and Gerber (1979), most notably. According to these vitalistic interpretations, sport and physical education must contribute to authentic human existence and fulfillment. Through "meaningful movement" individuals become aware of body-subject rather than learn about body-object. The body is not seen as an instrument to use or an object to overcome in movement, sport, and physical education. Rather it "opens" man to or makes possible an experience of self through movement, sport, and physical education. As Meier (1975) suggests,

> Sport, as a vibrant form of human endeavor capable of manifesting and transmitting affective stages and meanings, may be viewed both as a symbolic medium and as a potentially artistic enterprise capable of releasing and celebrating the creative subjectivity of the participant. (p. 179)

CONCLUSION

From this one is led to the question of the relevance of the humanistic view of the mind-body relationship for sport and physical education. A culture's regard for and practice of sport and physical education are fashioned, in large measure, by the views it holds of the body and its relation to the mind. An objective and instrumental regard for the body, body-object, views the body as something to be used in sport. According to this view, sport and physical education are to be devoted to increasing the efficiency of the body-object. A subjective and intrinsic

---

[2]This is not to suggest that all resolutions of the problem within sport and physical education have been of a humanistic sort. The realistic-tending view, for example, has been advanced by Eleanor Metheny (1968) in *Movement and Meaning* and Paul Weiss (1969) in *Sport: A Philosophic Inquiry*. The spiritualistic-tending view has been advanced by Eugen Herrigel (1971) in *Zen in the Art of Archery*.

regard for the body, body-subject, views the body as an integral feature of a unified self. According to this view, sport and physical education are to be devoted, in the case of rationalistic humanism, to the development and expression of individual self-consciousness and, in the case of vitalistic humanism, to the experience and expression of self.

REFERENCES

Broekhoff, J. (1972). Physical education and the reification of the human body. *Gymnasion,* **9**, 4-13.

Gerber, E.W. (1979). My body, my self. In E.W. Gerber & W.J. Morgan (Eds.), *Sport and the body: A philosophical symposium* (pp. 181-187). Philadelphia: Lea and Febiger.

Husserl, E. (1965). *Phenomenology and the crisis of philosophy* (Q. Lauer, Trans.). New York: Harper and Row.

Kaelin, E.F. (1979). Being in the body. In E.W. Gerber & W.J. Morgan (Eds.), *Sport and the body: A philosophical symposium* (pp. 167-176). Philadelphia: Lea and Febiger.

Kleinman, S. (1979). The significance of human movement: A phenomenological approach. In E.W. Gerber & W.J. Morgan (Eds.), *Sport and the body: A philosophical symposium* (pp. 177-180). Philadelphia: Lea and Febiger.

Kockelmans, J.J. (1967). *The philosophy of phenomenology: The philosophy of Edmund Husserl and its interpretation.* Garden City, New York: Doubleday.

Mehta, J. (1971). *The philosophy of Martin Heidegger.* New York: Harper Torch Books.

Meier, K.V. (1979). Embodiment, sport and meaning. In E.W. Gerber & W.J. Morgan (Eds.), *Sport and the body: A philosophical symposium* (pp. 192-198). Philadelphia: Lea and Febiger.

Osterhoudt, R.G. (1973). An Hegelian interpretation of art, sport, and athletics. In R.G. Osterhoudt (Ed.), *The philosophy of sport: A collection of original essays* (pp. 326-359). Springfield, IL: Charles C. Thomas.

Osterhoudt, R.G. (1981). The mind-body problem in world intellectual history: The case of sport in personalistic monotheism. In U. Simri (Ed.), *Physical education and sport in the Jewish history and culture* (pp. 19-30). Natanya, Israel: Wingate Institute for Physical Education and Sport.

Thilly, F., & Wood, L. (1957). *A history of philosophy.* New York: Holt, Rinehart and Winston.

Singer, P. (1983). *Hegel.* New York: Oxford University Press.

Slusher, H.S. (1967). *Man, sport and existence: A critical analysis.* Philadelphia: Lea and Febiger.

Zaner, R. (1964). *The problem of embodiment: Some contributions to a phenomenology of the body.* The Hague: Martinus Nijhoff.

Teleology and fitness: An Aristotelian analysis

Cliff Balkam
The American University

THE STATUS OF EXERCISE

Until recently, the responsibility for studying and reflecting upon exercise and its product, physical fitness, has been divided by our society between two different groups: "phys ed majors," often student athletes more concerned with team sports and the pursuit of victory than with the meaning of these activities; and exercise physiologists, whose references to VO_2 max, oxygen dissociation curves, and body chemistry assure their being understood by few other than themselves.

However, this is changing. The running boom and the fitness revolution have now endured longer than the typical lifespans of fads in this country and appear to have become well ensconced in our cultural landscape. This means that there is a much greater demand for reflection on the exercising-for-fitness experience than before. More importantly, it means that there is a much broader substrate of human experience of this phenomenon, with all the components that make it up: physical, emotional, intellectual, psychological, and, some would maintain, aesthetic and spiritual. This broadening of the societal base of experience of exercise and sport is one of the conditions that make this conference both timely and possible.

In this context, then, I would like to pose and attempt to answer a question—What status does exercise, specifically exercise for fitness, have? Exercise for fitness is a specifically human experience, with all of the dimensions of humanity that theologians, philosophers, and poets are prone to reflecting upon: mind and body, human emotions, human psychology, the search for meaning, triumph and failure, the individual and the group, and the task of self-integration. In fact, the human experience of exercising for fitness is as suitable and noble a subject for philosophical reflection as all of the other subjects the philosophers have typically focused on over the centuries. The intimate involvement of the body may make exercise a superior vantage from which to pose the mind-body question that has so bedeviled the world's great thinkers.

ARISTOTLE: CAUSALITY AND TELEOLOGY

My task will be to apply some of Aristotle's notions to the phenomenon of exercising for fitness. I will do this by first using these notions to derive a definition of health, then a definition of fitness, which goes beyond and at times conflicts with health. I will then try to draw out some of the implications of these models of health and fitness for an understanding of the mind-body relationship.

It must be remembered that the *Physics*, where Aristotle adduced the four causes, comes from an era about 2,000 years before the emergence of what we call modern science from the "natural science" or "natural philosophy" that Aristotle helped invent. Aristotle, upon observing the world, or nature, found it profoundly intelligible. He found the regularities of nature translucent to rational understanding. Much of his natural philosophy, including the four causes, represents his effort to spell out, in rational terms, the intelligible patterns he found inherent in natural objects. Although he was a careful observer, Aristotle was certainly no strict experimentalist. Still, his efforts to lay bare the intelligible patterns of natural phenomena are useful to us today in trying to make sense of exercise as a human experience. We have what we need of scientific findings; it is Aristotle's broader effort at elucidating an intelligible pattern to physical phenomena that can show the way for a similar effort on our part.

Let us, then, review Aristotle's four causes and spend some time in particular on his idea of the final cause and the related notion of teleology. I will then use these to arrive at definitions of human health and fitness.

Aristotle's exposition of the four causes takes place in the *Physics*, a "scientific" treatise concerned with the motion, or change of physical things (Bambrough, 1963). In the *Physics*, Aristotle holds that all entities subject to change can be understood in terms of four causes: the material cause, the formal cause, the efficient cause, and the final cause. Aristotle did not understand cause solely the way we do, that is, as a force or entity provoking a change or effect. Rather, the causes are the inherent or underlying principles which account for an entity's having a determinate existence, or moving from one determinate form of existence to another determinate form of existence. To understand a thing is to understand its causes; to understand a thing's change is to understand its causes. The causes capture and define a thing's intelligibility, and as previously stated, Aristotle found the world profoundly and inherently intelligible. In review, the causes are as follows:

- *Material*—that out of which the thing is made, its "stuff" or substrate, or raw materials.
- *Formal*—that into which a thing is made, or the pattern or organization that characterizes it and makes it what it is, that is, a member of a particular group or species. When any thing is named, it is by referring to the formal cause it shares with other similar things.
- *Efficient*—that which makes the thing, the immediate source of change or "formation." Thus, the father is efficient cause of the child, or the painter of the painting. This is the sense of cause which prevails in our language.
- *Final*—that for which the thing is made, its purpose or end. In a way, the final cause is the realization of the possibilities that are implicit in the formal cause,

in that anything must operate within the limits of its own nature in realizing its potentialities. The final cause is easy to grasp when man-made objects or human activities are considered. Thus, the clothing is made for warmth or modesty, the chair made to support the body at rest or at work. Similarly, with activities, a person walks to go to the store, plays a game to relax or for health. It is neither difficult nor controversial to identify the purposes or ends of these entities or activities.

The difficulty arises when the final cause is applied to natural objects (as Aristotle does). It appears that Aristotle is imputing to nature the purposefulness we normally attribute only to intelligent beings. This seeming personification or anthropomorphic treatment of nature has caused difficulties for later philosophers (see Cohen, 1931/1978), and I have neither the scope nor the skill to solve them here. On the other hand, many biologists admit that the best way to characterize the behavior of living organisms is as purposive, where the ultimate purpose is to preserve or promote life (Rensch, 1971). However, there can be no disputing that Aristotle held a teleological, or end-oriented, understanding of nature. Actually, Aristotle's teleological understanding of nature appears to anticipate Darwin's secular or agnostic teleology, the doctrine of natural selection. In the *Physics*, speaking of how different parts of the body have developed, Aristotle (Bambrough, 1963) observes:

There is the problem of knowing what there is to keep nature from acting without a purpose, and not because things are best as she does them....What is to keep it from being of necessity, for instance, that one's front teeth come up sharp and suitable for cutting things up, and that the molars are flat and useful for grinding food? One would then say that these things did not happen purposely, but came about by accident. It is the same with all the other parts in which purpose seems to be present. On this view, all things that accidentally turned out to be what they would have become if they had had a purpose were preserved spontaneously, once they had come together in a suitable fashion; things that did not turn out this way perished, and continue to do so....

This argument, and others like it, are the ones that might make one at a loss to know whether there is a purpose in nature; but it is in fact impossible for things to be like that. For these and all natural objects either always or usually come into being in a given way, and that is not the case with anything that comes to be by chance or spontaneously....If, then, we think that things happen either by accident or for a purpose, and if it is not possible for them to happen by accident or spontaneously, then they must happen for a purpose....Thus, there is purpose in things that come to be and exist by nature. (pp. 224-225)

Aristotle seems to be holding that as we observe the regularity or orderliness of nature, the "laws of nature," we are seeing the teleological aspect of nature at work. By this account, knowing nature and its laws means knowing nature's purpose or ends.

Modern science, on the other hand, takes the same orderly behavior of natural objects and seeks to account for this orderly or predictable behavior while expunging the teleological interpretation as systematically as possible. The closest thing to a teleological account of nature found in modern science is the Darwinian doctrine of natural selection and survival of the fittest found in his theory of evolution. This account of evolution is agnostic at best on the question of purpose in nature, if not antithetical to teleology.

For all of the precision and accuracy science gains by its rigorous method, still it gives something up. This something concerns the individual who like us is trying to assess the human meaning of the human experience that science can measure and describe. Thus, in the case of exercise, the exercise physiologist can tell you, in stunning detail and with remarkable accuracy, the changes taking place in your body during and after exercise. However, the scientist can only be silent at the question: "What does this exercise mean to me, as an intelligent embodied person?" It is to attempt an answer to this question that Aristotle's notion of a natural teleology can be fruitfully applied; while Aristotle's causes are not rigorously scientific, they can serve as tools in a peculiarly human attempt to uncover the intelligibility in a distinctively human activity, that is, exercising for fitness.

TELEOLOGY AND A MODEL OF HEALTH

Before considering fitness, it should be helpful to apply the Aristotelian notion of teleology to the body, its organs and systems, and see how this enables us to construct a model of health. This will serve as a point of departure for discussing fitness which will be seen as existing further down a continuum of human bodily function at some remove from health.

A teleological analysis of human organs and systems is, at first glance, embarrassingly simple. It consists of asking of the liver, the skeletal muscles, the brain, for example, "What is the organ's purpose, what is it for?" Thus far, this question differs little, if at all, from the question posed by the physiologist, "What does this organ *do*, and how exactly does it do it?" The only difference appears to be that the physiologist expunges the teleological content from the question; the answer will be virtually the same. Increasingly, scientists give impressively precise and detailed answers to the questions of function, or physiology, that they pose for themselves. One of their findings is that virtually all human organs and systems have a range or continuum of possible function, from little or no function to an exceptionally high level of function, with numerous gradations in between. By studying large populations, scientists have been able to assign statistical distributions to these different gradations of bodily function. This sort of enterprise has been the special concern of the exericse physiologists, who can tell you that only "x"% of the population has a VO_2 max of 68 ml O_2/kg/min or that only "x"% of the male population can deadlift two times his body weight. Similarly, the distribution of average resting pulse, aerobic capacity, and body fat composition throughout the population can be determined. These measurements can form a statistical model of normal function and, in a somewhat primitive sense, of health itself, where too great a deviation from the norm is to be thought unhealthy or exceptionally healthy.

Further, the scientists study bodily functions in minute detail, down to the cellular level and farther, to the chemicals whose reactions appear to drive many processes at a larger or macro level. A certain normative definition of bodily function comes from this sort of examination as well, not to mention an understanding of what is happening when things go wrong in the body. Thus, disease as a departure from normal function comes to be defined and studied.

Any Aristotelian-inspired effort to understand the purposes of human bodily functions would ignore these scientific findings at its peril. In fact, Aristotle's contribution to philosophy, it might be argued, was to encourage the freest rein for intellectual inquiry while uncompromisingly acknowledging the reality of physical and sensible beings. Thus, this philosophical attempt to grasp the purpose of bodily organs and systems must incorporate the physiologists' definitions of function at the micro level, and the range of possibilities for the function of those organs and systems at the macro level.

We are now ready to reformulate the question with the appropriate input from science: "What are the purposes of these organs and systems which function within scientifically defined parameters *for me*, an intelligent, embodied person who makes choices about how I live my bodily life?" This question acknowledges that there are purposes inherent in the design or structure of bodily organs and systems, and that these can be described in detail by physiologists. But there is more to the question. Unlike animals, who invariably live out the narrow range of possibilities implicit in their bodily structures, we humans have a wide range of choices and possibilities as to how to live out our bodily existence. In a word, we can in part choose our own purposes rather than having them assigned us solely by our biology, as they are in animals.

It is here, in the arena of human purposes and choice, that the question of human health arises. Physiological integrity and absence of injury or disease are not health per se, but the necessary conditions for health. Given these, health emerges from the relationship of human purposes expressed in behavior and bodily purposes inherent in the design and function of human organs and systems. Optimal or normative health consists in a harmonious relationship between behavior and bodily function. Put in more teleological terms, health consists of a congruence between human purposes and the purposes implicit in how our bodies are designed and function. Conversely, ill-health consists in a poor match or conflict between behavior and bodily function.

To illustrate this, consider the phenomenon of muscle atrophy. If muscles are not used, they wither away. Clearly, muscles are made to contract; they lose their power (their very being, it could be said) when they are not called upon to contract. As another example, consider the liver's function in the catabolism of alcohol. It seems the normal liver can digest 1 to 2 oz of alcohol daily. If a person assigns his liver three or four times that amount, the liver will eventually break down under the excess load. For these, as for most other organs, sufficient use and appropriate use are necessary for the attainment of health. How we use our body and its components is a matter of behavior and, we must admit, a matter of the choices that are implicit in the habits we accumulate.

While the functions of our organs and systems are given in our genetic inheritance, what we do with those functions is a matter of behavior which is itself a matter of choice. Health is not a given; the conditions for its attainment, that is, physical integrity, absence of injury or disease, may be given, but health itself is an achievement. It can be achieved only by intelligently choosing behaviors compatible with the purpose built into our bodies. The ongoing achievement of health is the answer to the question, "What is the purpose of these organs and systems for me?"

FITNESS AND THE CONFLICT WITH HEALTH

At first glance, fitness appears to differ from health in degree, but not in kind. The healthy person can jog five miles in an hour; the healthy person aspiring to fitness wants to run eight or nine miles in an hour. Surely fitness represents merely a "place" further down the continuum of bodily function than that occupied by the healthy person. In statistical terms, the fit person seeks the position 2 standard deviations from the mean, while the healthy cluster around the mean. In terms of measurable bodily function, this model of the fit person being more healthy than the merely healthy person is correct. However, there are two reasons why this model is wrong, forcing us to conceive fitness as differing from health in kind, not degree.

First of all, it must be noted that health is the optimal mode of human being. It is the appropriate, intelligently chosen realization of potencies implicit in bodily design and function. It is the harmonious state of being resulting from the mind choosing purposes expressed in behavior that are consistent with the purposes inherent in bodily function. Health is the happy state of enjoying bodily existence. As such, it is an end in itself, a desideratum for no other reason than the sheer happiness that attends it.

Fitness, on the other hand, is a bodily state of being that has some extrinsic goal, usually a performance goal, as its object. The person striving for fitness has not the state of fitness or physical capability as an end. Rather, it is the ability to attain some physical accomplishment like running a 6-min mile, beating an opponent at a physical game, or winning a ballet competition that is the goal. In sum, health terminates in a harmonious state of physical well-being; fitness goes through conditioning to a state of physical capability and terminates in some performance goal or activity, often a competitive one. Thus, health and fitness differ in their goal-orientation, or in the choices made by the individuals pursuing them.

Secondly, health and fitness normally differ in kind in the actual physical state which is pursued. Where health seeks a harmonious relationship between human purposes and bodily functions, the pursuit of fitness introduces disharmony and outright conflict into this relationship. This is so due to the extrinsic and fleeting nature of the goal that is sought in the pursuit of fitness. One cannot possess a playing field victory or a world record in one's body the way one can possess good health in one's body. Those goals are achieved by means of the body's having been brought to a certain condition, but they are still extrinsic to the body.

In other words, pursuing the extrinsic goals of fitness makes the body and its condition a means to an end. This contrasts with the state of health, where the harmonious relationship of bodily function and intelligently-chosen behavior is an end in itself. Clearly, then, the athlete with an extrinsic fitness goal strives for a bodily condition much farther down the continuum of bodily function than that with which the person merely seeking health would be content. The higher the level at which the athlete would compete, the farther along this continuum he must go.

This pursuit of excellence has its price, however. The fitness-oriented athlete, by making his body a means to an end, puts his health at risk. It is quite common for the competitive athlete to injure himself in the course of training for competition, as well as in competition itself. Frequently, the injury results from placing a greater workload on an organ or system than it is yet able to sustain, as in the example of alcoholism cited earlier. Training for fitness exceeds the appropriate use that is the norm for the pursuit of health. Thus, traumatic or overuse injuries are the normal by-product of the pursuit of fitness goals, where the magnitude of the end exceeds the capabilities of the bodily means of its attainment. Ironically, the athlete has in common with the alcoholic, the glutton, and the drug abuser the overuse of an organ or system which results in some form of breakdown. Thus, the pursuit of the extrinsic goals of the athlete is in principle at odds with the pursuit of health. Once the athlete is injured, whether in training or competition, this conceptual or potential conflict between health and fitness is realized in fact. Injury is the scandal of pursuit of fitness.

This is not to say that athletes pursuing certain fitness or competitive goals are unhealthy by virtue of this pursuit. On the contrary, many of them are exceptionally health, at least in terms of the bodily functions the physiologists can measure. The point is that the good health they enjoy is a by-product of the finely honed physical condition they are trying to achieve. Being in good health is incidental to being in physical condition to attain the performance goal. When uninjured, the athlete is in better physical condition than the merely healthy person. However, the athlete's health is always at risk: the healthy athlete is the athlete who, at the moment, is free of injury. The athlete who remains injury-free usually is not training as hard or competing as vigorously as his rivals, nor will he probably be as successful. Thus, risking injury is the price of success in competition.

Why are so many people willing to go to such lengths in training and competition at such risk to their health? Although exploring this question could be the basis for another chapter, we can advert to one aspect of this Aristotelian analysis that answers this question in part. The sheer pleasure that comes from physical movement in dance, sport, and various forms of locomotion is the existential discovery that the body is made for movement. Movement–swift, graceful, strong, elegantly controlled movement is the end, or *telos*, of our skeletons and musculatures. The pleasure we derive from running, cycling, rowing, and swimming comes from the inarticulate realization that this is what we are for, that bodily, we were made for this. Similarly, when we witness a gravity-defying drive to the basket, a magnificently executed touchdown pass, or a deeply moving *pas de deux*, we realize, for our species, that we were made for *that*.

In this exuberance of movement we know ourselves, and the magnificent images evoked by professional athletes spur many of us to test ourselves further in training and in competition. Even if healthy, we cannot but wonder how much speed, strength, grace, or force is still hidden in our hearts and muscles. Of course, there is only one way to find out, and that is to train and compete, if only with ourselves.

From this perspective, the mind-body problem is not such a problem, at least not existentially. The exercise of the body results in joy or happiness, the proper fulfillment of the soul. In pursuing health, the mind or soul makes intelligent choices about behavior, acknowledging the purposes implicit in the body and helping the body attain those ends. Health itself consists of a sort of body-soul harmony, that is, between behavior and bodily functions. By definition, there is no mind-body problem here. I think that by examining and resonating more deeply with our own experience of health, or embodied well-being, and fitness, or the bodily exploration of human possibilities, we will come to a greater appreciation of our beautiful, composite nature.

REFERENCES

Bambrough, R. (Ed.). (1963). *The physics: The philosophy of Aristotle* (J.L. Creed, Trans.). New York: Mentor Books.

Cohen, M. (1978). *Reason and nature.* New York: Dover Press. (Original work published 1931)

Rensch, B. (1971). *Biophilosophy.* (C.A.M. Sym, Trans.). New York: Columbia University Press.

Cultural narcissism and the resurrection of the indecent fitness machine: Problems and possibilities

Candace J. Norton
Georgia Department of Education

The world of exercise, once framed in a caste system of mammoth men playing football and anorexic girls dancing, is elbowing for room to expand its paradigm and allow for diverse, varied, and exchanged roles in participation. We are experiencing a return to the sincerity of living and experiencing our own bodies. One manifestation of this return is the resurrection of fitness.

Part of what this expansion is about is returning to our personal power, our center, our harmony. However, our "cement-condominium" consciousness will not allow the narcissim of the '70s, the "Me Decade," to come to such a simple next step. The personally liberating and enriching fitness experiences of today are intermingled with and cannot be easily separated from numerous ways of separating mind from body, intention from action, and object from experience: for example, commercialism and mass marketing, the tyranny of slenderness and the politics of fat, obsessions with youth and the spectacle of the body, cosmetic fitness, and the rehabilitation of body-objects including heart muscles, bustlines, gluteals, and waistlines.

In this chapter I discuss conceptions of fitness in physical education: the wellness renaissance, holistic conceptions of fitness, and mutual problems of East and West regarding the body and fitness such as obsession with body weight, eating disorders, and compulsive exercise. I conclude with ideas concerning revisioning the concept of holistic fitness in physical education.

THE FITNESS/WELLNESS RENAISSANCE

Physical education has been concerned with the teaching of sport, dance, and exercise forms in multiactivity, broadly based programs encompassing three primary themes: "Fitness is our focus, sport is our substance, and movement is our meaning" (Ulrich, 1979, p. 3). Fitness activity through various exercise forms is one of the oldest and most developed themes of education. We have returned to the fitness theme in our profession. Two decades ago, Eleanor Metheny described these periodic returns as follows:

> At each stage in the development of educational thought, physical education has tried to move forward; but at each stage, we have found it necessary to retreat and fire our old biological guns to ward off both real and imagined attacks made by other educators. We have made good use of our Nineteenth Century muskets. We have trained them on state legislatures to win many battles for laws and requirements; and, recently, we have triggered them with evidence that European children are more adept than American children in touching their toes, and won for physical fitness a quasi-cabinet post in our national government. At the moment, it appears that the wheel set in motion by the physical trainers of the Nineteenth Century has come full circle. We are back where we started from a hundred years ago, and the tattered old biological banner of physical fitness is again waving triumphantly from our educational battlements. (Metheny, 1965, p. 101)

The fitness experiences of today are not the same as those in the traditional "nineteenth century musket" approach. The fitness approach of today has been redirected into a positive health/wellness theme. The fitness renaissance cannot be easily separated from the wellness movement. Wellness is defined as more than the absence of disease. It is the presence of high-energy levels, fitness, alertness, self-assertion, freedom from destructive habits, self-awareness, confidence, creativeness, and satisfaction with basic life decisions. Wellness assumes that each individual can manage his or her health by increasing self-responsibility, longevity, and improving the quality of life.

FITNESS AND THE BODY: PROBLEMS

Conflicting concepts of holistic fitness

The primary advocates of the health-fitness or wellness theme are exercise physiologists, fitness buffs, and health promoters, falling on a continuum between "paramedics" and "gurus." All intone a vision of well-being based on a viewpoint of holistic or total fitness. Problems stem from conflicting conceptions of the terms *total* and *holistic*. The paramedics wear white lab coats, are certified by the American College of Sports Medicine (ACSM), give graded exercise tests, pinch fat, extract blood, plunge bodies into underwater weigh tanks, prescribe exercise, take blood pressure, rehabilitate heart patients, and charge fees for services rendered.

Despite the term *total fitness*, most research and programming is on the body-object. Most physical educators rarely consider the body in any way "but as a thing in the environment to be dissected, manipulated, treated, improved and utilized as an instrument for achievement" (Gerber, 1973, p. 16). Some think that holistic means attention to differing camps of separate parts within a time unit. Some of these camps variously consist of (a) components of fitness, such as cardiovascular endurance, flexibility, and body composition; (b) approaches to wellness, such as health risk factor appraisal, stress management, smoking cessation, physical fitness prescription, and nutrition analysis; and (c) domains of personal experiencing, such as cognitive, affective, and motor.

The gurus promote exercise as a panacea, taking us from darkness into light, from depression to euphoria, from "before" to "after," from sloth to Richard Simmons, from yoga tennis to inner skiing. A heavy emphasis is put on feeling in the sensory rather than the emotional sense. On the other hand, the paramedic approach to fitness is rather like engineering in that it quantifies fitness. The guru approach encourages consciousness of sensations such as the stretch reflex and awareness of how the sensations are personally meaningful. This leads one to suspect that the guru method is just another manifestation of Christopher Lasch's "New Narcissism." "It requires that the athlete focus on internal states to a degree that more conventional athletic thinking regards as downright self-indulgent" (Jerome, 1980, p. 301).

This contrast between the paramedic and guru path to holistic fitness illuminates one facet of a parallel ideological battle between the mystical and nonmystical in sport. There is a strong Eastern influence in sport today coming primarily from the martial arts. This influence emphasizes balance, economy of motion, centering, harmonious use of the body, and various other unusual states of mind and body. Proponents include Michael Murphy, Esalen's co-founder, Timothy Gallwey, and George Leonard. The traditional school in sport, the nonmystical, always views itself as proudly no-nonsense. "Cut the bull....Get the job done, knock off the stuff about nonordinary states of consciousness, and execute the fundamentals, harder, faster, and let the chips fall as they may" (Jerome, 1980, p. 302). The new athlete is more curious and accepting of new ideas and possibilities and is willing to use the processes of self-absorption, self-reflection, and awareness.

Attitudes toward the body and fitness

These conflicting conceptions of holism in fitness and sport are an extension of the oldest cultural issue, the mind/body problem. This problem, at least 2,000 years old, has appeared in our time in two forms: body as adversary of mind and spirit, and body as decorated and decorative object. "As the adversary of mind, the body must be overcome, disciplined, so that the intellect can devote itself to the pursuit of ideas and ideals" (Naess, 1981, p. 53). Exercise the body because a sound mind needs a sound body to exist within. But keep the body in its place.

> Prune it like a garden, walk it like a pet, keep it neat and trim and odor free and control it....As an aesthetic object, the body must be transformed to reflect present standards of beauty and become an appealing, subtle, well ordered shell, the suitable vessel for the rational, civilized mind to inhabit or use. (Naess, 1981, p. 53)

Consistency of attitude exists in Buddhist and Christian thought toward the body. Early Christian writers reviled the body, and the struggle to dominate the body still remains in the mainstream of Western culture. Although much of Buddhist thought reconciles so many of the opposites that we take for granted in the West and the Buddhist tradition idealizes the body, much of the training of the Buddhist monks reveals the opposite point of view. In his book on Buddhism, Conze (1959) refers to the education of monks who are taught to "view the material body as negative, repulsive, offensive, and disgusting." "Like the Christian, the Buddhist is not expected to delight or take pride in the body, but is taught to feel shame and disgust" (Chernin, 1981, p. 58).

Manifestations of mind/body problems

Several problems related to fitness currently exist as present day manifestations of the mind/body problem: obsession with body weight, eating disorders, and compulsive exercise. The obsession with body weight and the occurrence of eating disorders are becoming more prominent. Both disorders are primarily problems of females. Ours is an age fixated on food and bodies. In the recent decade of feminism, it is ironic that no serious effort has been focused on the obsession with slenderness as a form of oppression of women. This was also a time period when fashion proclaimed the ideal feminine beauty as boyish and childlike, for example, Twiggy, Brooke Shields, and Christine Olman. Marilyn Monroe of 1959 was, by current standards, fat!

During the 1960s, public awareness increased concerning the incidence of *anorexia nervosa*, that is, self-inflicted starvation. Hilde Bruch (1978), in her book entitled *The Golden Cage*, wrote that anorexia nervosa had increased tremendously in the last 20 years and that "one might speak of it as an epidemic illness, only there is no contagious agent; the spread must be attributed to psycho-sociological factors....I am inclined to relate it to the enormous emphasis that fashion places on slimness" (p. 27). Extreme thinness is valued in industrial societies where food is plentiful. Chernin (1981) postulated that during periods of history when women were without personal power and tied to their nurturing roles, they were allowed to appear more female. On the other hand, in times of supposed liberation, the ideal is one of slimness, even boyishness.

Bulimia, sometimes called *buliamarexia*, was defined in 1974 and became popularly known as the binge-purge syndrome, that is, periods of extreme gluttony followed by laxative abuse and/or self-induced vomiting. Schwartz, Thompson, and Johnson (1982) reported the following data: 56% of women aged 24 to 54 years diet; 76% of dieting women acknowledge doing so for cosmetic rather than health reasons; 70% of all 18-year-old girls feel fat; 25 to 50% of adolescent females in Western countries perceive of themselves as fat even though they are not; and 10 to 30% of women on college campuses engage in eating disorder behavior at some time during their college years. Nylander (1971) reported the incidence of anorexia included approximately 10% of adolescent girls in Sweden, and Ikemi et al. (1974) identified 5% of adolescent girls in Japan as anorexic.

Eating disorders seem to be increasing in many groups: adolescents as well as older women, men, and in many cultures, classes, and races. One interesting note is that males constitute 20% of the number of hospitalized anorexia patients in Russia and only 7% of similar patients in Europe and United States (Garfinkel & Garner, 1982). "No reports of anorexia have come from underdeveloped countries where the dangers of starvation and famine exist" (Bruch, 1973, p. 13). During other times in history, cultural attitudes toward physical appearance have resulted in disability, such as footbinding in China, which did not die out completely until the early 1920s (Lyons & Petreucelli, 1978).

L.M. Vincent (1980), a physician and dancer, in his book *Competing with the Sylph*, wrote about the many impressionable young dancers forced into destructive eating patterns by the weight obsessive dance subculture. It has been estimated that two thirds of eating disorder patients have some form of interest in sport, dance, or exercise to the degree that "the concentration on the body and the perfection of the body led them to express their difficulties in anorexic fashion" (Amdur, 1983, p. 30).

Physical fitness is described, as is physical attractiveness, in a subtly different way for females than for males. The flat belly and thin thighs are all. Vigorous, compulsive exercising aimed at burning calories is as common a problem with adolescent females as eating disorders. Compulsive exercising is a recent problem among middle-aged males. An article (Yates, Leehy, & Shisslak) in the February 1983 *New England Journal of Medicine* pointed out the similarities in personalities and conflicts between patients with anorexia nervosa and a group of male "obligatory" runners. The obligatory runner was one who ran 50 miles or more per week, was diet conscious, and had an above average need to control himself and his environment.

"Nowadays, overweight, aging, and ill health are considered moral lapses that one ought to 'do something about.' We hear: 'It's a disgrace the way she let herself go!' 'Don't eat that—you'll get fat and ugly!' " (Gross, 1982, p. 9). The prevailing belief is that no price is too high for thinness, including our health, and with this belief we must ask ourselves several questions: Have we allowed ourselves to become engrossed in the fitness renaissance without examining

- our role in the increased objectification of the body?
- the obsession with slenderness resulting in damaging disorders?
- the "spa mentality" of blatant commercialism?
- the compulsion to exercise to the point of negative addiction?
- our obsession with the cardiovascular system?

Does the value of self-responsibility espoused by the wellness movement invoke the necessity of feeling guilt for aging, illness, and obesity? Have we examined and explored the "somatic" dimensions of exercise sufficiently? Or do we continue to focus primarily on increasing our knowledge about exercise and on the instrumental values of exercise?

FITNESS AND THE BODY: POSSIBILITIES

Revisioning holistic fitness

Revisioning the concept of holism in fitness holds tremendous possibility. The evidence and respect for the body of life, what Hanna (1980) has termed the *somatic realm*, is a new cultural value. And if, as a culture, we have become fanatical about direct, subjective, personal experience (our cultural narcissism), "it is the antidote to centuries of conforming to external standards where the life of our bodies has had no decent place" (Naess, 1981, p. 54).

One key aspect of revisioning is to create an environment supportive of positive health practices. Fashion and diet industries and their impact on the symbolic illnesses of eating disorders can best be understood from a cultural point of view. A conscious struggle is necessary to acquire an imagery which speaks against our contemporary vision of our bodies, particularly women's bodies. We need to search for a vision "that will help us live comfortably within our own bodies, an imagery that is part of our effort to reclaim our bodies from a culture that has alienated them, along with so many other sources of our power and pleasure" (Chernin, 1981, p. 76).

Today, the average person finds physical activity inconvenient after his or her school years. Most are victims of the sedentary, overindulgent, emotionally stressful, affluent society that we have created. By early adulthood, aging effects and sedentary living have produced various syndromes: obesity, chronic low-back pain, weak abdominal muscles, high-neuromuscular tension, high-pulse rates, shortening of ligamentous tissues, and increased susceptibility to cardiovascular diseases, primarily hypertension and coronary heart disease (Falls, Baylor, & Dishman, 1980). A reasonable fitness program "based on individual needs and interests" is a logical step to a "solution for overcoming the harmful health effects from living in a highly mechanized and technical society" (Getchell, 1983, p. 9).

George Sheehan proposed two types of fitness programs. "One is the rational, practical, and physiological; the other, non-rational, mystical, and psychological" (Sheehan, 1978, p. 55). Personal fitness programs need to represent all aspects of fitness to be successful. They should include aspects of the disciplinary knowledge about exercise, aspects of exercise used to achieve instrumental values attributed to participation in exercise such as enhanced health, and aspects of the intrinsic values of exercise forms. More focus needs to be given to the intrinsic aspects of experiencing exercise for its own sake. "If movement is to be conceived of as being more than just a portion of reality to be studied or as a means to serve purposes extrinsic to itself, it must be entered into for its own sake" (Arnold, 1979, p. 178).

Steps toward holistic fitness

In order to increase possibilities in creating a holistic conception of fitness, changes must be made. Methods of achieving this goal are suggested as follows:

1. Promote self-integration and not fragmentation. Search for meaning and a sense of unity and well-being. Engage in theory-practice relationships in a more personalized and autobiographical manner. "Science cannot deal with ultimate meaning" (Macdonald, 1981, p. 135).
2. Emphasize wellness and strength. Focus on more than the prevention of coronary heart disease, low-back syndrome, and obesity. More people have died in our culture from trying to get thin than from being too fat.
3. Create an environment for fitness which supports long-term involvement and positive health practices, as well as systematic adherence. Focus on skills and support systems as well as knowledge.
4. Modify current behavior from a cultural rather than individual basis. Focus on family, work, and social organizations.

More specifically, we should incorporate a lifestyle which includes the following:

- physical fitness
- risk reduction including environmental hazards
- educated eating
- emotional well-being (lack of interpersonal skills is the largest form of stress)
- drug decision making (37% of people still smoke)
- occupational enrichment (70% lack fulfillment in work life)
- stress management skills (50 to 80% of visits to physician are stress related)

CONCLUSION

Complete body life, holistic fitness experience, comes not from reading books or listening to speeches about the body and physical activity; nor does it come from "getting into" a certain exercise form or from eating correctly. "It comes from a deeper inner listening to body-felt experience and a deep respect for body messages, a respect wholly equal to that given to messages from books, media, people and ideas" (Naess, 1981, p. 56). It is possible for all of us because it is a way of being as well as a way in which mind and body are one. Insight without corresponding action is impotent, yet characteristic of our cultural present. Our culture is imprisoned in its head. The time is right to get in touch with the soma, to increase our possibilities, to come home.

REFERENCES

Amdur, N. (1983, March 6). The toll conditioning can take on athletes. *The New York Times*, pp. 29-30.

Arnold, P.J. (1979). *Meaning in movement, sport and physical education*. London: Heinemann.

Bruch, H. (1973). *Eating disorders: Obesity, anorexia nervosa, and the person within*. New York: Basic Books.

Bruch, H. (1978). *The golden cage: The enigma of anorexia nervosa*. Cambridge: Harvard University Press.

Chernin, K. (1981). *The obsession: Reflections on the tyranny of slenderness*. New York: Harper and Row.

Conze, E. (1959). *Buddhism: Its essence and development*. New York.

Falls, H., Baylor, A., & Dishman, R. (1980). *Essentials of fitness*. Philadelphia: Saunders.

Garfinkel, P.E., & Garner, D.M. (1982). *Anorexia nervosa: A multidimensional perspective*. New York: Brunner/Mazel.

Gerber, E.W. (1973, December). *My body, my self*. Paper presented at the meeting of Texas Association for Health, Physical Education and Recreation, Dallas.

Getchell, B. (1983). *Physical fitness: A way of life* (3rd ed.). New York: Wiley and Son.

Gross, M. (1982). *Anorexia nervosa*. Lexington, MA: Collamore Press.

Hanna, T. (1980). *The body of life*. New York: Alfred A. Knopf.

Ikemi, Y., Ago, Y., Nakagawa, S., Mori, S., Takahashi, N., Suematsu, H., Sugita, M., & Matsubara, H. (1974). Psychosomatic changes under social changes in Japan. *Journal of Psychosomatic Research*, **18**, 15-24.

Jerome, J. (1980). *The sweet spot in time*. New York: Summit Books.

Lyons, A.S., & Petreucelli, R.J. (1978). *Medicine: An illustrated history*. New York: Harry N. Abrams.

Macdonald, J.B. (1981). Theory-practice and the hermeneutic circle. *The Journal of Curriculum Theorizing*, **3**, 130-138.

Metheny, E. (1965). *Connotations of movement in sport and dance*. Dubuque, IA: Wm. C. Brown.

Naess, J.L. (1981). The dancer's body. *Dance Scope*, **15**, 52-56.

Nylander, I. (1971). The feeling of being fat and dieting in a school population: Epidemiologic interview investigation. *Sociomedicine Scandinavia*, **1**, 20-36.

Schwartz, D.M., Thompson, M.G., & Johnson, C.L. (1982). Anorexia nervosa: The sociocultural context. *The International Journal of Eating Disorders*, **1**, 20-36.

Sheehan, G. (1978). *Running and being: The total experience*. New York: Warner Books.

Ulrich, C. (1979). Tones of theory revisited. In A.E. Jewett & C.J. Norton (Eds.), *Proceedings of the curriculum theory conference in physical education*, Vol. 1 (pp. 3-13).

Vincent, L.M. (1980). *Competing with the sylph*. New York: Andrews and McMeel.

Yates, A., Leehey, K., & Shisslak, C.M. (1983). Running: An analogue of anorexia. *The New England Journal of Medicine*, **308** (5), 251-255.

SECTION III

The Eastern view and its challenge

In the first essay of this section, Scott Duncanson points out that Eastern philosophy was not free from controversy. Separation of, and commitment to, either the inner or outer world was an issue confronting Confucians, Buddhists, and Taoists in the 13th century. Wang Yang-ming in his teaching and personal life "demonstrated that self cultivation is pointless unless it is applied to real world problems." He contended that "inner and outer learning are inseparable." Wang's unity of knowledge and action is remarkably like the Western phenomenological view: Every act is a physical manifestation of thought and intention.

David Ch'en maintains that the use of symbols in the martial arts is evidence of man's desire for unity with nature. Man's intentional and decision-making powers of motion and imagination bring "forth the metaphysical reality of the animal image in all the martial spirit and power it stands for. And then the desired unity of nature in man is consummated...this is the secret of mind-body transcendance."

In "The Importance of Being Stationary," Tetsunori Koizumi cautions us against an overcommitment to the Cartesian paradigm which causes us to "lose a sense of unity with nature" by treating it as "an object of rational inquiry separate from ourselves." The eastern concept of "no-action...is a way of acquiring knowledge while preserving that sense of belonging to nature." Koizumi's essay demonstrates a marvelous utilization of Eastern and Western thought and action presenting artistic examples of an aesthetic which moves us beyond art to a way of viewing ourselves and life.

Richard Schmidt and Michael Canic are the first two authors who bring us into the martial arts studio. Schmidt gives us a description of the origins of the martial arts, their pedagogical principles, the training environment, and the relationship of master to student. The objective is one of self-realization through the form; and thus, the experience may be regarded as spiritual education for the practitioner. Canic briefly recounts the development of Zen, tracing its roots from India to China and ultimately to Japan. In Zen the path to enlightenment is through meditation. The movement practiced in the development of skill may be regarded as a form of meditation. The role of the teacher is primarily that of demonstrator with little or no verbalization. "Words exist because of meaning; once you've gotten the meaning, you can forget the words." The role of the learner is to practice with a detached mind, a meditative mind in order to realize the essence or unity underlying the task. Learning is a nonrational process not grounded in a rational conception of space and time. Realization and enlightenment constitute an intuitive leap.

Angelika Förster and Adam Hsu alert us to some of the problems which emerge when attempts are made to place the martial arts in a Western setting. Förster states that the use of Western principles and practices will impose and inevitably alter the foundation upon which the Eastern form is built. This will result in a fundamental shift in the theory and practice of these forms. Therefore, she cautions us against a piecemeal and semiliterate knowledge of the Eastern movement forms and their philosophical bases.

Adam Hsu provides us with a good explication of the Chinese martial arts, their derivation, and their principles. A clear distinction is made between Eastern and Western approaches to activity and the difficulties involved in transmitting Eastern conceptions to Western practitioners.

The utilization of one Eastern form to enhance the practice of another is recommended by Lynda Mitchell in "The Role of Hatha Yoga in the Martial Arts." Mitchell points out that the martial art forms have yoga roots. Therefore, yoga principles not only are applicable, but enhance the martial arts objectives. Stretching, relaxation, breathing and awareness techniques emphasized in yoga will improve performance in the more combative martial art forms.

Gregory Olson and Norman Comfort III's paper on aikido provides us with insight into one of the most recently developed martial art forms. A brief history of aikido's development is followed by a statement of principles and an exposition on the purpose of technique. The *aikidoka* (student) practices more than a method of defense. The student aspires to harmonizing with nature, achieving a mind-body unity beyond "demonstrable physical laws (to a) way of life."

Paul Linden in "The Art of Aikido: Philosophical Education in Movement" goes beyond description and offers some strong recommendations both for education and physical education. Aikido's use of awareness and breathing techniques reveal and enable one to take a philosophical stance. Because of this, Linden concludes that physical education may be seen essentially as philosophical education. "Only when tasks are used primarily as vehicles for self-examination through movement will students have the opportunity to learn to use movement as a means of philosophical growth." A physical education based on this view would take on a new look. It would include such areas as the Eastern movement forms and movement awareness techniques such as those developed by Alexander, Feldenkrais, and Laban.

Lisa Hofsess and Mark Wheeler provide us with access to Eastern movement in the form of dance rather than in the martial arts. Each explores the relationship between Eastern and Western dance in her or his own way. An interesting contrast is drawn by Hofsess between Japanese Kabuki and American jazz. The cultural roots of each reveal many of the factors operating which cause such distinctions to emerge. It remains to be seen what effect the mixing of our cultures will have upon the traditional movement and dance forms. Hofsess' paper, in a way, echoes a basic theme pervading this entire volume.

Mark Wheeler traces the appropriation by modern dance of Eastern styles both literally and essentially. For example, while Ruth St. Denis copied the form, the technique of Martha Graham utilizes the concept and practice of breath as it is practiced in yoga and t'ai chi. In a sense, this is analogous to the way larger cultural changes are manifested. We seem to be moving from appropriation to dialogue. This in turn may be indeed the preliminary to "mutation" and finally to the paradigm shift currently underway. The authors of this section seem to be trying to provide us with a glimpse of this new world.

Unity of knowledge and action: The thoughts of Wang Yang-ming

Scott Duncanson
Georgia State University

The problem before us in thinking about sport and movement is the relationship between polar opposites—mind and body, thought and movement, inner person and outer performance, or knowledge and action. Because so much thought is divorced from action and so much action is devoid of thought, the disconnection of the two is a real dilemma in sport and movement, as it is in everyday life. The same dilemma was a central concern of the philosopher Wang Yang-ming in his role as a government bureaucrat, in his teaching, and in his personal development.

In Ming Dynasty China during the 13th century, a great gulf existed between practitioners of the orthodox Confucian model of strict literary study and "investigation of things" versus believers in the heterodox Buddho-Taoist ideal of contemplation upon natural virtue. The so-called Realists advocated worldly activity in service to the Emperor and to civilization, while the so-called Idealists tended to shun the trappings of social relations in favor of solitary meditation. Wang's greatest contribution to the neo-Confucian convergence of these polarized traditions was his assertion that inner and outer learning are inseparable and that one is impossible without the other if any genuine learning is to occur.

Several things about Wang Yang-ming's notion of the unity of knowledge and action merit our attention. First, he refused to accept the false dichotomy that divided his peers and refused to be labeled as a member of either camp. In short, he sought to reconcile a polarized situation among the scholarly community. Second, he actively reconciled the same kind of polarity in theory and in practice. Wang's personal adventures as a poet, bureaucrat, soldier, exile, courtier, hermit and teacher demonstrated that self-cultivation is pointless unless it is applied to real-world problems, and that the only way to confront social and political difficulties in an informed manner is to simultaneously confront oneself at every turn in seeking self-realization as a sage. Wang (Chan, 1963b, p. 30) said, "Knowledge is the beginning of action, and action is the completion of knowledge."

Third, the convergence of opposing schools of thought in Ming China provides us with a convergence of Asian and European philosophies. Wang's "unity of knowledge and action" is remarkably like Husserl's "life-world" and a whole range of phenomenological Western thinkers (Jung, 1965, p. 615). Although there are probably as many phenomenologies as there are phenomenologists, their fundamental position of encounter—where one acts in, on, and toward the world—seems to be in perfect agreement with Wang's.

The pivotal idea in this East-West convergence is *intentionality*. The Chinese word *yi* is translated as "thought," yet it refers also to "intention," as the Chinese language does not separate the operations of the intellect from those of the will. Aaron Gurwitsch (1964, p. 167) defines phenomenology as a theory of knowledge which is "concerned with phenomena...not with things and objects simply, but with things and objects as they appear through acts of consciousness." This active and interactive function of a consciousness engaged in events is an important link between Eastern and Western thought as well as between inner thought and outer activity in the individual.

Intention, that is, the act of consciousness, is what "connects" an athlete with his or her performance, game, or event. When there is true unity of knowledge and action, we witness a highly developed performance. A basketball player, for example, leading a fastbreak looks for an opening, and the act of looking constitutes a movement toward the opening. The decision to pass off is a movement toward a teammate, and the teammate's shot is intention itself, as the ball is willed toward the hoop.

Wang Yang-ming (Chan, 1963b, p. 93) said, "Knowledge in its genuine and earnest aspect is action, and action in its intelligent and discriminating aspect is knowledge." When we see an athlete's movement as a single event which fuses the polarities of thinking, knowing, acting, and completing a movement, we alter the artificial separation of knowledge *of* the phenomenal field from action *upon* the phenomenal field. That is what a dance instructor means when the dancers are merely showing technique, and she demands that they "Be there!" It is what a martial artist means when he says the mind broke the brick.

It should be noted that this fusion of knowledge and action is not just the idealized goal of an extraordinary performance. It is the common property of gifted athletes and weekend duffers because intentionality pervades our everyday thoughts and actions, for good or ill. Just as mental practice innervates the muscle fibers appropriate to the movement being imagined, extraneous thoughts in the midst of practice disrupt and detract from the performance by introducing extraneous physical movements. A pebble dropped into the pool of the mind creates ripples that expand outward. This ripple effect implies that every thought has its physical manifestation, and only if the thought is appropriate to the movement does its intentionality have a positive result.

The applications in the world of sport and movement are clear. A gymnast must maintain single-pointed concentration in order to direct his or her every intention toward precisely controlled interactions with the floor, bars, beam, rings, or horse. Runners are most unified, most at peace, and most effective when their thoughts reside in the striding of the legs, the pumping of the arms and the rhythm of breathing. We sometimes tend to take an engineering approach to performance, yet the first and last objective of an athlete must be unification in the physical.

We might find some implications for training, as well, in the teachings of Wang Yang-ming. To the degree that concentration can be taught, we should be teaching techniques for concentrating the mind on the activity at hand. We might employ the breathing techniques of yoga and t'ai chi ch'uan to literally inform an athlete's body and activity with additional energy, power, and purpose. Above all, we might try to instill the knowledge that knowledge is action, that action is knowledge, and that everything we do on both sides of the equation makes a difference.

In the traditional Chinese conception of being, mind-and-heart (*hsin*) is the seat of intention (*yi*). Mind-and-heart functions as both a receptive, prereflective agent of perception and learning, and as a creative instrument of volition. It is interesting that we are not narrowly talking about the brain, but the nervous system and the *heart*, as the center of knowledge and action that is engaged in events. Wang Yang-ming was talking about education in the physical.

Never straying from his concentration on the unifying thread running through diverse interests and responsibilities, Wang recommended sport and the arts to his students as an avenue for harmonizing intellectual pursuits with the real world. The state of engagement with events is central to making one's inner life concrete and one's outer life meaningful. "What is it that is called the person?" Wang (Chan, 1963a, p. 664) asked rhetorically. "It is the physical functioning of the mind."

REFERENCES

Chan, W.-T. (Ed.). (1963a). *A source book in Chinese philosophy*. Princeton, NJ: Princeton University Press.

Chan, W.-T. (Trans.). (1963b). *Instructions for practical living and other neo-Confucian writings by Wang Yang-ming*. New York: Columbia University Press.

Gurwitsch, A. (1964). *The fields of consciousness*. Pittsburgh: Duquesne University Press.

Jung, H.Y. (1965). Wang Yang-ming and existential phenomenology. *International Philosophical Quarterly*, **5**, 612-634.

Natural symbolism in Chinese martial arts

David Y. Ch'en
The Ohio State University

"Heaven evolves with unfailing force, therefore the superior man must strengthen himself without cessation," so says the sage in *The Book of Changes*, the oldest Chinese work on the philosophy of nature and human life (Wang Pi, 1967, p. 1b). This statement presents nature, here represented by the concept as well as the phenomenon of "heaven," not only as a source of inspiration of man's moral conduct but also as a model for his physical activities. In fact, the phrase "self-strengthening without cessation" has become frequently cited motto for physical education and a familiar inscription on trophies in sports in China. The enormous impact of this classic on Chinese thought and life is manifold, including the development of an intricate and extensive system of natural symbolism which has embellished and enlivened the Chinese civil and martial arts for more than 3 millennia.

PHYSICAL RESEMBLANCE OF NATURE

Concerning man's view of his relationship with nature, there was an early Chinese notion that a physical resemblance exists between the universe and man. This has been expressed in a popular creation myth that when P'an Ku, the first man who was born and lived in chaos, died, the members of his body were transformed into heavenly bodies and geographical formations, and his spirit manifested in atmospheric effects and climatic changes. From this the concept that the human body is a miniature universe is derived; this concept forms an essential part of the underlying metaphysical principle shared by the medical sciences and the martial arts of China. Chinese medicine and the art of individual combat known as *wu-shu* are twin disciplines, both specializing in the welfare of the human body, and the ultimate goal of both is to achieve the unity of nature and man.

In Chinese medicine, a unique aspect is the use of celestial symbols in physiological terminology, such as the naming of numerous acupuncture points on the human body. It is interesting to note that the acupuncture points system, which is essential to the physician's needle-healing techniques, is also utilized by the wu-shu practitioner of digitipunch techniques to temporarily disable or instantly destroy his opponent with finger tips. In both practices, although their purposes are diametrically opposed, natural symbolism plays the role of designating the vital parts and points of the human body with analogous objects or phenomena of nature.

IMITATION OF NATURE

Besides the physical similarity between the universe and man with which ancient Chinese interpretation of the structure and function of the human body is associated, another important concept in this philosophy of nature is man's benefit from his imitation of nature. This concept springs from the principle of "following nature" of Taoism, as found in the emergence of wu-shu systems. Shapes and postures, motions and maneuvers, contacts and interactions of myriad things in the creation have long inspired wu-shu masters in designing their systems of functional and effective forms of movements for the defense and the offense, for the empty-handed combat and the use of weapons. The naming of such terms, therefore, often contains natural symbols which reflect the imitation of movements of living things and the concept of unity of nature and man in those original designs.

ANIMAL SYMBOLISM

Among the natural symbols designating dramatic imitation of nature's action in all wu-shu systems, animal symbols play a major role. The earliest Chinese exercise for health and fitness, which paved the way for the rise and development of wu-shu practice, is the Five Animal Plays designed by the famed physician Hua T'uo of the 3rd century. Hua T'uo mimicked the characteristic postures and movements of the tiger, the deer, the bear, the ape, and the bird for the benefit of the human body. The motivation of his creation of the animal-imitating exercise is given in these words: "The ancient immortals engaged in the *tao-yin* method of breathing and exercise by imitating the bear's climbing the tree and the hawk's turning its head, stretching the body and moving the joints, in search of the way to everlasting youth (Chao Yeh, 1967, 9.65b-66a). This idea was derived from the earlier observation of Chuang Tzu (4th century B.C.), the Taoist philosopher, about the ancient practice "to exhale and inhale, to expel the exhaust air and receive the fresh air, and to imitate the bear's climbing the tree and the bird's spreading its wings and stretching its legs, in order to achieve longevity" (Kuo Hsiang, 1967, 6.114-115). In the complex systems of wu-shu that evolved in ensuing periods, animal play in theory and practice was closely followed, and symbolic animal names remained predominant in the terminology of styles and movement forms of various wu-shu systems and became more and more prolific and poetic as those systems developed.

For example, the creation of the T'ai-chi Ch'üan, perhaps the most popular of wu-shu styles in practice today, has been attributed to Chang San-feng, the 12th-century Taoist master and the alleged founder of the Wu-tang School. His fighting techniques were said to have been inspired by the struggle between a snake and a crane he chanced to watch in the mountain. Through centuries of evolution of the T'ai-chi system, such movement forms as "the white snake sticking out its tongue" and "the white crane spreading its wings" are still preserved. Much of the founding of the Wu-tang School and indeed of many other wu-shu schools may be labeled legendary due to the paucity of written records. Yet the undeniable fact remains that such pugilistic forms consistently and convincingly reflect man's imitation of animal behavior and its registration in animal symbolism in those early body movement designs.

Another leading wu-shu school, the Shao-lin, is even more deep-rooted in animal symbolism. The popular belief that Boddhidarma, the first patriarch of Chinese Ch'an (or Zen in Japanese) Buddhism, initiated the Shao-lin system in the 6th century is perhaps as debatable as the origin of the T'ai-chi. It is more reliably documented that in the 12th century, Pai Yü-feng, a noted layman wu-shu expert, converted to Buddhism, choreographed the famous Shao-lin system of five pugilistic styles, all named after animals: dragon, tiger, leopard, snake, and crane. During the same age, Yüeh Fei, a patriotic general fighting the invading Tartars in the North, brought forth a much larger version of animal plays for training his soldiers. It is a 12-set system in imitation of various beasts, birds, and reptiles—dragon, tiger, monkey, bird, camel, cock, hawk, swallow, snake, pigeon, eagle, bear—known as the Form and Mind School. Other varieties of animal plays can also be recognized in the Praying Mantis Style and the White Crane Style, each carrying a sort of inherited totemic emblem of its origin.

Wu-shu styles and their movement forms using animal terms fall into two categories: They may be *animal-related*, that is, the performer as dealing with the animal; or they may be *animal-modeled*, that is, the performer as the animal. To illustrate the two types of animal terms, one set of movements is called *taming the tiger*, an animal-related term; whereas a single movement in another style, with the right fist attacking the chest of the opponent from underneath the high-arched left arm, is called *the black tiger stealing the heart*, an animal-modeled term. Both refer to the same animal. Turning to the T'ai-chi, we notice that the very first movement in any variation of the system is called *retaining the sparrow's tail*, which is animal-related. Other such movement terms include *carrying the tiger back to the mountain, reaching up for the horseback*, and *drawing the bow on the tiger*. On the other hand, the forms described as *the mustang spreading its mane, the golden cock standing on one foot*, and *chased moneky stepping back* well illustrate the category of animal-modeled movement forms.

COMBAT IN ANIMAL SYMBOLS

The art of fighting with weapons in the Chinese tradition is just as abundant in animal symbols as the art of empty-handed combat. An interesting story of the Spring and Autumn period (722-481 B.C.) tells about the superb sworsdmanship of the Maiden of Yüeh, who was summoned by the king to advise him on martial arts. On her way to the royal court, she met an old swordsman who introduced himself as Master Yüan and who challenged her to a match. With due respect and humbleness, she accepted the challenge. Master Yüan snatched a bamboo branch and attacked her with it, and she responded with all her skills. In the end, Master Yüan suddenly jumped onto a tree and took leave. This mystifying episode seems to suggest that the Maiden of Yüeh was able to perfect the art of the sword with simian dexterity, flexibility, and unexpectedness she had learned from an ape, so that no swordsman in her days was her rival. This is known as the Maiden of Yüeh Sword Style; its authentic art is lost, but its original name has been preserved and always associated with Master Yüan, the ape.

Of animal images that are incorporated into the name of weapons, each associated with either the shape of the particular weapon or the style of its movements, the tiger, traditionally the foremost symbol of bravery, seems to claim almost the lion's share. So we have the *tiger's head hook*, the *tiger's tail club*, the Five Tigers Spear Style, and even the dramatic term of Tiger-Falls-on-a-Flock-of-Sheep Staff Style. The dragon, often taking the lead in the sequence of animal plays, by virtue of its symbolic royal stature fortunately is not forgotten in weaponry, but is only occasionally reflected in such a term as Coiled Dragon Staff Style. Among the single-edged swords, there are the *cow's ear sword*, the *elephant's trunk sword*, and, for a rather romantic diversion, the *mandarin duck's double swords*.

If we take a closer look at one weapon-fighting style, for example, the T'ai-chi Double-edged Sword, we are immediately aware of a number of movements designated with animal names. Some are *the phoenix spreading its wings*, which is a wide swing of the blade from low to high in the right, and *the mustang jumping over the mountain stream*, which is a forward and downward thrust with a jump and with both hands holding the sword. Apart from these animal-modeled forms, a perfectly illustrative form of animal-related movement is slicing left and right with the body leaning forward and advancing; it is termed *parting the grass to track down the snake*. This term, by the way, relates the animal symbol of snake with the plant symbol of grass. Another animal-plant combination term is found in *the white ape presenting a fruit*, described as holding the hilt with both hands and pushing the blade forward and upward, aiming at the opponent's throat—a thrust home.

Plant symbols, though not as frequently used as animal symbols, are also present in wu-shu terminology, especially in weaponry. For example, the spear, owing to the tassel fastened around the base of the spearhead, is called *flowering spear*. When the spear is in motion, the tassel will swing and spread like a huge flower in full bloom. Hence the southern school of Plum Blossom Spear, and in case the tassel is white, the northern school of Pear Blossom Spear. A narrow-bladed sword is known as *willow leaf sword*, mostly adopted by women by virtue of its lightness. One system of the double-edged sword is named *green duckweed sword* perhaps for its light, easy movements that suggest the buoyancy of floating water plants. The flora, however, being immobile and inactive by nature, yields to the fauna in the role of natural symbolism in the wu-shu arena of bodily movement.

The persistent use of animal symbols in the history of wu-shu may be superficially explained as a traditional way of describing those movement forms that resemble animal actions. Also, certain movement forms, especially those of later creations, have been named with familiar animal imagery as a matter of convention. But the deeper meaning of the symbolic language of wu-shu reaches beyond mere analogy of behavior between animals and man; for behind the physical resemblance, there is a metaphysical reality. We have now arrived at the point of paramount importance in our investigation of wu-shu as a martial art, and it calls for elucidation.

METAPHYSICAL REALITY

Notwithstanding that the Chinese wu-shu practitioner's mimicry of animal actions is initially conceptual, the mimetic acting itself is realistic. Mankind in its advancement of civilization has certainly unbashfully learned useful things from other members of the animal kingdom. The inventive ideas of an aircraft, a ship, a submarine, or a tank perhaps would not have ever been conceived without animal prototypes. The fact that in the Chinese wu-shu tradition human actions are associated with a host of fanciful animal images is not incidental, but rather it has sprung from a primitive need for survival commonly felt throughout the entire animal kingdom.

To the animal, to make certain vitally necessary movements in crucial moments of life, either defensive or offensive, is instinctive and limited by nature-endowed attributes in terms of the structure and function of the body; whereas to the wu-shu practitioner as martial artist, to adopt animal-imitating movements in a combat is intentional and benefited by his abilities of selection, modification, and combination of animal movements of various species. Hence, complex and competent fighting styles and movement forms have been designed which have proved effective in coping with diverse belligerent situations. Furthermore, each animal-imitating movement of an accomplished wu-shu master is not simply aping an animal action; it is a fresh, human kinetic creation with the dexterity of the body that is supported by accumulated inner energy and the concentrated power of the mind as a result of self-strengthening of the superior man.

Thus, motion and imagination together, through a long and painstaking process of contemplative and empirical experiences, eventually bring forth the metaphysical reality of the animal image and all the martial spirit and power it stands for, so enacted, and nature itself in a particular form, so recreated, in man. Then the desired unity of nature and man is consummated at a dramatic moment of human existence. This, I believe, is the secret of mind-body transcendence of the age-honored wu-shu tradition of Chinese martial arts, long codified in the system of animal symbols.

Finally, a certain beauty is witnessed in this art form that is adorned with such an enchanting symbolic language. Just imagine that the black tiger is to steal one's heart, or the white ape is to present one a fruit; the strike may be fatal, but the style is positively poetic.

REFERENCES

Chao Yeh. (1967). *Wu Yüeh ch'un-ch'iu* [The Spring and Autumn annals of Wu and Yüeh] (*Ssu-pu ts'ung-k'an* ed.). Taipei: Commercial Press.

Fan Yeh. (1967). *Hou Han shu* [The history of Later Han] (*Po-na* ed.). Taipei: Commercial Press.

Kuo Hsiang. (Anno.). (1967). *Nan-hua chen-ching* [The book of Chuang Tzu] (*Ssu-pu ts'ung-k'an* ed.). Taipei: Commercial Press.

Wang Pi. (Anno.). (1967). Chou Yi [The book of changes] (*Ssu-pu ts'ung-k'an* ed.). Taipei: Commercial Press.

The importance of being stationary: Zen, relativity, and the aesthetics of no-action

Tetsunori Koizumi
The Ohio State University

Creating tension between action and no-action, between motion and rest, plays a vital role in all forms of Japanese art. How such tension is created, needless to say, differs from one form of art to another. In the performing and martial arts, which involve bodily movement, the artist deliberately resorts to no-action in the literal sense of the word. In fact, mastering the art of controlling one's body and mind at the critical moment of no-action when all motion is frozen is generally regarded as a mark of highest artistic achievement.

There is no reason, however, why the aesthetics of no-action should be limited to the performing and martial arts; a state of no-action would not command the aesthetic value that it does in Japanese art if it were employed in only those forms of art which involve bodily movement. Although the word *no-action* needs to be interpreted in a figurative sense, the same artistic ideal is pursued in other forms of art as well. A master artist is one who, regardless of the artistic medium employed, is able to convert a state of no-action into one of high drama, full of imagery and suggestion.

An outstanding example of the effective use of no-action in visual art is Hokusai's woodblock print, "The Great Wave." As is true with any work of art which is recognized as a masterpiece, this work is never short of those qualities which appeal to our sensibility. Some may be awed by the sheer immensity of the wave, which is about to break and engulf precariously floating boats. Others may feel sympathy towards the people who are helplessly clinging to the swaying boats. Still others may be struck by the lively composition of the scenery highlighted by the use of bold lines.

"The Great Wave," to be sure, evokes all these feelings and sensations. But what is most remarkable about it is the skill with which Hokusai managed to create tension between action and no-action, between motion and rest, which is vital to Japanese art. For what Hokusai so masterfully captured is a movement temporarily frozen, a drama which is temporarily halted. As a result, we, the viewers, are thrust right into the uncharted space which lies between hope and despair, between life and death. Indeed, this work reminds us of the unsettling condition of our existence, of our frail endeavors against natural forces. All this existential anxiety crosses our minds in a flash as we view this world of wind, waves, and clouds—we are mere bubbles in the cosmic sea of mutability! How much, indeed, this work tells us about ourselves!

Hokusai's masterpiece thus exemplifies what the aesthetics of no-action is all about. For one thing, the aesthetics of no-action expresses an artistic ideal which cherishes economy of effort on the part of the artist in bringing out the maximal effect. More importantly, however, it reflects a state of high artistic achievement in which the artist, by recreating reality, becomes one with reality. But what does the aesthetics of no-action mean to us moderns who have long lost touch with such an intuitive mode of comprehending reality? This is the question we hope to explore in this chapter.

ZEN AND THE AESTHETICS OF NO-ACTION

Aesthetic principles of the Noh play

No form of Japanese art incorporates the aesthetics of no-action more explicitly than the Noh play. This is so not only because the Noh performance deliberately blends action and no-action, but also because Noh as an art form is founded on a definite set of aesthetic principles. We can infer what these principles are, thanks to Zeami, the principal figure in the development of Noh, who left us a number of critical essays on his art.

The main aesthetic principle underlying Noh, according to Zeami, is *yūgen* which roughly translates into "mystery" or "profundity." To be more specific, yugen is the term that characterizes the state of highest achievement in the Noh play as embodied in the beauty of form and movement. In Zeami's (1958, p. 295) own words, yugen refers to "a degree of artistry which is of that middle ground where being and nonbeing meet."

The influence of Zen Buddhism is apparent in these words. Noh, as a performing art, tries to recreate human drama which invariably involves tension between the pain of life and the stillness of death; this tension defines the middle ground between being and nonbeing, between life and death. How, then, does the Noh performance propose to guide the audience into this middle ground? This is where the aesthetics of no-action comes into play, as we find in the following words of Zeami (1958):

> Dancing and singing, movements and the different types of miming are all acts performed by the body. Moments of "no-action" occur in between. When we examine why such moments without actions are enjoyable, we find that it is due to the underlying spiritual strength of the actor which unremittingly holds the attention. He does not relax the tension when the dancing or singing comes to an end or at intervals between the dialogue and the different types of miming, but maintains an unwavering inner strength. This feeling of inner strength will faintly reveal itself and bring enjoyment. However, it is undesirable for the actor to permit this inner strength to become obvious to the audience. If it is obvious, it becomes an act, and is no longer "no-action." The actions before and after an interval of "no-action" must be linked by entering the state of mindlessness in which one conceals even from oneself one's intent. This, then, is the faculty of moving audiences, by linking all the artistic powers with one mind. (p. 291)

We can infer from these words that the moments of no-action acquire their importance, in the first place, from the importance of integrating the body and the mind. While the body engages in all kinds of actions in the performing arts, the mind unifies these actions by interspersing them with moments of no-action when the body is at rest. This is the way in which the tension between action and no-action, between motion and rest, is created in the Noh play. As a matter of fact, Zeami goes a step further by suggesting that the moments of no-action are the most enjoyable part of Noh. Here we find further evidence of Zen influence in which the mind is interpreted as the unifying principle of the cosmic process. To see how Zen philosophy underlies Noh, we must examine in more detail some of the characteristic features of Noh as a performing art.

There are many features of Noh which we can easily identify as Zen elements. First, there is the idea of simplicity which regulates the staging of the Noh play. Although the costumes worn by the Noh actors are colorful and elaborate, reminiscent of the artistic ideal of *miyabi* which characterized Heian court life, the Noh stage itself is a simple, rectangular structure. Moreover, the stage is usually left completely bare except for small gadgets called *tsukurimono* which are employed in some plays. This is one way of conveying to the audience that Noh relies heavily on the power of suggestion. The simplicity of the setting is reinforced by the simplicity of the actions themselves. Unlike the ballet dancer, the Noh actor, as a rule, is not expected to stand on tip-toe or leap in the air. The whole performance is one of graceful restraint, suggesting the stillness beyond this world. In fact, the Noh actors often wear the masks of ghosts, indicating that the audience is being invited to glimpse into another reality. The drama itself usually evolves around the theme of existential anxiety which is created by the tension between the pain of life and the stillness of death.

There is another interesting feature of Noh which reminds us of the Zen emphasis on the mind as the fundamental unifying principle. In Noh plays, the Buddhist priest plays the major role in pacifying the spirits of the ghosts who, having failed to find salvation themselves, return to this world to haunt the people with whom they used to associate in their former lives. The priest, with his enlightened mind, guides the ghosts to attain salvation as the drama draws to a conclusion. From a psychological point of view, Noh actually offers an interesting resolution of the conflict between animus and anima in the human mind by introducing three archetypal roles—the warrior, the woman, and the old man. In this triad, the old man, often appearing as a Buddhist priest, embodies the archetype of the wise old man in Jungian psychology. It is, therefore, possible to give a psychological interpretation to the aesthetics of no-action in Noh in terms of Jungian psychology as invoking "Self," the all-embracing aspect of the working of the unconscious mind (Jung, 1969).

If the mind is indeed the unifying principle in Noh plays, then the audience is expected to appreciate the world of yugen staged by these accomplished actors by participating in the drama with their own minds. As Zeami (1958) states, "What the mind sees is the essence; what the eyes see is the performance" (p. 302). In that the ghost plays a major role, *Hamlet* comes closest to creating the world depicted in Noh, especially in those Noh plays which are called *mugennoh*. Recall how Hamlet's mind's eye was able to see his father in that middle ground where being and nonbeing meet. If the aesthetics of no-action carries an epistemological implication, it thus comes down to this simple statement: What the mind sees is the essence; what the eyes see is the performance. Then, did not the fox remind the Little Prince (Exupéry, 1971, p. 87), "It is only with the heart that one can see rightly; what is essential is invisible to the eye"? In the state of mindlessness which characterizes the moments of no-action, Noh actors can guide the audience into that middle ground between being and nonbeing. For it is the mind that links all things—being and nonbeing, life and death, past and present.

No-action in other art forms

What is true in Noh is also true in other forms of art. The aesthetics of no-action as an aid to knowledge explains why the ink-brush painting called *sumie* makes copious usage of empty space. The empty space, unlike the negative space in Western painting, carries positive meaning, as the space of no-action. It is here in the empty space that the painter appeals to the power of suggestion to draw our attention to the things which are not depicted in the painting. Moreover, a master painter like Sesshū skillfully employs a flexible perspective to guide us right into that middle ground between being and nonbeing. Take a look at any one of Sesshū's landscape paintings. The whole scenery evokes such an eerie sensation that we are made to feel as if we are floating in the air, travelling over mountains and waters. This must be the kind of sensation which Wordsworth (1936) experienced when he wrote,

> I wandered lonely as a cloud
> That floats on high o'er vales and hills. (p. 149)

By letting our minds escape into the scenery painted by a master painter, we are guided into the middle ground between being and nonbeing and rewarded with "the bliss of solitude" which flashed upon Wordsworth's inward eye.

In literature, the aesthetics of no-action involves inferring the hidden meaning between the lines. What is left out between the lines in the space of no-action often becomes more important than what is actually written. This explains why the Japanese have elevated *haiku*, a poem consisting of only 17 syllables, into one of the highest forms of art. To appreciate what is expressed in a haiku, we are expected to project ourselves into the world the author creates within and beyond the span of 17 syllables. The more we are able to infer what is left unsaid, the more we are able to experience the totality of reality which covers both the space of action, and of no-action. Here again we are reminded of the all-important epistemological implication of the aesthetics of no-action: It is the mind that links all things—being and nonbeing, life and death, past and present.

RELATIVITY AND THE AESTHETICS OF NO-ACTION

The aesthetics of no-action as an artistic ideal lends itself to a natural interpretation as expressing the importance of economy of effort on the part of the artist. In the performing and martial arts which involve bodily movement, this interpretation has an obvious linkage to the physics of the body in motion. Does the aesthetics of no-action as an aid to knowledge, which has to do with the working of the mind, have a similar linkage to the physics of the body in motion? To make any sense out of this question, it may be useful to rephrase the question as follows: What does it mean to say that something is in a state of no-action, or rest?

Implications of relativity

A little reflection should convince us that there is no such thing as something being absolutely in a state of no-action. Consider, for example, the case of the Noh actor who is in a state of no-action when all his dancing and singing come to rest. To the audience this state of no-action of the Noh actor is perceived as a state of no-action relative to the stage on which his performance is taking place.

But what if the Noh play in question is being staged on a boat moving on a lake? To the audience who is on the moving boat watching the performance, a state of no-action of the Noh actor continues to be perceived as a state of no-action. However, to a person standing on the shore, the same state of no-action would no longer appear as a state of no-action, for the stage, or the boat on which the Noh performance is taking place, is moving relative to the shore on which this person is standing. Is the person standing on the shore, then, in a state of no-action? By now it should be clear that the answer has to be, "It depends." If we define his act of standing with respect to the shore, or the earth, he is in a state of no-action. However, neither he nor the earth would be in a state of no-action relative to the sun around which the earth revolves. Even the sun, if we follow this line of reasoning, will not be in a state of no-action relative to some galaxy.

This is exactly the kind of reasoning, it may be recalled, that led Einstein (1916) to formulate his theory of relativity. It is not difficult to see why this kind of reasoning leads to a notion that the only motion in the physical universe is motion relative to something else. Einstein developed this notion into his special theory of relativity because he found it difficult to accept, in the face of the Michelson-Morley experiment which confirmed the constancy of the speed of light, the old Galileian notion about the existence of a body of reference which is physically at rest. If he was to rescue the principle of relativity, which guarantees that the same laws of nature apply in all bodies of reference moving uniformly relative to each other, he had to abandon the Galileian transformation in favor of the Lorentz transformation. All this, of course, is well known to the student of the history of science. What concerns us here is the question, What does the Einsteinian special theory of relativity, which has to do with the physics of the body in motion, have to say on the aesthetics of no-action, which has to do with the working of the mind in the state of mindlessness?

The nature of the relationship between the special theory of relativity and the aesthetics of no-action may become clearer if we go back and examine the meaning of two basic postulates of the special theory: the principle of relativity and the law of propagation of light. The principle of relativity says that the laws of nature are the same in all bodies of reference moving uniformly with respect to each other. Because the only motion in the physical universe is motion relative to some body of reference, the principle of relativity implies that there is no way of distinguishing between uniform motion and nonmotion. The law of propagation of light, on the other hand, says that the velocity of transmission of light in a vacuum is the same in all bodies of reference for all observers moving uniformly relative to each other. The law implies that the instruments used to measure distance or time change from one body of reference to another in such a way that the speed of light always appears to be constant at 300,000 km/s. How a given moving object will appear to an observer will therefore depend on whether the observer is stationary or moving with the object. To a stationary observer, a moving object measures shorter, distancewise as well as timewise, as its velocity increases.

Implications for no-action

These implications of two basic postulates of the special theory of relativity have corresponding implications for the aesthetics of no-action. That a state of no-action is, as was already argued in the case of the Noh actor, only relative to some body of reference follows from the principle of relativity. To the performing artist, therefore, a state of no-action means that the artist is at rest relative to the stage on which the performance takes place. However, because the stage itself is also moving relative to some body of reference, it follows that the artist in a state of

no-action can actually experience being in a state of motion. To those in the audience who are watching the performance, the same state of no-action provides
an opportunity to duplicate the artist's experience by projecting themselves into
the same space of mindlessness, as they are encouraged to do in the Noh performance.

That appearances are relative, on the other hand, follows from the law of
propagation of light. If appearances are relative, then it is up to the mind to discern
the reality behind changing appearances. In fact, in the case of the performing
and martial arts which involve bodily movement, the artist's mind and body must
be in harmony if he is to experience, firsthand, that to be in a state of no-action
is to become a part of the cosmic process. Dōgen (1958), the founder of the Sōtō
School of Zen in Japan, also talks about the importance of integrating our body
and mind if we are to discern the reality behind the veil of relativity:

> When you go out on a boat and look around, you feel as if the shore were
> moving. But if you fix your eyes on the rim of the boat, you become aware
> that the boat is moving. It is exactly the same when you try to know the
> objective world while still in a state of confusion in regard to your own body
> and mind. (p. 252)

The special theory of relativity, which has successfully integrated two basic
postulates, has further interesting implications. First, there is the equivalence of
mass and energy expressed by the celebrated formula: $E = mc^2$. The formula says
that mass and energy are different manifestations of the same thing, that mass
is nothing but a form of stored energy. Because energy is released with action,
the equivalence of mass and energy has an interesting implication for the aesthetics
of no-action. In particular, it implies that a state of no-action corresponds to a
state in which there is no kinetic energy due to velocity. This, then, provides us
a physical basis for the statement that the aesthetics of no-action involves economy of effort on the part of the artist.

Another interesting implication of the special theory of relativity follows from
Einsteinian body of reference, or coordinate system, which involves the concept
of a four-dimensional space-time continuum. This concept provides us with a
physical basis for the importance of here and now. Carried to its extremity, the
concept implies that here contains there and everywhere, and now contains past
as well as future. A state of no-action here and now, in the light of the concept
of a four-dimensional space-time continuum, thus carries a far-reaching epistemological implication as holding a key to knowledge. T.S. Eliot (1971), with his
characteristic flair for rhythm, beautifully expresses what this knowledge is all
about:

> Time past and time future
> Allow but a little consciousness.
> To be conscious is not to be in time
> But only in time can the moment in the rose-garden,
> The moment in the arbour where the rain beat,
> The moment in the draughty church at smokefall
> Be remembered; involved with past and future.
> Only through time time is conquered. (p. 16)

Zen Buddhists, too, emphasize the importance of here and now, for Zen is
not so much an abstract system of thought as an idea that every act in living holds
a key to knowledge. As a practical method of acquiring knowledge, however,
Zen Buddhists have come to stress the importance of meditation, for meditation

in the act of sitting, for example, helps us to guide ourselves into the state of mindlessness. The Zen emphasis on meditation also reflects their conception of the mind as the unifying principle of the cosmic process. But this does not mean that the body can be neglected. On the contrary, the body plays an equally, or probably more, important role in reaching enlightenment as Dōgen (1958) explains in the following words:

> So long as one hopes to grasp the Truth only through the mind, one will not attain it even in a thousand existences or in eons of time. Only when one lets go of the mind and ceases to seek an intellectual apprehension of the Truth is liberation attainable. Enlightenment of the mind through the sense of sight and comprehension of the Truth through the sense of hearing are truly bodily attainments. To do away with mental deliberation and cognition, and simply to go on sitting, is the method by which the Way is made an intimate part of our lives. Thus attainment of the Way becomes truly attainment through the body. (p. 255)

The aesthetics of no-action thus lends itself to an interesting physical interpretation whether we look at it as a phenomenon associated with the physics of the body at rest or the psychology of the mind in the state of mindlessness. Historically speaking, the aesthetics of no-action in Japanese art has evolved out of Zen philosophy and, therefore, expresses the Oriental ideal about the importance of being in tune with the cosmic process which is also found in Taoism. The Taoist concept of *wu wei*, which is usually translated as "non-action," does not mean, therefore, doing nothing. Rather, it means action in harmony with the ongoing cosmic process. This is what Lao Tsu (1972, p. 39) means when he says, "Tao abides in non-action, yet nothing is left undone." In the final analysis, the aesthetics of no-action is thus an outgrowth of a worldview which emphasizes the need for human existence to be in harmony with the cosmic process.

CONCLUSION

The aesthetics of no-action as an artistic ideal cherishes economy of effort on the part of the artist in bringing out the maximal effect. To the extent that art imitates life, the aesthetics of no-action thus incorporates a notion of "economy" which is to be cherished in conducting our lives. To be more specific, the notion implies that our lives must be in tune with the cosmic process, that a true economy lies in maintaining an organic harmony with nature.

The aesthetics of no-action as an aid to knowledge, on the other hand, suggests a holistic approach to comprehending reality. It is holistic, first, in the sense that both the mind and the body are involved in the acquisition of knowledge about the world around us. This is in sharp contrast to the Cartesian dichotomy in which the body is dispelled from the realm of rational inquiry. It is holistic also in the sense that it offers a valid alternative to the Cartesian paradigm, which employs a reductionistic methodology based on an arbitrary segmentation of reality. The aesthetics of no-action explicitly recognizes the ecological nature of reality which includes ourselves as part of the cosmic process. While the Cartesian paradigm tries to understand nature by separating nature from ourselves as an object of our rational inquiry, the aesthetics of no-action tries to comprehend nature by placing us right in the midst of the cosmic process. While the Cartesian paradigm guides us to study the laws of nature which govern the cosmic drama, the aesthetics of no-action guides us to learn the ways of nature by participating in that drama.

Our comment here is not to be construed as a rejection of a reductionistic approach to knowledge as represented by the Cartesian paradigm. Because reality involves complicated patterns of ecological interaction, an artificial segmentation of reality becomes a useful device of acquiring knowledge about different aspects of reality. By doing so, however, we tend to lose sight of reality as an organic whole of which we are a part. If we moderns have come to lose a sense of unity with nature, it is partly because we have relied too much on science as an aid to knowledge which treats nature as an object of rational inquiry separate from ourselves. By separating nature from ourselves, we have lost the sense of belonging to nature, which comes from the realization that we, too, are the product of the cosmic process.

The aesthetics of no-action, in contrast, is a way of acquiring knowledge while preserving that sense of belonging to nature. By using art to recreate reality, we are trying to create the mirror of perception in our own minds, which would reflect ourselves as part of that reality. The aesthetics of no-action is thus intended as an aid to developing the mind necessary to reach enlightenment by overcoming the constraint which the body imposes on us by confining ourselves to here and now.

Finally, the aesthetics of no-action, as it relies on artistic symbolism, is patently a nonlinguistic mode of representing reality. Any attempt to represent reality by a linguistic mode is, in the final analysis, limited by the cardinality of the language which is employed to describe reality. Science is no exception in this regard. The aesthetics of no-action, on the other hand, explicitly recognizes the importance of comprehending reality in toto, which is beyond the cardinality of any language. According to Lao Tsu (1972, p. 39), "The Tao that can be told is not the eternal Tao." Our own endeavor to describe what the aesthetics of no-action is all about now finds itself in a state of no-action where words no longer suffice. With Hamlet, we conclude, "The rest is silence."

REFERENCES

Dōgen. (1958). Body and mind. In R. Tsunoda, W.T. de Barry, & D. Keene (Eds.), *Sources of Japanese tradition* (p. 255). New York: Columbia University Press.

Dōgen. (1958). Realizing the solution. In R. Tsunoda, W.T. de Barry, & D. Keene (Eds.), *Sources of Japanese tradition* (p. 252). New York: Columbia University Press.

Einstein, A. (1916). *Relativity*. New York: Crown.

Eliot, T.S. (1971). Burnt Norton. *Four quartets*. New York: Harcourt, Brace and World.

Exupéry, A.S. (1971). *The little prince*. New York: Harcourt Brace Jovanovich.

Jung, C.G. (1969). *The archetypes and the collective unconscious*. Princeton, NJ: Princeton University Press.

Lao Tsu. (1972). *Tao Te Ching* (Gia-Fu Feng & Jane English, Trans.). New York: Vintage Books.

Wordsworth, W. (1936). I wandered lonely as a cloud. In T. Hutchinson (Ed.), *Poetical works* (p. 149). Oxford: Oxford University Press.

Zeami. (1958). On the mind linking all powers. In R. Tsunoda, W.T. de Barry, & D. Keene (Eds.), *Sources of Japanese tradition* (p. 291). New York: Columbia University Press.

Zeami. (1958). The Book of the way of the highest flower. In R. Tsunoda, W.T. de Barry, & D. Keene (Eds.), *Sources of Japanese tradition* (p. 302). New York: Columbia University Press.

Zeami. (1958). The nine stages of the No in order. In R. Tsunoda, W.T. de Barry, & D. Keene (Eds.), *Sources of Japanese tradition* (p. 295). New York: Columbia University Press.

Japanese martial arts as spiritual education

Richard J. Schmidt
University of Nebraska at Lincoln

The purpose of this paper is to describe how Japanese martial arts and ways serve as vehicles for spiritual education (*seishin kyōiku*) or self-realization (*jitsugen*) for practitioners from both East and West. In defining the role which the martial arts and ways play, an analysis is presented concerning the moral, ethical, and philosophical origins of martial arts and ways, martial pedagogy, the training environment, and the relationship between disciple and master. Although the earliest forms of martial arts (*kōbujutsu*) were utilized solely for military and naval combat, some of their modern cognate forms known as the martial ways (*budō*) are practiced the world over as methods of sport, physical education, aesthetics, meditation, and self-defense. As the martial arts and ways differ widely with respect to purpose, technique, and method, the underlying intrinsic martial ethos of both remain essentially the same (D.F. Draeger, personal communication, November 4, 1981). Their most salient characteristic, however, is to serve as systems of education for cultivating in the individual the values and virtues reminiscent of and idealized in the samurai legacy of feudal Japan (Dann, 1978; Herrigel, 1971; Jackson, 1975; Lebra, 1976; Rohlen, 1973).

SELF-CULTIVATION "PATHS"

Within Japanese culture, in order to develop what is considered to be a mature and complete human being, one must undergo training, education, and self-cultivation (Dann, 1978). Japanese culture contains a multitude of activities that are devoted to the development and maintenance of spiritual education. Some of those more familiar to the Westerner are the tea ceremony (*chadō*), calligraphy (*shōdō*), and Zen meditation. The new martial ways (*shinbudō*) of *karatedō*, *kendō*, *iaidō*, *aikidō*, *kyudō*, and *naginata* are a group of activistic disciplines that focus on self-cultivation via the combative mode. The *dō* suffixed to the aforementioned arts suggests that they are "ways" or "paths" to travel throughout one's life. From a metaphysical viewpoint, the do (*Tao/michi*) are understood to be moral, ethical, philosophical, and self-actualizing paths that are unending and profound and filled with "numerous technical difficulties" (Draeger, 1973b, p. 24). They are methods of self-cultivation that ultimately lead to self-perfection or enlightenment (*satori*) in the Zen sense.

> All of these disciplines are complicated, intricate challenges in the pursuit of a better way of life and are based on the firm conviction that no man is as complete a human being as he can be after sufficient experience with the 'do,' (Draeger, 1973b, p. 25).

SELF-ACTUALIZATION IN THE MARTIAL DISCIPLINE

In Western terminology then, we may say that the Japanese martial disciplines help to foster the process of self-actualization. Although very much concerned with the combative application of various techniques, the martial disciplines are deeply rooted in human psychology and character development through self-actualization. They recognize the martial exponent as a wholistic individual with latent abilities and potentialities to be realized given the proper training environment. From a phenomenological perspective as well as from the standpoint of Zen teaching, the exponents of the budo believe that to understand the body is to understand its existential being in the world. Treated as an ethic, self-actualization "affirms the view that to discover one's essence and to develop what talents one has is both incumbent and good" (Arnold, 1979, p. 91).

In an effort to understand the significance of self-actualization in the martial disciplines, it is necessary for us to examine the central concept of *seishin kyōiku* and the major root of bushido which is known as *seishi o chōetsu suru* or "transcending thoughts about life and death." Concerning this concept, Dann (1978) has stated that

> Meeting or confronting one's death has been a central teaching in the martial ways and continues in a muted form today. Budo's use of death, consistent with its classical heritage, has been to treat it as a spiritual metaphor for the 'killing' of desire, weakness, and other disharmonies created by the 'small self' (jishin) or ego. (p. 130)

Because the budo are concerned with the nurturing of seishin kyoiku, they utilize introspection and exorcism of self to attain that end. Introspection allows critical examination of one's innermost self, one's emotions and beliefs, one's center or *kokoro* (heart) as it is known in Japanese, for the purpose of bringing about a harmonious ordering of one's actions with one's beliefs as well as those of his or her social nexus. Mental exorcism is another facet of self-cultivation that is concerned with inner purity and is not considered complete unless it eliminates all inner anxieties and frustrations which prevent the mind-body complex from functioning in a natural way. "In this sense, purity is associated with self-contentment, serenity, and tranquility, and ultimately leads to the Buddhist ideal of empty, detached self" (Lebra, 1976, p. 162). The concept of mental exorcism has as its roots the purification rituals of Shinto.

Diligent practice of exorcism and introspection is believed to give rise to a self which emanates great potency (Lebra, 1976). The source of this potency is the *hara*, or the central torso region, the vital center of the body. Certain types of practices within the martial disciplines, such as intense repetitive execution of techniques to the point of fatigue, prolonged sitting in *seiza* (formal sitting position), special training sessions held during extremes of heat and cold, and the general perseverance through pain and bruises, are all thought to test, nurture, and refine the ability to concentrate one's physical and mental efforts. "The underlying belief is that through such concentration one can achieve anything one undertakes" (Lebra, 1976, p. 163).

The unification of the body-spirit complex takes on a quasi-religious nature as exemplified by the principles of *tairyoku-shugi* (body-power principle) and *taiatari-shugi* (principle of direct body attack) in the direct exposure of the live self to a hazardous situation without external help" (Lebra, 1976, p. 164). In the combative arts this is represented via the mode of one-on-one combat where one undergoes a symbolic death.

PHILOSOPHICAL, MORAL, AND ETHICAL ORIGINS OF THE JAPANESE MARTIAL DISCIPLINES

Because the budo are quasi-martial in nature, they reflect, to a degree, what has become to be known as the "fighting spirit of Japan." It is this warrior ethos, infused with the religious, moral, and mystical beliefs of Shinto, Taoism, Chu Hsi Confucianism, neo-Confucianism, and Zen and Mikkyo Buddhism that is promulgated in the traditional teaching of the martial arts and ways today, and that serves as the basis of the budo as a vehicle for seishin kyoiku.

The warrior ethos consisted of a code termed *bushidō*, literally "the way of the warrior." To this code, which has subtly affected all of Japanese culture, Shinto imparted the worshipping of nature, ancestors, and heroes. On a deeper level, Shinto is involved with the budo in promoting the Japanese aesthetic ideal of naturalism (*shizen-shugi*) and a universal system of morals and values (*dotokū*). Mikkyo, Taoism, Chu-Hsi Confucianism, and neo-Confucianism all stress morals and ethics to a certain degree. Zen Buddhism contributes feelings of subtle serenity and calmness as well as fosters the idea of quietly accepting the realities of one's life and resignation to the inevitable. Interestingly enough, it is the metaphysical teachings within the Japanese martial disciplines which are based upon a fusion of Buddhist and Taoist concepts formalized by Zen that receive the primary emphasis today for facilitating self-actualization.

Martial arts pedagogy
The learning process is characterized by a protracted apprenticeship under a master teacher (*sensei*) whose function is to serve as the interpreter and transmitter of the techniques and philosophies of his particular martial tradition (Dann, 1978). The sensei serves as the model for the trainee to emulate. Long and difficult hours of intense, repetitive training in prescribed movements punctuated at times by physical and verbal abuse by the sensei is the mode of instruction (Befu, 1971). Learning the martial arts and ways embodies the idea that suffering and hardship are necessary parts of life that need to be experienced if one is to become a "whole" person, imbued with the quality of a mature and wholesome inner enlightenment. It is considered to be a process of seishin kyoiku where mind and body undergo spiritual forging (*shinshin tanren*) via the combative mode to foster the development of a mature and self-actualized human being at harmony with oneself, the social order, and the cosmos.

Reflective of the Zen method of training, the emphasis is on a nonverbalized, intuitive approach rather than rational intellection. The trainee is encouraged to "think with his body" and not with his mind, and to develop his two-fold sight of gaze and perception (Draeger, 1973b). In the Zen sense this entire educational paradigm is known as *kufū*. "Generally, it means to seek the way out of a dilemma" (Suzuki, 1973, p. 178). It is the total involvement of one's physical and mental powers to unceasingly struggle for the solution to a problem. It is an altogether personal and individualistic endeavor that grows out of one's inner self.

The progression through the mastery of technical competence and self-cultivation in the budo may be elucidated by the process of gyo, shugyo, jutsu, and do (Draeger, 1973b). The *gyō*, or introductory, stage represents the initial level of training where the *budōka* is introduced to his chosen martial art, its customs and etiquette, his teacher and seniors, as well as his training hall, the *dōjō*. The trainee learns that the budo techniques must be practiced assiduously. At this level, training is a process of trial and error. The teacher is overly critical of the trainee, and great will and perseverance are needed by the trainee to carry him through endless repetitions of basic movements. Silent communication is valued by the teacher, who often does not give the trainee verbal instruction. The teacher rarely speaks—he demonstrates. Training at the gyo level is a "blood, sweat, and tears" process and either "makes or breaks" the trainee (Draeger, 1973b).

Through perseverance and self-discipline the trainee progresses to the second level of training known as *shugyō*. Shugyo is a Buddhist-derived term for religious austerities; hence, practice in the budo takes on distinctly religious overtones (Dann, 1978). Considered to be the austere training level where uninterrupted training takes place, this is the stage involved with the resolution of kufu, a process that is more spiritual than mechanical. At this level, the trainee attempts to effectively reproduce the actions of the master teacher. Using a technique from Zen instruction, the master teacher presents the trainee with physical *koans*, or dilemmas, which force the trainee to attempt to solve the various conceptual problems associated with this particular art (Draeger, 1973b).

The third stage is the *jutsu* or art level. At this level, the trainee has acquired a mastery of the basic skills but still senses an incompleteness in his techniques. Movements once requiring conscious thought processes are now fully internalized and executed automatically.

The fourth stage is known as the *dō*. This is the state of the "artless" art where the expert, who has transcended the outer forms, is both master of himself and the art. This level is the final and ultimate stage of self-realization, the do, the equivalent of Zen enlightenment, or satori. "Attainment of the 'do' represents, beyond mere perfection of motor skills, a self-perfection in which old habits of dependence upon mechanics are thrown away and restrictive thought, or awareness of 'I' or 'I am doing' is lost" (Draeger, 1973b, p. 59).

The dojo

The hall in which the martial arts are practiced is called a dojo. Dojo is the name given to a place devoted to religious exercises, and its original Sanskrit meaning, *bodhimandala*, is the place of enlightenment. Because the Japanese martial tradition is indissolubly tied to Shinto, most dojo in Japan maintain a Shinto shrine and often a Japanese flag. Dojo which are run by Zen Buddhists, other religious groups, or local community organizations will not have this altar. Usually these dojo, as well as most dojo in the West, will replace the shrine with some other form of an appropriately spiritual nature. Due to its religious atmosphere, the dojo is simple and without ostentation and reflects the Japanese aesthetic values of *wabi* (simplicity) and *sabi* (tranquility).

The focal point of the dojo is the *kamidana* or deity shelf. It is here that the *mitama* (spirits) of the deities reside and under whose cognizance the exponents diligently train in hope of seeking their approval. For this reason the dojo is considered to be a *shinsei*, or sacred space. All actions within the dojo are conducted according to a strictly prescribed code of etiquette known as *reigi saho*. These forms of etiquette serve as outer forms of self-cultivation, the purpose of which is to bring order and harmony to the social nexus.

From a physical standpoint, what is considered to be the front of the dojo is known as the *shōmen*. This is where the deity shelf resides and all factors and references take place in relation to the kamidana. To the left of the kamidana is the *jōseki*, or upper side, where the senior ranking students sit for the opening and closing salutations. To the right is the *shimoseki*, or lower side, where the lower ranking students sit. The instructor is seated in front of the dojo, near the *kamiza*, signifying not only close physical contact with the *mitamas*, but spiritual as well. The students, being situated toward the rear of the dojo (*schimoza*), signify their distance, both physically and spiritually, from the mitama located in the kamidana. Salutations (*aisatsu*) in the form of bowing and verbal greetings toward the shrine, instructors, senior students, and each other occur before, during, and after training and are considered to be a physical behavior motivated by inner convictions of humbleness of one's spirit and respect for the status-oriented vertical societal hierarchy.

Master-teacher/discipline relationship

The relationship that exists between the sensei and student is paternalistic in nature and based on personal loyalty and a complex system of reciprocal obligations (*ōn*). Its organizational structure is reflective of the feudal *iemoto* system still extant today. The sensei acts as the exemplary model which the student aspires to attain. Acting as the transmitter of the technical, philosophical, and cultural aspects of his particular martial tradition, the sensei attempts to provide educational experiences for the learner's self-discovery. The sensei's obligation exists toward his teacher, the discipline, and his country in general. Faithfully teaching his followers is deemed as sufficient in repaying his obligations. As for the student, diligent training and personal acceptance of what the sensei presents to him is considered as sufficient in repaying his debt. The sensei, who is in an *emic* position, accepts the student, who is in an *etic* position, because of the latter's desire to learn the art and progress along the path of spiritual education following traditional methods.

The trainee is expected to exhibit *nyūnanshin* (pliant-heartedness) so as to be able to readily accept the teachings of his martial art and undergo the spiritual forging process. Patience, diligence, respect, and perseverance in training are the hallmarks of a dedicated trainee. The student is expected to have a feeling of gratefulness (*kansha*) toward his teacher and his martial art for the instruction received.

SUMMARY

This chapter was to describe how traditional Japanese martial arts and ways serve as systems for self-cultivation among practitioners of both East and West. Protracted experience in the budo serves to enhance one's sense of wholeness and human-beingness through the process of seishin kyoiku. Confrontation of self through the combative mode of the budo will cultivate in oneself those qualities that will enable one to more effectively face the challenges of modern-day life.

REFERENCES

Arnold, P.J. (1979). Intellectualism, physical education and self-actualization. *Quest*, 31, 87-96.

Befu, H. (1971). *Japan: An anthropological introduction*. San Francisco: Chandler.

Dann, J.L. (1978). *Kendo in Japanese martial culture: Swordsmanship as self-cultivation*. Unpublished doctoral dissertation, University of Washington, Seattle, WA.

Draeger, D.F. (1973b). *Classical budo*. Tokyo: John Weatherhill.

Draeger, D.F. (1974). *Modern budo and bujutsu*. Tokyo: John Weatherhill.

Herrigel, E. (1971). *Zen and the art of archery*. New York: Vintage.

Jackson, G.B. (1975). *Kendo: On a psychology of Japanese life*. Unpublished doctoral dissertation, University of California-Irvine.

Lebra, T.S. (1976). *Japanese patterns of behavior*. Honolulu: The University Press of Hawaii.

Rohlen, T. (1973). Spiritual education in a Japanese bank. *American Anthropologist*, 5, 1542-1562.

Suzuki, D.T. (1973). *Zen and Japanese culture*. Princeton, NJ: Princeton University Press.

An Eastern approach to motor skill acquisition and performance

Michael J. Canic
University of British Columbia

My use of the designation "An Eastern Approach" in the title of this chapter implies that there is no single approach which is representative of Eastern world thought. Hinduism, Buddhism, Confucianism, Taoism, and Shintoism, for example, each possess a distinct view of the world. With this in mind, a Zen Buddhist approach to skill acquisition will be investigated in this paper.

Zen, historically, has been allied with physical activities (e.g., the martial arts, swordsmanship, archery), and it does serve to represent *general* Eastern views as a whole. The seeds of the Zen school are found, of course, in Indian Buddhism. After Buddhism was introduced into China, the "Ch'an school" (which was the Chinese precursor of Zen) emerged and began to carve an identity for itself. The subsequent interaction of Ch'an with Japanese culture ultimately yielded the Zen Buddhism that we know today. Thus, perhaps more than any other system of thought, Zen is truly an "Eastern" philosophy, having been influenced by Indian, Chinese, and Japanese thinkers.

Any approach to motor skill acquisition is dependent upon underlying philosophical assumptions. These assumptions reflect how we structure and represent the world around us. More specifically, they help to provide us with some type of answer to fundamental questions such as, What is the nature of reality? Of the universe? Of being? Of knowledge? and How is it that we may acquire knowledge about things? Accordingly, in this chapter, the task is to investigate these assumptions in the area of skill acquisition within the context of Zen.

I have structured the topic according to the following common divisions in the field of motor skill acquisition: (a) the nature of the skill, (b) the role of the instructor, (c) the role of the learner, and (d) the nature of the learning process. The distinctions suggested by this structure are demonstrated as only one representation of Reality, and further, an illusory representation to one who has become "skilled" in the Eastern context.

THE DEVELOPMENT AND FOUNDATIONS OF ZEN

Before an Eastern approach to skill acquisition can be outlined, it is first necessary to address the philosophical foundations of that approach. The Japanese term *Zen* is an adaptation of the Chinese *ch'an*, which is phonetically derived from the Sanskrit *dhyāna*, which means meditation (Chan, 1973, p. 425). To understand the development of the basic philosophies of Zen, we must first investigate the development of Ch'an Buddhism in China. It is with the origin and development of Ch'an that the central philosophies readily identified with Zen came into existence. Ch'an Buddhism, simply put, developed out of the synthesis of Chinese Taoism and Indian Buddhism, which began in the 1st century A.D. and continued through the 7th century A.D.

Taoism is a philosophical system based primarily on the teachings of Lao Tzu, who is believed to have lived in the 6th century B.C., and Chuang Tzu, who lived in the 4th century B.C. *Tao* is a term which may be translated as the ''Way'' (Chan, 1973, p. 136nl), but more accurately may be described as the natural flow and order of the universe.[1] The ideal of Taoism, the Taoist sage, is one who acts in harmony with nature and is at one with the United Ultimate Reality. He is selfless and without ego; therefore, the great Tao is able to act spontaneously through him. The life of the Taoist sage is a simple life. He realizes that the Ultimate Truth, which lies in the Tao itself, is a truth beyond words.

Buddhism is an Indian religious/philosophical system based on the teachings of Siddhārtha Gautama (b. 563 B.C.?) who, after attaining Enlightenment at the age of 35, became known as the Buddha or ''Enlightened One.'' The core of Buddhist teachings is found in the Four Noble Truths which were expounded by the Buddha. These truths are as follows:

- All life is suffering.
- Desire is the cause of suffering.
- The cessation of suffering comes with the attainment of *Nirvāna*.
- The Way to Nirvāna is through the ''Middle Path.''

Underlying the Four Noble Truths is a specific view of Reality. This view is explained by Derk Bodde in an introduction to the section on Buddhism in Fung Yu-lan's (1953) monumental two-volume work, *A History of Chinese Philosophy*:

> There has been no single act of divine creation that has produced the stream of existence. It simply is, and always has been, what it is....Thus the wheel [of life and death] is permanent and unchanging in the sense that it goes on eternally. It is impermanent and changing, however, in the sense that everything in it is in a state of flux. This means that phenomenal ''existence,'' as commonly perceived by the senses, is illusory; it is not real inasmuch as, though it exists, its existence is not permanent or absolute. Nothing belonging to it has an enduring entity or ''nature'' of its own; everything is dependent upon a combination of fluctuating conditions and factors for its seeming ''existence'' at any given moment. This is the Buddhist theory of causation. (p. 237)

---

[1]Although literally translated as ''the Way'' and regarded as such by all schools of Eastern philosophy, the more detailed implicit meaning of the term, *Tao*, varies depending on the school of philosophy which employs it. For example, Confucians regard the Way as, ''the path of man's moral life'' (Runes, 1980, s.v. Tao). I have given a description consistent with the Taoist view because it was the Taoist concept of *Tao* which was integrated into Ch'an Buddhism.

That all life is suffering arises out of the mismatch between Ultimate Reality and desired Reality. Thus, desires are the root of all misery. Desires and their manifestations in action are called *karma*. The karma of each being in successive past existences determine what he or she is to be in existences to come. These rebirths constitute the wheel of life and death.

The only escape from this wheel of suffering and the continued operation of karma is through the attainment of Nirvāna. Nirvāna is the state of oneness with the Ultimate Reality. Being at one with the Ultimate Reality, the desire for change is extinguished. Being at one with the Ultimate Reality is to live totally in the here and now—the present. Having reached Nirvāna signifies the ultimate attainment of Buddhahood or Enlightenment.

To truly know this Unified Ultimate Reality, we must break down the conceptual distinctions that characterize our normal, everyday conscious minds. Nirvāna may be attained by following the Middle Path. The Middle Path avoids the two extremes of existence: the first the search for happiness through the pleasures of the senses; and the second, the search for happiness through self-denial or asceticism. Although the exact nature of this Middle Path varies among schools within the Buddhist tradition, it is always characterized by this avoidance of extremes. The Zen school advocates almost exclusively the practice of meditation as the path to be followed towards Enlightenment.

Kumārajīva (344-413), an Indian who was brought to the Chinese capital of Ch'ang-an in 401, was one of the great figures in the historical development of Buddhism in China. In a period of 10 years, he translated 72 Buddhist works into Chinese (Chan, 1973, p. 343) with the use of Taoist terminology. Through endeavors such as this, Indian Buddhism was synthesized with Taoism leading to a Chinese form of Buddhism.

Kumārajīva also introduced the important *Mādhyamika*, or Middle Doctrine School of Nāgārjuna (ca. 100-200), into China where it became known as the Three-Treatise school. The main tenet of this school was the Ultimate Emptiness (Sanskrit: *sūnyatā*; Chinese: *k'ung*) of Reality. That is to say, the phenomenal world is, in reality, Empty because the contents of the phenomenal world are not only changing but are also ultimately impermanent. This conceptualization was a vital precursor of Ch'an Buddhism.

Seng-chao (384-414), who was a student of Kumārajīva, wrote several essays on Buddhism which clearly incorporated Taoist ideas and, as a result, contributed to the foundations of the Ch'an school. The most important of these was his essay "On *Prajñā* Not Being Knowledge." (*Prajñā* is Sanskrit for "sage-wisdom".) In his work, he argued that because true understanding transcends distinctions, most importantly the subject/object distinction and because conventional knowledge must have an object which it is about (i.e., to know X), then one who has achieved true understanding has acquired knowledge that is not conventional knowledge. Because this knowledge transcends the subject/object distinction, it cannot be communicated through words. This anticipated the movement of the Ch'an school away from the traditional emphasis on scriptural study.

This knowledge is not a product of desire as manifested in intentful thought because this would only serve to create distinctions rather than to break them down. It is not a product of rational thought because rational thought itself is grounded in distinctions. Clearly, it is the distinguishing, conceptualizing mind that is being opposed here.

Ch'an was introduced to Japan by Ch'an missionaries during the time of the Chinese Sung dynasty (960-1279). However, it did not become established as a school until two native Japanese, Eisai (1141-1215) and Dōgen (1200-1253) separately brought the teachings back with them from China. This marked the beginning of Japanese Zen.

Japanese culture, due to its affinity with the arts and its sense of the aesthetic, allowed many avenues through which the Zen master could express him or herself. From the time of the establishment of Zen in Japan, throughout the succeeding centuries and up until today, these avenues have been explored. The subtlety of floral arrangement, the ritual of tea ceremony, the flow of calligraphy, the simplicity and clarity of poetry, and the effortless grace of the martial arts can each be an expression of this approach to life. As will be seen, this same understanding can be expressed in an approach to motor skill acquisition and performance.

THE NATURE OF THE SKILL

The term *skill* has been used several ways in Western motor performance literature. It has been used to designate a continuum, ranging from high to low, along which one occupies a place with respect to one's ability to perform. For example, one might ask, "What level of skill has that person attained?" It has been used to specifically designate a high level of ability or capacity to perform well. This meaning would be implicit in the question, "Is this person a skilled performer?" Finally, the term has been used to refer to the specific processes or activities that constitute the performance itself as in, "What skill is it that this person is performing?" It is this last use of the term *skill* which will be the focus of this paper. The term *motor skill* as opposed to, for example, a *cognitive skill* (such as the memorization of a list of words) indicates the necessary involvement of the motor system or, in other words, that part of the nervous system responsible for the control of the muscles.

Skill possesses quite a different meaning in the context of Zen. Recall that the primary concern of the Buddhist and thus the Zen disciple is spiritual cultivation in order that he or she might attain Enlightenment. As a disciple, all living activities are directed toward this spiritual cultivation. Therefore, one concludes that skill performance is activity directed toward spiritual cultivation. D.T. Suzuki in the introduction to Eugene Herrigel's (1971) classic book, *Zen in the Art of Archery* writes:

> One of the most significant features we notice in the practice of archery, and in fact of all the arts as they are studied in Japan and probably also in other Far Eastern countries, is that they are not intended for utilitarian purposes only or for purely aesthetic enjoyments, but are meant to train the mind; indeed, to bring it into contact with the ultimate reality. (p. v)

For one who has attained Enlightenment, the performance of a motor skill becomes an outward expression of the Enlightened state, the higher understanding. Clearly, the Skill that is being performed in Zen—the underlying Skill, the real Skill—is the Skill of spiritual cultivation and expression, the Skill of life. This skill goes far beyond the mere perfecting of specific responses to given sets of environmental conditions. The vehicle for the practice of this Skill, whether in archery, sworsdsmanship, floral arrangement, or tea ceremony, is unimportant as long as the proper path (the Middle Path) is followed to the proper destination (Nirvāna).

The focus in the present context then, is on the process, the approach to the motor skill, the internal or *how* it is done as opposed to the product, result of the motor skill, the external or *what* is done.

THE ROLE OF THE INSTRUCTOR

Unlike Western approaches where the instructor actively assists the learner by structuring the environment, setting goals and objectives, directing attention to relevant cues, and providing feedback, the task of the Zen master is simply to help the student follow the Tao, and to realize his or her own true nature as that of the universal stream. The instructor may help the student acquire the Zen Skill through the instruction of a motor skill.

The role of the instructor, with respect to how he or she teaches a motor skill (and thus the Zen Skill), is a subtle one. The instructor teaches primarily through the use of demonstrations. This allows the student to visually interpret the Zen Skill. A demonstration may have much more effect than a dialogue between teacher and student. By excessive verbalization, the instructor would only serve to modify the student's deluded concept of Reality by providing more distinctions to which it might cling. The instructor cannot help the student to master a motor skill by explaining it any more than he or she can make the student aware of the Ultimate Truth by telling him or her.

However, the limited use of words may serve a purpose if the student understands that the words are intended only as a vehicle, a vehicle that can ultimately be dispensed with when the student achieves true understanding. A passage from the Taoist classic, the *Chuang Tzu*, serves to illustrate this point:

> The fish trap exists because of the fish; once you've gotten the fish, you can forget the trap. The rabbit snare exists because of the rabbit; once you've gotten the rabbit, you can forget the snare. Words exist because of meaning; once you've gotten the meaning, you can forget the words. Where can I find a man who has forgotten words so I can have a word with him? (Watson, 1968, p. 302)

It is important that the instructor convey an attitude that denies distinctions as much as possible. For example, an environment must not be created where the student perceives that an object/teacher is going to demonstrate a skill to a subject/self. Rather, the instructor must convey an attitude that one is a mere instrument through which the great Tao is acting. Credit must not be taken or possessiveness displayed toward one's actions. The student must realize that through destruction of the ego, he or she can also become an instrument through which the Tao is manifested.

What Zen emphasizes is the intuitive knowledge that results from direct, firsthand experience. Thus, the instructor allows the student the freedom to make errors and self-discoveries. In this way, the student does not become overly dependent upon the instructor for technical instruction or spiritual guidance. The instructor may come to evaluate performance through intuition—the same way that he or she acquires prajñā (Sage-Wisdom). As one who is in harmony with the Ultimate Reality, the instructor possesses a sensitivity to the disruption of that harmony. This sensitivity, like the prajñā acquired, is beyond reason; it is purely intuitive and is a result of the training process.

In the Zen sense, the pinnacle of instruction is the point where true understanding is gained and the student no longer needs the instructor. At this point, the instructor's role is fulfilled.

THE ROLE OF THE LEARNER

In a Zen approach to skill acquisition, the learner is not only the focus but the essence of the skill acquisition setting. How is this so? The skill that is learned, the Zen Skill, is not something external to the learner; rather, it is found within the learner. Given the importance of the learner in the skill acquisition setting, one might guess that the role of the learner is also a very complex one. This is not the case, however. Essentially, the learner has only to overcome the conceptualizing mind and to extinguish desires in order to realize the Zen Skill. Though not complex, this often proves to be a very difficult task.

A Zen approach to motor skill performance may be thought of as "meditation in movement." The meditative mind is a clear and detached mind, and it is this mind which the learner attempts to realize. The realization of this mind results in action that is spontaneous and not a product of conscious desires. To place the mind anywhere in particular is to remove it from the natural flow of the universal stream and thus to lose awareness of the ever present here and now. To consciously place the mind anywhere is to create a conceptual distinction which perpetuates the notion of a distinct self. When the mind is attached to anything, it loses touch with the Ultimate Reality.

The Zen master Takuan (1573-1645) wrote in depth about Zen and the art of swordsmanship, in general, and about the placement of the mind, in particular, in a famous letter to Yagyū Tajima no kami Munenori:

> The thing is not to try to localize the mind anywhere but to let it fill up the whole body, let it flow throughout the totality of your being. When this happens you use the hands when they are needed, you use the legs or the eyes when they are needed, and no time or no extra energy will be wasted. (The localization of the mind means its freezing. When it ceases to flow freely as it is needed, it is no more the mind in its suchness.)....
>
> The mind is not to be treated like a cat tied to a string. The mind must be left to itself, utterly free to move about according to its own nature. Not to localize or partialize it is the end of spiritual training. When it is nowhere it is everywhere. When it occupies one tenth, it is absent in the other nine tenths. Let the swordsman discipline himself to have the mind go on its own way, instead of trying deliberately to confine it somewhere. (Suzuki, 1973, pp. 107, 108)

By practicing with a detached mind, a meditative mind, one may realize the essence or unity that underlies a motor skill setting. In the case of archery, for example, one comes to realize the unified and indistinguishable nature of archer, bow, arrow, and target. This is the essence of that learning environment. At this point, performance of the motor skill reflects mastery of the Zen Skill in that setting.

THE NATURE OF THE LEARNING PROCESS

What is the importance of time in the learning of a motor skill through a Zen approach? Is there a learning "process" as such? Recall that Zen recognizes the metaphysical unity of space and time. To make spatial or temporal distinctions is to cling to the phenomenal world and, thus, to inhibit the spontaneous flow of the mind with the Tao (natural stream of existence). Therefore, for a student to ask "How long will it take to learn?" or "How far have I progressed up to now?" is to pose meaningless questions to the Zen master.

The very act of asking questions concerned with time or progress indicates a lack of true understanding on the part of the student. It may take many years to reach Enlightenment, or it may take a very short time if one has a mind that is near to the true nature of Reality. Mastery, however, does not depend on the amount of practice, but on the nature of the practice. This is colorfully illustrated in the following anecdote:

A young boy traveled across Japan to the school of a famous martial artist. When he arrived at the dojo he was given an audience by the sensei.
"What do you wish from me?" the master asked.
"I wish to be your student and become the finest karateka in the land," the boy replied. "How long must I study?"
"Ten years at least," the master answered.
"Ten years is a long time," said the boy. "What if I studied twice as hard as all your other students?"
"Twenty years," replied the master.
"Twenty years! What if I practice day and night with all my effort?"
"Thirty years," was the master's reply.
"How is it that each time I say I will work harder, you tell me that it will take longer?" the boy asked.
"The answer is clear. When one eye is fixed upon your destination, there is only one eye left with which to find the Way." (Hyams, 1979, p. 95)

Enlightenment is not something detached from the individual in time, and it is not something that is distinct from the individual in that he or she does not "possess" it. The seed of Enlightenment is within the student here and now. The student has only to realize his or her own Buddha—nature. This realization occurs with the breakdown of conceptual distinctions and the extinction of desires. Thus, contrary to the conceptual construct that for learning to occur something must be acquired, a Zen approach implies just the opposite. That is to say, the path towards Zen Skill is not characterized by what is acquired, but rather by what is dropped.

The entire context for skill acquisition, which is set by the instructor, is grounded in the nonrational knowledge with which the learner cannot initially come to grips. As what is perceived in the phenomenal sense to be the learning process continues, the conceptualizing mind becomes more and more confused due to its inability to rationally resolve this context. Eventually, the confusion becomes so great that the conceptualizing mind tires, unable to comprehend the context for skill acquisition and no longer motivated to do so. It is at this point that the mind is "ripe" for Enlightenment. The Enlightenment experience itself is sudden and forceful. It is a great realization, an intuitive leap. Once Enlightened, the learner can finally be described as a "Skilled" performer.

CONCLUSION

It may now be asked what it is that ultimately results from a Zen approach to motor skill acquisition and performance. In the true spirit of Zen, a master might reply, "Nothing." To recall that the Ultimate Emptiness (Sanskrit: sūnyatā; Chinese: k'ung) of Reality is a prime tenet of Buddhist metaphysics is to realize that it is exactly "nothing" which results. And in this lies everything.

REFERENCES

Chan Wing-Tsit (Trans. & Comp.). (1973). *A source book in Chinese philosophy*. Princeton, NJ: Princeton University Press.

Fung Yu-lan. (1953). *A history of Chinese philosophy* (Vol. 2) (D. Bodde, Trans.). Princeton, NJ: Princeton University Press.

Herrigel. E. (1971). Zen and the art of archery. New York: Random House.

Herrigel, E. (1974). *The method of Zen* (H. Tausend, Ed., & R.F.C. Hull, Trans.). New York: Random House.

Hyams, J. (1979). *Zen in the martial arts*. Los Angeles: J.P. Tarcher.

Runes, D.D. (Ed.). (1980). *Dictionary of philosophy*. New Jersey: Littlefield, Adams.

Suzuki, D.T. (1973). *Zen and Japanese culture*. Princeton, NJ: Princeton University Press.

Watson, B. (1968). (Trans.). *The complete works of Chuang Tzu*. New York: Columbia University Press.

The nature
of martial arts
and their change
in the West

Angelika Förster
Universität Karlsruhe

The interest in Eastern martial arts has recently found its manifestation in the philosophy of sport and in the practice-oriented integration of Far Eastern exercises into traditional Western sports. However, an analysis of the philosophical background and practice which forms the basis for sufficient comparison of Western and Eastern physical culture is more or less missing. Particularly suitable for such an analysis are the Japanese *budo* disciplines. (Budo is the Japanese "generic" term for the martial arts.) The budo disciplines are fully integrated into the Japanese educational system and have found widespread support in the Western world during the last decades. The Japanese martial arts belong to the so-called *do* disciplines (i.e., judo, karatedo, tea-ceremony, etc.) and have a highly developed teaching tradition and philosophy which vary fundamentally from the Western combat forms such as boxing and fencing.

THE NATURE OF EASTERN MARTIAL ARTS

The concept of do (way)
The emphasis of do is inherent in all the arts which are influenced by Zen-Buddhism. The origin of this do concept goes gack to Chinese sources and has the following meaning: It is important to follow a certain path, to pursue it assiduously and unswervingly, and thereby to lay special emphasis on the inherent maturing process. It is not important which path is chosen, for every path has its own worth. Most significantly, it is not the final result or the success which counts, but the experiences gathered in the pursuit of the path. This concept emphasizes inner attitudes and self-knowledge in the sense of the Zen tradition.

One of the most remarkable aspects of this tradition is that by following the special path, excellence is not excluded. It is rather the result of long, unswerving exercise which constitutes the basis of inner perfection. Do does not imply the renunciation of achievements nor does it exclude an orientation toward a certain goal: It goes far beyond this. Achievements are possible on a different level and are seen as an integral part of the path. What counts is the *way* of achieving the goal, not the goal itself. Thus, many Western practitioners of noncompetitive martial arts harbor the misconception that do totally excludes achievement or competition (Leonard, 1975).

Western sports overvalues competition and overrates the so-called competitive spirit. In contrast, if we adopt the do concept, the idea of winning and losing, of victory and defeat does not have the same significance; competition is only a by-product, an intermediate step within the longer and more important maturing process. In view of the humanization of sports (Lenk, 1977), the athlete may follow his "path" for a lifetime regardless of the physical and psychical conditions, regardless of whether or not he may attain high-level achievements.

The "paradox" of martial arts

The do orientation of the martial arts formed budo in such a way that defeating an opponent is not the common aim or goal (Förster, 1983, pp. 219-223). Recent analysis shows, for example, "that Eastern 'combat sports'...tend to reduce violent tendencies and curb them" (Becker, 1982, p. 21). Fighting and aggression need not be connected or interdependent. On the contrary, full fighting force and use of inner energies are only possible if aggression and the initial aim-orientation are eliminated. This "emptiness" enables the fighter to achieve the highest quality of movements, and the necessary state of quiet and alertness. In this stage, the opponent can barely hit or tax the "empty" fighter. Does this mean that the rejection of fighting and aggression are only the means to create a fighting superiority? Not at all! The fact still remains that highest fighting force is only attained when the "paradox," the full rejection of fighting, is reached. (Goal-seeking sometimes occurs, but not for long.) Ultimately, philosophy and ethics present in the practice of budo prevent the undermining of the "paradox" (through rituals of respect toward the opponent, rules of conduct, and nonaggressive behavior, etc.). Even the "toughest" martial art demonstrates this markedly (Förster, 1983).

Unfortunately, this regulating factor is often lost in the adoption of Far-Eastern methods which have brutalized the martial arts. The impulse to fight can only be overcome by the martial art and fighting *practice*! Even the engaged Westerner may not grasp the complexity of the "paradox," which, in turn, leads to deep misunderstandings about the tough, more competitive disciplines (Leonard, 1975), or to self-deception and over-estimation concerning one's own degree of mastery.

The essence of exercise in do

Western philosophy of sport clings to self-fulfillment through sports. Due to a "concern for excellence" (Weiss, 1969), the athlete tries to excel and to overcome the daily routine. In an educational sense, this form of experience is very important, but as an isolated conception, it has many disadvantages. In high-performance sports such disadvantages are reflected in the obsessive hunt for records and outstanding performance with all its negative implications and excesses (i.e., doping). Unique striving for achievement deprives the athlete of essential inner dimensions of the experience. Competition and high-level performance are only a small part of the whole sport experience. Why should it not be possible to achieve self-assertion independently from external success and external dynamics, and thereby derive deep enjoyment from daily practice? In other words, why should it not be possible to emphasize the internal maturing process of the athlete?

Western sports are fixed on skills, abilities, and physical strength which lead to an artificial separation of body and soul. In the martial arts, technical skills and abilities are secondary; rather, they are the means to give stability to the "path." Exercise is more enriching and satisfying in martial arts because it is based on a wholistic concept, that is, a unity of physical and mental elements.

Kihon (basics)

Kihon is the term used to describe the process of learning and mastering the techniques. The trainee repeats the basic techniques in the optimal form to the best of his or her ability and with full mental concentration no matter how often they are repeated. On a more advanced level, the trainee perceives the difference while executing the movements. The ultimate object is not to reach a degree of automatization. In other words, the purpose of the exercise is not to achieve an effortless and complete mastering, but, instead, to use the mastering achieved to transcend the purpose. At this stage, the student only has to attend to the inner factors such as anxiety or fear. Attention is directed away from the technique and toward the inner state; the technique is a mirror of this inner state of mind. Thus, in practice, the hit that does not score is not the result of a lack of skill but is caused by the inner state. The trainee uses the technique as a medium to explore his inner self and thus to train his mental abilities.

Kihon is also used to attain fringe experiences. The effort is so great that when the trainee reaches his limits, he can only rely on his own will power and self-conquest. To reach these limits, it is most helpful to train in rhythm with a group using fighting cries which encourage development of a fighting spirit.

Kata (form)

Kata are inseparable parts of the large variety of exercises. They are combined defense and attack patterns under the assumption that a number of enemies are attacking from different directions. The inherent fighting principles and techniques have been handed down for centuries. Kata are fascinating combinations of movement patterns, concentration, and inner energy (*ki*) which show clearly the aesthetics of the martial arts. More than that, the movements of kata express its philosophical and ethical basis. Therefore, kata not only represent a form, but also a meaning. For example, each kata or *karatedo* (shotokan style) starts with defense (blocking). This shows the rejection of violent, aggressive behavior and the peace-loving character of this art. The wish for harmony with nature and cosmic principles (*yin* and *yang*) manifests itself in the imitation of animal movements, waves, and rhythms. Without meaning, the value of the form would be lost and again would be no more than mere skill without inner orientation.

As well as evaluating the importance of form (and technique), the mastery of the practitioner must be taken into consideration. When Becker (1982, p. 23) claimed "that in martial arts the form of the movement is more fundamental than any other results," it showed an incomplete understanding of form in the martial arts. An interesting dialectic exists in the sense that through the emphasis of the inner meaning of form in do, at some time or other the form itself becomes unimportant. For that reason, the teaching tradition demands that the advanced student "break off," not cling to the form, and transcend technique. A real master is able to act spontaneously, to free himself from all forms, and even in hazardous situations, is able to find the simplest solution, to not use complicated forms or techniques; and perhaps is able even to renounce the fight. Thus, masters of the highest degree revert to wearing the white beginner's belt, instead of the black master's belt.

Zhanshin and hara

Two principles are taught from the beginning of training and are correlated. *Zhanshin* means alertness, attention. The practitioner perceives his environment with full attention and concentrates on his own action without losing inner stability. It does not mean suppressing external stimuli. It is a relaxed awareness which enables the practitioner to remain fully active. Zhanshin is inseparable from body processes and feelings and is located in the lower part of the human body, a few inches below the navel. In Japanese culture the nucleus of body and soul, which is the center of personality, is called *hara*. Western culture is upper body oriented; feelings are located in the heart, and attention is in the head. Hara has a twofold meaning for the budoka because the physical center of gravity of the body (control of balance, safe stance) coincides with zhanshin and the inner body processes. The outward manifestation of hara is the earth-bound and "centered" stance of the fighter. It maintains openness and alertness and enables the fighter to control complex processes of activation and relaxation. For the Westerner, these Far-Eastern principles have great importance. They are related to carriage, proper breathing, the nervous system, and muscular tension and relaxation. It is interesting to note that these principles are an integral part of different therapies such as bioenergetics and breathing therapies.

The inner experience and the concept of no mind

Fringe experiences as they are sought at times in budo are found today in high-performance sports, especially sports with risk and endurance. The experiences and feelings (see "flow," Gabler, 1981) may be so intrinsically motivating they are repeatedly sought afresh. They correspond to general, but highly active states of trance. This may also be an explanation for the persisting fascination of these kinds of sports. During the "flow" experience, external stimuli are hardly noticed; attention is selective.

This experience differs in some ways from the quality of experience aimed for by daily exercise in the martial arts. Attention is not reduced, but increased. In this case, the fighter and the environment melt together.

The fighter becomes completely absorbed by the movement so that there is congruency between intention and execution. This new quality of reality is only possible when the fighter reaches a "loss of ego," free from an anxiety, success-bound orientation. The fighter may liberate inner forces which do not emerge by willpower. This concept of *no mind*, this unison which overcomes the rift between thinking and action, is felt positively due to the ease of movement and the different perception of time.

No mind, with body and mind in perfect harmony, is systematically taught but not limited to the martial arts or to high-level performance. It is only possible if thoughts do not plan the movements in advance. The response to a situation takes place without any thought about "doing it," but does not imply an absence of thinking. Thinking takes place within the action and after the action. Tiwald (1981) questions the usual concept that movement imagination precedes the movement experience. He contends the reverse is true: do orientation and no mind stress learning as an inductive process. The students learn by imitation and observation and have to be more self-critical. The techniques are acquired on the basis of a wholistic process, and in order to control possible dangers inherent in martial arts, it is necessary to strictly observe discipline and hierarchy (i.e., the concepts of shuhari, sensei-sempai-kohai, etc.).

THE EASTERN MARTIAL ARTS IN THE WESTERN WORLD

Obviously, some of the typical Japanese social structures and religious rituals (e.g., Shinto) could not be adopted. The transition of the martial arts to martial "sports" imparts a negative impact. Specialization supplants do orientation; commercialism paves the way into show business, and the worst result is the brutalization of the martial arts. Full-contact karate, most popular in the United States, is an example.

One positive consequence of the practice of martial arts is the rediscovery of meditative moments in the sport experience. Sport as a means of self-discovery allows the renewal of personal unity in the do sense. This coincides with the search for new methods for increasing this quality of performance. The inner game (Gallwey, 1974) offers such possibilities for the athlete. But the simple assumption of methods isolated from philosophical background and do practice with only partial understanding of the martial arts lead inevitably to a change of the method, and a failure to realize the enriching potential of Western sport.

REFERENCES

Becker, G. B. (1982). Philosophical perspectives on the martial arts in America. *Journal of the Philosophy of Sport, 9*, 19-29.

Förster, A. (1983). Neue perspektiven für den sport durch die philosophie and praxis der fernöstlichen kampfkünste. In H. Lenk (Ed.), *Topical problems of sport philosophy* (pp. 211-240). Schorndorf: Hofmann.

Gabler, H. (1981). Fringe experience in high-performance sport from the psychological viewpoint of motivation. In *Olympic performance, ideal, conditions, limits. Meetings between sport and science* (pp. 248-264, 466). Cologne, West Germany: Bundesinstitut für Sportwissenschaften.

Gallwey, W. T. (1974). *The inner game of tennis.* New York: Random House.

Lenk, H. (1977). Humanisierung im hochleistungssport. In H. Lenk (Ed.), *Handlungsmuster leistungssport.* Schorndorf: Hofmann.

Leonard, G. (1975). *The ultimate athlete.* New York: Viking.

Tiwald, H. (1981). *Psycho-training im kampf und budo-sport.* Ahrensburg: Czwalina.

Weiss, P. (1969). *Sport: A philosophic inquiry.* Carbondale, IL: Southern Illinois University Press.

Chinese martial art: Bridging the cultural gap between East and West

Adam Hsu
Chih Ke Kung Fu School

Chinese martial art is often referred to as *kung fu*, a generalized term for any skill attained through hard work over a long period of time. This term is associated with the martial arts of China because years of dedicated practice are required to reach a level of mastery. Like other cultural traditions such as dance or literature, kung fu is a mature art that represents the accumulated knowledge and experience of generations of practitioners.

Although the East and West are less isolated from one another today, the people and culture of China remain a mystery to most Westerners. The complex character of the Chinese people and the ancient philosophy that underlies the culture are woven into the fabric of traditional kung fu. Thus, learning kung fu can help to bridge the cultural gap between East and West.

Learning kung fu is not an easy task, however. The cultural context from which kung fu derives is vastly different from Western tradition, and the fundamental principles of kung fu are difficult for Westerners to understand and to incorporate in their training. By examining the evolution of traditional kung fu and the principles of technique and usage, the path that one must follow to cross from West to East can be more clearly defined.

ORIGINS OF KUNG FU

Kung fu was developed to satisfy practical needs of the ancient Chinese. It was not developed for sporting competition or as a performing art, but for defending oneself and one's family, village, or country. The authentic kung fu that has endured into the 20th century reflects the ingenuity of a people dependent on fighting skill for survival. Indeed, kung fu was shaped by the grim realities of warfare and must be considered in this light to grasp the essence of the art.

In general, the development of fighting technique into a sophisticated art coincided with the evolution of Chinese civilization. As people's occupations became more specialized, professional martial artists became prevalent, devoting all their time and effort toward refining their fighting skills.

FIGHTING TECHNIQUES

Arm usage

Because the hand is such an important part of the human fighting apparatus, martial artists first concentrated their efforts on improving this feature. Many hand techniques were developed involving distinctive hand formations such as the open hand, fist, and hook, and different parts of the hand were used including the palm, fingers, and knuckles.

But those techniques designed primarily for the hand were still very limited. The ancient Chnese martial artists were determined to surpass those limitations and developed the usage of the entire arm as a basis for more sophisticated fighting techniques. They expressed this idea in a saying, "The whole arm is the fist."

This principle is applicable regardless of hand formation; the hand is comparable to a drill bit and the arm to a drill motor. Using the whole arm (from the shoulder to the hand) gives one a larger area with which to attack or defend, and enables one to attack and defend simultaneously. For example, a strike can be countered by sliding the arm along the opponent's attacking arm, using the forearm and elbow area to deflect the attack as the fist strikes the opponent. Also, the different areas of the arm can be used interchangeably; if one's fist is parried, the elbow or shoulder can succeed the initial attack.

This approach to fighting brought a different mentality to Chinese martial art; the possibilities for technique were greatly expanded, and the dynamics of usage became more adaptable and flexible. If one is trained to focus all attention and technique on using the hand only (single-point technique), one is likely to be in a vulnerable position if the initial attack fails. If, however, the whole arm is considered the fist, a fist attack can be followed naturally—like the connected cars of a train—by the forearm, elbow, upper arm, and shoulder. This is a major difference between kung fu and other martial arts. In kung fu the fist is considered *a* striking surface, not *the* striking surface.

Whole body usage

Over the centuries Chinese martial artists developed the concept of the "arm is the fist" even further. Realizing that the arm is actually an extension of the body, they began to see techniques in terms of the whole body. Eventually, they revised their concept to say that the "whole body is the fist."

The whole body approach to martial art is rooted in the psychological heritage of China. The *lung*, a mythological creature that symbolizes good fortune in Chinese culture, is a composite of many animals: a horse's face, eagle's claw, ox's nose, snake's body, deer's horns, lion's tail, and fish's whiskers. This creature reflects the adaptable, complex character of the Chinese people, who were able to create such a unique way of using the body. When the whole body is coordinated as a functional unit, any part can be used to inflict damage. This kind of complex, multiple-attacking usage requires an ability to concentrate on and use several parts of the body simultaneously. One must be able to adapt and to change continuously like water flowing until the ultimate goal is achieved— destroying the opponent.

The kung fu way of using the whole body as a weapon is quite different from single-point fighting techniques. In learning kung fu, Westerners must develop a more flexible mentality that enables the mind to focus on more than one area of the body at once; then the body parts can be orchestrated to execute the kung fu techniques correctly. This training process requires patience and dedication, and a willingness to modify ingrained patterns of thinking.

Opening the door

Close-in fighting techniques are predicated on being able to reach the opponent. Kung fu experts devised a simple concept with which to analyze this tactical problem. They visualized a spherical space around the body consisting of nine interrelated doors, subdivided into three sets of three doors. The main entrance (front of the body) and two side entrances (left and right sides of body) constitute one set of doors. The upper, middle, and lower portions of the body make up another set of doors, and the three distances relative to the body—far, middle, and inner—constitute the last set of doors.

For example, one might approach an area such as the middle level of the side door and try to enter and move into the opponent's upper-level inner door. If that particular approach is untenable (the door is closed), one must try an alternative approach. Also, the opponent must be approached in a way that does not leave one's own door open and vulnerable to attack. This strategy is best accomplished by finding a "leak" in the opponent's defense and attacking that specific area (door). One must use speed, timing, and technique to take advantage of such an opportunity. Oftentimes one must "create" a leak to open the door by using fakes, applying pressure, or trading blows. Once the opponent's door is open, the conflict is nearly finished.

For Westerners, the main and side doors and the upper, middle, and lower doors are not difficult to comprehend. The far, middle, and inner doors, however, are not well understood by Westerners.

From the position of the far door, for example, one must use the body position to pressure the opponent, without touching, circling the opponent like a wary cat. One must be able to slam the door— to stop an attack—almost before it happens. The far door involves farsightedness, the ability to plan more than three movements in advance as in a chess match, along with having the capability of adjusting automatically to changing circumstances. If one thinks that it is possible to reach and totally destroy the opponent according to a specific plan, one will not be seduced by opportunities to inflict only partial damage.

Westerners, on the contrary, are more apt to grab the first opportunity to attack, to try to force in the door if possible. This aggressive mental attitude is a good quality, but it must be tempered with intelligence and skill. In modern society there is a tendency to hurry forward for fear of letting any chance go by. The Chinese take a broader view of life. Their thinking is shaped by a long history and by philosophies that include Confucianism, Taoism, and Buddhism. They see life in terms of generations, continuity, and cycles. Patience, waiting for a decisive opportunity, is considered a great virtue by the Chinese.

The step

The Chinese say that one should attack the door first and then attack the opponent. The only way to bring the whole body to attack the door is the step. The step is used to situate the body in relation to the target (shortening or lengthening the fighting distance). Of course, using the arms is necessary to protect oneself and make contact, but the step is more important. A kung fu expression relates that the arm may inflict the damage, but the step creates the opportunity.

This area of usage is little known, even among kung fu practitioners. Many kung fu experts rarely taught the real use of the step; they considered it so crucial that they did not want to teach their technique to someone who might use it against them.

In kung fu, the outcome of a fight depends primarily on leg usage. In general, usage involves 30% arm and 70% leg usage. Leg usage does not mean kicking; it refers to using the steps and stances. The Chinese sometimes call steps and stances "dark" or hidden kicks because every one is a potential kick or leg maneuver, such as a lock or sweep, that can put one inside the opponent's door.

Most leg usage is low and not as obvious as high kicks. This fact demonstrates another facet of the Chinese character—indirectness. The more direct, impulsive approach prevalent in Western culture is not characteristic of kung fu. In kung fu, the less obvious parts of the body are frequently used to inflict the most damage or control the opponent. Because one is not committed to any fixed pattern of movement, the opponent cannot easily predict where the attack will come or what part of the body will be used.

Issuing power

All martial arts have special methods that train one to issue the power. The Chinese developed a method of issuing power to facilitate using the entire body for complex, multiple attacking. Technique and the way of issuing power are completely interwoven so that any part of the body can be used to issue power instantaneously. This method is known as *chan szu ching* (silk reeling) because its application resembles the movement of a silk thread as it is pulled from a cocoon.

Chan szu ching involves increasing the working distance of the body. A child learns early on that in order to throw a ball far, he or she must start the throw from behind the shoulder. By initiating the movement from that point, the ball is thrown much farther than if it were merely flicked with the wrist or thrown solely with the power of the forearm and elbow. Similarly, in martial arts, one is limited by the relative size and mass of the body. Therefore, we try to heighten our power. Some martial arts rely mainly on a muscular strength and momentum gained through speed within a framework of movement to issue power.

Chan szu ching uses the intrinsic energy of the body to increase power. All the body's joints are applied in a highly disciplined twisting action (see Figure 1). For example, in striking with the fist, the power comes from the effect of all the joints, tendons, muscles, and bones—beginning with the foot, ankle, knee, hip, waist, back, shoulder, elbow, wrist, and finally the hand—working together as a single unit (see Figure 2).

The entire body must be relaxed and grounded until the moment of impact when all the accumulated energy is focused on and delivered to the target. The

Figure 1. Chan szu ching creates a spiraling or corkscrewing action that increases the working distance available from which to issue power.

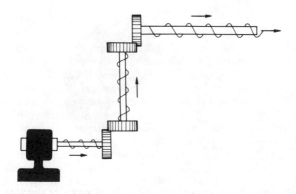

Figure 2. Similar to a set of interlocking gears, the joints of the body, beginning at the rear heel and progressing to the hand, coordinate to use the intrinsic energy of the body to issue power.

actual working distance is from the rear heel to the hand, but this distance is not measured in a straight line; it is measured via the curved line of the spiral. Chan szu ching implements a corkscrewing action that unifies the straight and the curved. As the body moves forward in space (like a thread of silk), it simultaneously revolves on its own axis (like the rotation of the cocoon as the silk reels), creating a force much greater than that which is dependent on strength and speed alone.

Chan szu ching is not a natural way of moving. Learning this skill is difficult and requires great patience and a step-by-step approach. The first step is becoming aware of old patterns of movement learned from conventional sports and other activities. One must shed these habits to make way for the kung fu way of moving. As the ancient Chinese philosopher Lao Tzu (Sih, 1961, p. 13) states, "In gathering your vital energy to attain suppleness, have you reached the state of a new-born babe?"

Initially, one must practice without power, cultivating a relaxed awareness. This type of training will make someone who is young and strong feel very awkward and weak. However, "investing in loss" is essential to realizing the goal of the training. Chan szu ching training can teach Westerners a great deal about themselves and give direct experience of the values of patience and hard work that are such an integral part of Chinese culture.

EAST-WEST DIFFERENCES

Yin and yang

These multiple fighting techniques can also be explained in terms of ancient Chinese philosophy. The theory of yin and yang was developed as a practical way of describing and classifying the universe. Yin and yang represent complementary opposites such as day and night, male and female, in and out, fast and slow, and hard and soft. The Chinese convey this relationship graphically in a circular shape that expresses the interaction and complementary nature of opposites (see Figure 3). The curving line that connects the two entities expresses the basic idea underlying the theory of yin and yang—change. Yin and yang, therefore, symbolize the process of flux in nature: day (yang) is always changing

Figure 3. The tai chi diagram graphically represents the interaction of yin and yang.

into night (yin), and night is always changing into day. Not only do yin and yang continuously interact, but the yin always contains some yang, and the yang contains some yin. The essence of this idea is found in the Chinese saying, ''Yang reaches its limit and gives birth to yin; yin reaches its limit and gives birth to yang.''

In Western culture ideas are more fixed (black and white), as evidenced in Western styles of martial art by the more rigid conception of usage and technique. It is difficult for Westerners to conceptualize existence as an interplay of complementary forces in a state of continual change and to apply the concept to martial art. The concept of yin and yang is completely absorbed within kung fu—the whole body is continually moving, turning, and twisting, adjusting spontaneously to the demands of the situation.

Many of the older generation kung fu experts were illiterate and could not explain their art, but their kung fu naturally conformed to the principles of yin and yang. Understanding the theory of yin and yang can give Westerners insight into the depth and sophistication of both Chinese philosophy and kung fu.

Body type

Body type is also an area that shows the physical and mental differences between East and West. The ability to use the whole body techniques of kung fu necessitates a strong foundation. If the legs are not strong enough, the techniques cannot be executed effectively. Like the roots of a tree, the bottom half of the body must be able to support the upper branches.

Western culture places more emphasis on upper body strength. The ideal male physique is characterized by broad shoulders and narrow hips, and the breath is carried high in the chest to assume a proud bearing as exemplified by soldiers in the military ''at attention'' pose. This creates a body structure similar to an inverted pyramid—broad at the top and narrow at the base.

Kung fu requires the opposite kind of structure—wide at the base and narrow at the top—and the breath must sink to the lower abdomen. When the weight sinks into the lower body, the foundation is naturally stronger and more stable. Asian people, due to their culture and physique, are more equal in terms of upper and lower body balance. Kung fu training cannot be adapted to suit Western body types. Therefore, Western preconceptions about the body must be revised, and students must follow the kung fu training to help restructure the body.

CONCLUSION

In this chapter, the fundamental principles of kung fu and some of the general differences between the mind and body of East and West were briefly outlined. Students who want to study kung fu or learn about Chinese culture must be willing to cross the bridge from West to East and open themselves to new ideas.

Kung fu was developed specifically as a fighting art, but it also teaches important moral and social principles that can be applied in everyday living. In today's modern society, qualities such as patience, honesty, devotion, and a serious attitude toward study can benefit humanity. For Westerners, kung fu is indeed a path filled with difficulty—following this path, however, can lead to a profound understanding of oneself and the Chinese people and culture.

REFERENCE

Sih, P.K.T. (Ed.). (1961). *Tao Teh Ching* (J. Wu, Trans.). New York: St. John's University Press.

The role
of hatha yoga
in the martial arts

Lynda D. Mitchell
Lynda Mitchell Yoga Studio

Upon entering the majority of martial arts training halls in the United States to-day, an observer immediately becomes aware of the sounds of physical activity. The most deliberate sounds are the purposeful karate yells, or the conscious expulsion of breath in conjunction with an executed technique. The observer sees arms and legs in various states of suspension—limbs extended, retracted, poised, or relaxed....And always the sound of breathing. The manifestations of energy, of movement and vitality show in occasional beads of sweat. A quivering leg or an unplanned shuffle of feet not only indicates the difficulty of a balanced recovery from a particular stance, but also reveals the experience level of the student. The focused gaze of a dedicated student expresses a high degree of concentration. Moments of inactivity are balanced against moments of action. The deceptive ease of movement of the advanced student exhibits the calm and stability sought in an Eastern art form.

The same observer, looking in on a hatha yoga class, sees similar manifestations of physical activity: extended limbs, concentrated gaze, and ease of movement. Conscious control of breathing and balance and the careful effort of coordinated body movement in slow and relaxed rhythms would set the pace of the class. Rather than the outward and direct expression of most martial arts activity, one sees an inwardly directed and static effort to control and balance the forces of tension between muscular resistance and muscular action. Silence and stillness sets the yoga studio apart from the typical martial arts training hall. But always, and most importantly, both are marked by an attention to proper breathing, without which the closely related disciplines of yoga and the martial arts would remain weak and ineffectual.

One may ask how or why the yogi might legitimately end up in a martial arts training class, where to many untrained observers, much of what is happening seems to be rough and ready violence in the television screen style of the black belt performer. How can the quiet and passive yogic creature reconcile him or herself to the potentially injurious display of power or violence of many of the martial artists in today's modern world? Perhaps opposites do attract and complement each other, or perhaps in order to attain strength and enlightenment, one must learn many ways and many techniques.

Only the student trained in the awareness of physical and mental states of activity can attain the ultimate control required by these specific Eastern disciplines.

The patience and slow progress of the yogic form leads one to a greater understanding of self and actions. The majority of martial arts students, so charged with energy and plans, never consider the importance of a still moment, and thus may never learn the value of a clear and relaxed mind.

The intention of this chapter is to demonstrate ways in which hatha yoga can assist the martial artist in reaching higher levels of perfection. To go to the yoga roots of the martial arts is to go beyond the techniques, beyond the way. It is to start when movement was codified in the Yoga Sutras of Patanjali, over 3,000 years ago in ancient India. The relaxed stretches, lifts, balances, and breathing exercises of yoga were designed to develop a meditative mind, as well as strength and agility. Legend has it that the yogic monk Bodhidharma transformed these yogic postures into fighting movements for purposes of protection and physical conditioning. Moving into China, these techniques took on local and national characteristics and evolved into more specific martial art forms from country to country as time passed.

VALUES OF YOGA FOR MARTIAL ARTS PRACTITIONERS

Postures

Most of us readily admit to the value of yoga postures in preparation for martial arts training. Bouncing and repetitive stretching movements have been largely replaced by the long static stretches of hatha yoga. Stretching enables muscles to relax and lengthen. Especially important for the martial artist are the stretches for the hips and pelvis which improve ease of hip movement because every defense receives its decisive force by turning away the hip. In yoga and martial arts, all action generates from the pelvis, which depends upon the limberness and strength of the spine. Special exercises are devoted to the back and spine because the yogis considered a limber spine crucial for smooth bodily functioning. Stretching also promotes limberness in the large motor muscles of the legs, thus further increasing range of movement. A limber body can transform movement into a graceful flow of coordination and rhythm, whether it is the body of a dancer, athlete, housewife, or businessman.

Relaxation

The ancient masters also knew that the swiftest motions were only possible when relaxed. They systematically taught their students many physical and mental techniques of relaxation. Although relaxation is important for quick, supple movement, utmost tension is needed at the moment of striking, and it is said that whoever is master of relaxation is also master of tension. Yoga stretches are designed in part to specifically target the release of suppressed and bound up energy in the body. Relaxed tissues dissolve tension, resulting in improved circulation and energy flow. Encouraged to concentrate during stretching, the student becomes aware of subtle changes within the body. Eventually, more dramatic transformation and awareness occurs as the body responds to daily practice and patience.

Breathing

Just as relaxation is essential to ease of movement, correct breathing methods are essential in concentrating power to display strength and confidence. The karate practitioner is instructed to yell from the diaphragm and to exhale along with the execution of a particular technique. Specific yoga breathing exercises isolate the breathing muscles so that the student becomes aware of the breathing mechanism. As always, breathing practice is slow and deliberate, requiring total concentration; all but the most basic exercises are complicated and involve conscious respiratory control. The intensity and exaggeration of the yoga breathing exercises lead to increased lung capacity and improved circulation through stretched and opened lung passages. Such practices eventually insure more efficient breathing patterns in both stressful and normal situations.

The importance of correct breathing cannot be overestimated, and without an adequate knowledge of breathing techniques, the martial artist may be considered partially handicapped. The martial artist knows that exhaling helps when tensing, and that one exhales at the moment of greatest force and release. In the East, yoga and the martial arts have been long regarded as a psychological development, and the breathing methods are a constant factor in the unification of mind and body. Specifically, the basic action of the diaphragmatic breathing exercise of hatha yoga bypasses normal stimulation to the vagus nerve which activates all sympathetic functioning. As the active system relaxes, so does the autonomic system, thus allowing the body an opportunity for deeper rest. Diaphragmatic breathing is normal when one is asleep or relaxed. The person consciously trained in diaphragmatic breathing generally has a reserve of energy and strength, an obvious benefit to the martial artist.

Balance

The balance postures of yoga, which develop steadiness and a unity of mind and body, eventually make possible a balanced position with very little muscular effort. Balance is the foundation of a martial art and can easily be learned through simple yoga practice. Confidence and focus are enhanced by performing such postures as the tree, the eagle, the stork, or any number of yoga balances. These postures also strengthen the legs and feet, and at the same time, place little strain on joints or muscles.

Isolating various muscle groups into contracted and relaxed states provides an awareness of the physical sensation of vitality and action. The eventual conscious control and balance develops the total body into a finely tuned instrument. At this point, relaxation becomes more important as the body becomes more sensitized. Yoga teaches an awareness and appreciation of the moment, an acceptance and ability to adapt or to become immune to outside disturbances. As the postures teach the body to bend without breaking, so the mind learns to empty without closing.

SIMILARITIES IN YOGA AND MARTIAL ARTS

The cumulative effects of yoga and martial arts practice lead to a build-up of power which requires tempering in light of the ancient doctrine of *ahimsa*, or nonviolence. In a Western culture accustomed to violence, such a concept may cause confusion in the minds and hearts of many an undeveloped martial art student. In the words of a Chou dynasty treatise on the martial arts called the *Sun-Tzu* (Oyama, 1965, p. 319), ''The ultimate good lies not in winning a hundred battles but in overcoming a man or an army without a conflict.'' To the immature student the words have only a vague and mystical sense. The yoga student quickly learns that one must overcome one's own desires and demands, whether of the body or of the mind. The real secret of the martial arts is to defeat the opponent without thought of victory. The secret of yoga is that the opponent is oneself, and what is important is to be aware of one's own self at all times. This consciousness, this heightened awareness, becomes the defensive weapon against attack, real or imaginary, external or internal. In both disciplines, release from the ego, the fostering of humility and tolerance, and detachment from any narrow perspective of thought are achievements requiring special skills and strengths. Thus the alert yet detached state of the warrior is required for both the temporal and the spiritual battle.

In both disciplines, one must come to know oneself; then comes knowledge of others, friend or foe. The words of the *Sun Tzu* repeat (Oyama, 1965, p. 319), "If we know the other man and know ourselves, there is no fear in 100 battles. If we know not the other man, but know ourselves, the odds are even. If we know neither the man nor ourselves, there is danger." (And so the Socratic dictum "Know Thyself" continues as a thread through both Eastern and Western philosophical thought.)

Ultimately, the expansion of a sixth sense determines the maturity of the martial artist. This perception or intuition can be systematically developed through the quiet and conscious practice of deep meditative or relaxed states. However, this discipline of mind and body is difficult to achieve if one does not possess proper muscular coordination. Conversely, the yogic and fighting masters tell us that if the spiritual side of the discipline is ignored, its physical aspect is meaningless. The yoga way of turning inward can help to make possible the refinement of the body and of the spirit. It is through the practice of meditation that a desired state of inner calm can give birth to strength of action and can focus the mind on positive and creative purpose.

Yoga is based on the premise that all action begins in the mind. An untrained mind in constant motion can frustrate the ambitions of any performer. Calm, directed action is impossible without a calm and focused mind. Ancient yoga techniques of visualization and concentration have become increasingly acceptable as modern research on mental states and physical behavior bears out the claims of the science of yoga. Yoga is a study of stillness, a study of silence. One first learns to control the body and mind through inaction, and then one contemplates and carries out actions.

CONCLUSION

The martial arts student benefits in many ways from yoga practice and will find that control and understanding of one's actions and feelings can lead to noble results. The passive ways of yoga, instilling methods of alleviating fear, ego, ignorance, attachments, and aversions are of inestimable value to the active ways of the warrior. The stretching and body lifting postures along with relaxation, breathing exercises, concentration, and self-observation can prepare the student to continue any martial art with equanimity and confidence. The ways of both sciences can only serve to better the life of the individual and, ideally, the life of society.

REFERENCE

Oyama, M. (1965). *This is karate*. Tokyo: Publications Trading Company.

Aikido: The art of human movement

Gregory D. Olson and
Norman D. Comfort III
Montana State University

The martial arts of the East—specifically of China and Japan—with their discipline, philosophy, and movement seem to capture the imagination of many people. In what way can movement forms of the martial arts contribute to sport-minded, analytical Western culture? The art of human movement is exemplified emphatically through the martial art aikido. Aikido embodies a way of defense, a way of movement, and a way of life. An informative look at the Japanese martial art aikido, which provides an excellent alternative supplement to the physical education programs of the West is presented in this chapter. Included is a historical account of aikido and its founder as well as thoughts on intuitive and scientific paths to learning as demonstrated by aikido and the movement dynamics of aikido within its philosophy of movement.

A RECENT MARTIAL ART

Historically, aikido is a relatively modern martial art; its founder, Morihei Uyeshiba (1883-1969), while in his youth, studied many of the traditional martial ways and arts of Japan. For 86 years Uyeshiba's existence seemed to be devoted entirely to the development and continuous refinement of aikido: He studied three different *jujutsu* (unarmed self-defense) schools (the Kito, the Daito, and the Shinkage schools); Japanese swordsmanship from the Yagyu school; spear techniques; and was experienced in the modern way of judo. All of these arts greatly influenced and provided Master Uyeshiba with a very strong physical foundation on which to base his own ideas in developing a new martial way.

Although Uyeshiba was certified to teach several of the arts he had studied and mastered, he felt that something was missing. Was it necessary to study the martial ways and arts of ancient combat traditions in today's modern society? What would the chances be of ever being attacked in the modern world? So he asked himself—Why? What else could provide the answers?

He searched for his answer in the study of philosophy and religion. The concepts of Zen were studied in the Shingon school of Buddhism and the religious school of Omoto-ko. Master Uyeshiba deeply sought the secrets of the martial ways and now had a philosophical spiritual dimension with which to build and integrate with the physical dimension. Master Uyeshiba's enlightened synthesis of the mind and body, the philosophical and physical, finally produced his martial way—aikido—the way of harmony with nature and energy.

In 1925, Master Uyeshiba started his own *dojo* (training hall, or gymnasium) for the study of aikido in Tokyo. Although the beginning period for his dojo was very difficult, it has grown to one in which hundreds of people from all over the world train daily, and now has many branch dojos in Japan and throughout the world.

DIFFERENCES BETWEEN AIKIDO AND OTHER MARTIAL ARTS

Compassion

How then does Uyeshiba's aikido differ physically and philosophically from its predecessors and other martial arts? Physically, the techniques may lie anywhere on a continuum from not touching to totally devastating an attacker. Philosophically speaking, this provides the *aikidoka* (practitioner or student of aikido) with a wide range of choices in dealing with a violent attack. The fact that there are choices suggests another continuum in regards to a philosophy of defense. At the upper end of the spectrum lies the choice of compassion, whereby the aikidoka chooses to meet an intended violent attack with love, harmonizes with the aggressor, and neutralizes the attack with the least harm to the attacker and virtually no harm to him. The other end of the spectrum holds the choice for complete disregard for human life. The choice for compassion gives aikido something many martial arts and ways cannot attain. Uyeshiba saw love as the heart of martial arts in which harmony instead of resistance and the resolution of conflict instead of the propagation of violence were practiced.

Noncompetitive

Aikido differs greatly from the modern sport versions of traditional martial ways in that aikido is not a sport. Although aikido is usually practiced in groups of two, there is no competition, only mutual cooperation. For example, let us compare the sport of judo with aikido in basic structure and philosophy. In 1882, when Jigaro Kano founded judo, he realized that Japan was turning to the West for its skills. As a prominent figure in the Japanese educational system, having earned his doctorate in physical education, Professor Kano (later called the father of Japanese physical education) required all students to study either judo or *kendo* (Japanese fencing). Judo was derived from the unarmed combat form jujutsu as a sport in order to make it a safe and acceptable activity for the general population. The result of taking a combative form and deriving a sport from it is the removal of all potentially hazardous techniques that could maim or injure.

The new sport form must also have game boundaries, rules and regulations, judges, and a winner and a loser. The philosophical side to this issue means that the thinking of the practitioner is focused on winning, often resulting in practitioners lowering themselves to a "win at all costs" attitude. The rules become their foundation, winning is everything, and the individual becomes lost in the competition.

The founding of aikido as a noncompetitive martial way avoided the shortcomings and problems of a sport. The aikidoka trains toward a perfection of the self. There are no rules, boundaries, or judges; therefore, the only competition one has is with his own ego. If one can drop the ego, the rationalization process between reality and self, one realizes the beauty of harmony with nature—enlightenment!

THE PATH TO SELFLESSNESS

Zen skin

In Uyeshiba's aikido are three different levels of awareness that the aikidoka experiences on the path to selflessness. The first of these levels (sometimes referred to as *Zen skin*) is considered the technical level; the aikidoka trains in the *Kihon Waza* (basic or foundation techniques) to build a basic "vocabulary." Repetitious practice and study of basic movements and specific techniques provide the content for the aikidoka's vocabulary. Through many repetitions, the aikidoka becomes aware of the if-then syndrome, thinking that *if* a particular attack, *then* a specific corresponding technique must be applied.

Although this reasoning is incompatible with the upper levels of aikido training, it is an unavoidable part of beginning practice. This basic beginner level is often characterized by the students' overeagerness intellectually to understand techniques and results in extensive analysis and rationalization (sometimes referred to as a scientific approach). While scientific analysis of techniques and their movements can provide useful insights, it does not provide the complete way to study aikido. Book learning produces similar results, useful information, and study in foundation techniques, but this level can only provide a superficial coverage. The aikidoka must move on.

Zen flesh

Zen flesh is the second level of attainment for which the aikidoka strives, learning to see and feel the rhythm of movement. The underlying foundation of all movement, particularly the martial arts, is correct breathing. The correct breathing process produces a rhythm that is analogous to a rhythmic flow of energy. Inhaling, drawing air in, is seen as a drawing of energy from the surroundings into the aikidoka's center; exhaling, expelling air out, is viewed as an extension of directed energy from the aikidoka's center back into the environment. This energy, with its close connection to breathing and an individual's center, is referred to in the martial arts as *ki*. Through the experience and understanding of the rhythm of breathing (the flow of energy) comes the understanding of the rhythm of movement and energy flow within an attack. Practicing this level of awareness is the aikidoka's second major step in understanding the way of aikido.

Zen bones

The third level of awareness is that of *Zen bones*. As a new learning process begins, technique and rhythm are forgotten. An aikidoka is the movement and the movement is the aikidoka. At this level of attainment, all movement which had its foundation in Zen skin and Zen flesh is forgotten. The attack and defense, the mind and the body, no longer exist as separate entities; there is only the harmony of the pattern of movement. All movement is art, and art is the expression of self-actualization.

As previously stated, aikido is a way of defense. The attacker–defender relationship is at the root of the original martial art purpose and serves as a means of studying aikido's principles. Aikido, as a method of self-defense, has no apparent offensive actions, only calmness. Defense in aikido is to recognize the "mind of attack" in the opponent. If the mind of attack is not present, then there is no technique; however, if the intent (mind) to attack does exist, then the fact of the attack will provide an opening or weakness through which a technique can occur to neutralize the attack.

Mind of attack

The three levels of awareness experience—Zen skin, Zen flesh, and Zen bones—may be examined in another way through the example of recognizing the mind of attack and the concept that to attack produces an opening or weakness in the attacker. The first level the aikidoka experiences in training is to see an opening, then consciously choose and execute a technique. This is known as *Sen*: See the opening, *then* execute the technique.

Sen no Sen is the second level, in which the aikidoka is cognizant of doing a technique at the same time the opening developed and was seen: See the opening, executing the technique. In the third level, *Sen Sen no Sen*, all openings and techniques (as in Zen bones) are forgotten. Self is forgotten: See the opening, the technique is already completed; the opening and the technique occur simultaneously without conscious thought. This is the level of intuitive reasoning: The aikidoka feels the total situation, the reasons for the attack, and the justifiable action resulting. Feeling the environment, the aikidoka can act accordingly without emotion to color his actions. Intuition can therefore lead to compassion.

BRIDGING THE EAST-WEST GAP

The traditional Eastern approach to learning the martial arts seems to be based on intuition. This abstraction of thought, nurtured by body control oriented experiences designed to develop the inner awareness and perception of the mind, teaches the mind to respond through the body without evidence of conscious rational thought. Thus, what is produced is a heightened kinesthetic sense between mind and body acting as one intuitively.

The Western view of movement forms, particularly sport, has taken on new dimensions in scientific research and analysis. Human movement and biomechanics can now be systematically analyzed through high-speed cinematography and computer-assisted equipment. Highly skilled athletes are being introduced to such terms as *center of gravity* and *angular momentum*. Sport techniques are now being taught in relation to principles of movement and the physical laws of nature.

The gap between intuitive reasoning and scientific analysis can be bridged by aikido. Aikido allows a conceptual-visual analysis of the physical laws of nature and an understanding through a demonstrable efficiency in movement. At the same time, Aikido allows the opportunity for the mind to "let go" and depend on an intuitive kinesthetic sense to feel a oneness between the mind and body and a oneness with the laws of nature.

Movement dynamics

The heart of aikido's defensive structure and learning experiences lies in movement dynamics. The essence of aikido lies in its philosophy of movement and philosophy of life. To learn aikido is to learn to move in correct response and balance to the physical laws of nature. Techniques work because the physical laws of moving bodies and motion work. Aikido's principles of movement are in agreement with the laws of nature, for aikido is harmony with nature. The aikidoka's strength in dealing with an attack lies not in muscular resources, but in the harmonization with nature's laws.

Training in aikido deals first hand from the very beginning with the concepts of center of gravity, angular momentum, velocity, acceleration and deceleration. The most efficient way to study and experience aikido's movement dynamics is in partner practice (two people in cooperation). Aikido has its roots in defensive self-protection skills (and retains its potency if the need arises) which dictates the manner in which the movement skills are practiced. Usually one person takes the role of the defender and doer of a technique (*nage*), while the other attacks and receives the technique (*uke*). This becomes a dynamic system in which two people experience the balance and flow of energy. It is a dynamic system of at least two different bodies, interacting with different levels of energy flowing at first in different directions; then it becomes one system, one center, one energy flow, and one purpose as one aikidoka harmonizes with the other in the execution of a technique.

Principles of movement in aikido

There are certain principles of movement in aikido that respond to the dynamics of human movement. To be centered and stable both in movement and in posture is one of the most significant principles. Human motion follows the principle of angular momentum, in that the largest body parts start the motion and then transfer the energy via angular momentum to the other body parts. The hips, considered the largest body part, are the center to which martial artists refer. To control one's center is to control one's motion and power. Aikido's principle of spherical circular motion allows the aikidoka to deal with the linear energy of an attack and redirect and control it by drawing the opponent's center into his, harmonizing in a circular pattern.

Two of the most basic motions and movement principles in aikido are entering (*irimi*) and turning (*tenkan*). These two principles are used to either enter or turn out of a line of attack in order to gain a strategic position to unbalance the opponent and avoid the attack.

The principle of extension is closely linked to the flow of energy and mechanical advantage. The aikidoka learns to extend power either physically or mentally in order to control, lead, or unbalance the opponent. Mechanically, extension forces an opponent to deal with the aikidoka's center, the entire mass, whether a wrist or both shoulders are grasped. In applying the principles to an attack, the aikidoka allows the technique and movement to complete itself, usually resulting in one of two finishing techniques: *nage waza* (throwing techniques) or *osae waza* (securing control techniques).

Although aikido techniques, as defined by the principles of movement, could exist in themselves as a superior form of self-defense, they only have real meaning as a way to understand the resolution of conflict and the harmony with nature. This understanding goes beyond the mind-body oneness or the demonstrable physical laws, for it has significance in many areas as a way of life.

The art of aikido: Philosophical education in movement

Paul Linden
The Ohio State University

By simply executing a movement, a person is making a philosophical statement; thus, it is possible to use movement education as a means of philosophical education. However, most people just move; that is, their movements exhibit their philosophical attitudes, but they are not *consciously* making any philosophical statements or elucidating their philosophies in or through movement. Physical education could become one of the primary humanities disciplines if it approached movement from the point of view that body use manifests a person's core philosophical beliefs and that changing people's body use changes their philosophies as well.

   Aikido (pronounced eye-key-doe with even emphasis on each syllable) takes this approach. Aikido is nonviolent Japanese martial art which uses self-defense practice as a vehicle for philosophical inquiry and development. By considering some exercises and principles from aikido, this chapter first elucidates the nature of the philosophical approach to movement education and then examines its implications for the profession of physical education.

PHILOSOPHICAL APPROACHES

The first question to discuss is what is meant by "philosophy" in this context. It is necessary to distinguish between two approaches to philosophy, the *methodological* and the *substantive* approaches. Methodological philosophizing is a formalized process of elucidating the nature of verbal/conceptual tools and maps which form the basis for organizing some subject matter. Methodological philosophizing does not in itself have anything to say; it is simply a way of attaining coherence and clarity in our thinking. In this, it is very different from substantive philosophizing.

   Substantive philosophizing is a process of mulling over human philosophical problems with an eye toward clarifying them and finding actual, satisfactory solutions for them. In substantive philosophizing, a philosophical question is an existential quandary, a problem which has to do with a person's feelings about his or her existence in the world. This is a felt disturbance in a person's life, an experiential problem rather than a merely theoretical problem. In dealing with this disturbance, the philosopher must first find a way to gain a clear experience of what he or she feels and how it affects his or her relationship with the world, and then must discover how to live in a more satisfactory way. The philosopher must solve substantive philosophical questions through personal changes which lead to experiential resolutions, and movement offers a power tool for doing substantive philosophy.

Intention and movement

How can substantive philosophy be done through movement? The key to this question lies in the concept/experience that an intention automatically organizes the body for the movements necessary to carry out that intention. In aikido, we say that intention is where the mind and the body intersect; that is, the intention to move leads immediately and automatically to the faint muscular beginnings of the movement and the gross movement follows.

The easiest way to explain what this means is to describe an exercise by which I illustrate it for my students. First, the students stand up and shut their eyes. Then I ask them to imagine that they have come up to an elevator with a package in their hands, so they must lean over to the side and push the elevator button with one shoulder. If the students really feel in their bodies the desire to do this, then they will find they involuntarily tip a little bit towards the imagined elevator button. Generally, this response is the result; however, some complications occasionally arise. For example, some students will *think about,* rather than actually *feel* a desire to push the button. This is different and will not lead to any movement. The point of this exercise is to let people experience that an intention leads to the setting of the muscles for the movement to accomplish that intention and that any normal movement is the result of a precursor intention. (Edmund Jacobson derived the same result through electromyographic studies in the early thirties, and it was on that basis that he developed his system of progressive relaxation.)

Thus, there is an equivalence between posture and intention. With the possible exception of such things as postural deviations caused by physical trauma, the way people carry themselves is the way they intend to carry themselves. (Note that I am counting unconscious intentions as being real intentions.) Posture is not a thing or a position. It is an activity, a process, something the person does with his or her muscles. What is important is that posture and body use are intentional activities—processes in which each event is a direct manifestation of the person's will to create that event.

Meaning in intention

The intentional nature of posture and body use is significant to us because intentions/postures have *meaning.* They are philosophical statements. On a gross level, it is obvious that a given posture will be better or worse as a starting place for a particular action. If I am bent forward at the waist, I am in a better position to bend over and pick up a pebble off the ground than I am to reach up to touch a leaf over my head. On a subtle level, given ways of carrying oneself will be more or less appropriate as starting places for different kinds of interactions with oneself, other people, and the world; this constitutes the meaning in body use. Posture is really an intention to relate to life in a given way, and that is exactly what a philosophy is.

Aikido and philosophical problems—an example
To clarify this, let us look at an example of how aikido deals with a philosophical problem in terms of the person's manner of being in his or her body. It will be important to keep in mind that this level of body use does not only involve gross positions of the body, but has to do with very subtle patterns of breathing, muscular tension and relaxation, body alignment, energy flow, and movement flow.

One of the important lessons people have to learn in aikido concerns their reactions to being attacked. An exercise I use helps my students identify and change their reactions: The students work with partners, and I instruct one partner to slap the other smartly across the face. (I make sure that they slap in such a way that there will be no risk of injuries and warn them that they should not try the exercise if they feel that it would be too stressful for them due to past experiences such as being mugged or molested.) Most of the students expect the slap to hurt, so they tighten up, gasp, and shy away as they see it coming. When they feel the slap, most experience pain and a sense of being invaded; they get alarmed, perhaps even angry, stiffen up, and then try to resist any further slaps by staying stiff. Students quickly discover that fear, anger, and resistance are inevitably accompanied by unevenness, stiffness, and constriction in breathing, posture, and movement.

After the students have felt this part of the exercise, I go on to show them a breathing practice in which they learn how to breathe deeply and softly in the abdomen. The skill involves learning how to exert a gentle self-control which enables them to keep breathing calmly and fully in spite of any external events. Students find that breathing in this free and open manner is incompatible with the whole constellation of physical and mental changes involved in fear, anger, and resistance and makes it possible to prevent or control these changes. Once they learn to inhibit these feelings, I ask them to deliberately stiffen and constrict themselves just before being slapped. When they do, they find they react with fear and anger again; in other words, they find that the physical and mental experiences of fear, anger, or resistance are equivalent, each leading to the other.

When the students can stay soft, they discover that the same slap they experienced before does not hurt as much as they had thought. In addition, in staying soft, they naturally sway and give with the force of the slap, so they actually lessen its impact. The implication of this exercise is that the students themselves created much of the pain they experienced originally and attributed to the slap.

The key issue is rigidity versus softness. The essence of being ready to meet the slap with resistance is a tense, armored body and jerky, tight movements. If people maintain this body style, they are carrying themselves—and are *intending* to carry themselves—in a way that will set them up for strained and painful responses to the slap. The way people hold themselves is an expression of what they expect the slap to be like, and by and large, their expectations will shape their experiences into just what they had been expecting. Not only that, but because people who fear the slap will create a genuinely fearful experience for themselves, they will find that their expectations were justified and will feel their reactions were reasonable. Hence, they will be caught in a vicious cycle.

The purpose of this example of how aikido teaches people to deal with being slapped is to show how posture and movement could be philosophical statements, that is, actions that carry *meaning*. The meaning is contained in the fact that posture is a readiness to relate to some aspect of life in some manner. In addition to showing how posture is a manifestation of philosophy, this example also indicates how philosophical change could be pursued through movement.

MEANS OF PHILOSOPHICAL CHANGE

Learning how to learn

The goal of practicing aikido defense techniques is not simply that of learning how to defend oneself. That is, of course, important, but the real goal of aikido practice is to learn how to learn. The goal is to find out how to use the training as a situation in which to create and direct philosophical change.

A given way of holding oneself will be a good way of reacting to life and shaping life in certain ways. Changing that way of holding oneself and moving will mean that one's experience of life will be different, and the different experience will give rise to new beliefs and feelings, which will in turn influence the person to move in new ways, and so on. The same lessons that people learn in finding out how to deal with being slapped apply to any type of pressure people face in their daily lives, and life's pressures include everything from falling in love, to paying taxes, to dealing with illness and death. If people go into a pressure situation with a feeling or belief that resistance is a useful way of dealing with pressure, they become tense and stiff. They are unable to react fluidly or creatively to the situation and are unable to find appropriate ways to deal with the problem to which they are subjected. By not tightening up, they stay soft and ready to move and thus can find effective ways of dealing with the pressure they face.

The key philosophical issue is rigidity versus softness. Broadly speaking, a rigid way of moving is an expression of some fear of life and shapes the person's experience so that he or she finds that life is indeed fearful. A soft way of moving is a free and accepting way of relating to life and leads to a much more satisfying way of living.

Being centered

There is an ideal of correct being and correct moving that underlies aikido practice. This ideal is called *being centered*. It manifests in the body as a firm, supple, balanced, and open body organization. In manifests in movement as freedom to move evenly, smoothly, and powerfully in all directions. It manifests psychologically as a calm, alert, fluid, and focused state of mind. And it manifests philosophically as a spirit of nonattachment, an ability to accept life as it is while at the same time working to change it to meet your wishes, not being overwhelmed either by getting what you want or by not getting it.

Being centered is at once a type of posture, a way of moving, a way of feeling, and a way of thinking. It is at once a philosophical and a postural ideal. The aikido class is really a laboratory for life. In the class, we can work with simple, explicit situations and discover by examining what we *do* (rather than merely what we say), what we really feel and believe in. Once we become sensitive to and aware of the changes that take place in our bodies and movements and understand how these changes relate to our attitudes toward the external events with which we are dealing, we can work toward learning new ways of moving, feeling, and acting. As we learn how to do this in class, we can begin doing the same in our daily lives.[1]

---

[1] It would be impossible in a short chapter to give more than a bare hint of what the actual training procedures involved in aikido practice are. Usually, learning these procedures demands years of arduous study. However, I have found that it is possible and very useful to separate the fundamental movement awareness elements from the combat techniques by which they are usually taught and present them in an explicit and succinct manner as a study in their own right. I teach this in a method I call *Being In Movement*; it gives people relatively quick and easy access to the material so that they can apply it in whatever areas may interest them.

IMPLICATIONS FOR PHYSICAL EDUCATION

Process orientation emphasis

What implications for the profession of physical education can be drawn from this consideration of the philosophical approach to posture and movement? To begin with, it would be possible to utilize a philosophical method of instruction in any sport or movement form. As an example, I recently taught an intermediate swimming class and concentrated on helping the students utilize practice of the strokes as a way of discovering how they perceived themselves and their capacities for action. As they learned how to pay attention to their movements, they began to understand the relation between themselves and the water. They learned how to learn a swimming stroke and thereby learned the strokes as well. In addition, from what they told me, they also started to apply the ideas they learned in swimming to other areas of their lives.

It is important to note that looking at movement education as a process of helping students develop self-awareness means that process orientation rather than goal orientation must be emphasized. When movement and the mover are evaluated on the basis of whether they were successful in performing some task, then the manner in which the person goes about accomplishing the task will be of relatively little importance—especially if the task is in fact performed successfully. If success is defined by external, goal-oriented criteria, then relatively little attention will be paid to the human element, that is, to what the person feels himself to be as he does the task. Only when tasks are used primarily as vehicles for self-examination through movement will students have the opportunity to learn to use movement as a means of philosophical growth.

Training in movement awareness

However, utilizing movement as a means of philosophical education means more than just *talking* about ideas and values in the context of sport participation. Doing philosophy in and through movement must be based on specific and concrete methods for relating body patterns and philosophical attitudes. Only with proper training can physical educators draw upon the methods included in aikido and other movement-awareness disciplines and incorporate them into their teaching.

One task that would be important in physical education would be to examine the movement requirements of various sports and the movement styles of teachers and coaches to determine what kinds of philosophical stances are inculcated by internalization of those movement patterns. In teaching students to get used to holding their bodies and moving in certain ways, we are also teaching them to feel certain ways and, therefore, to hold certain attitudes and philosophies. The question is whether we are conscious of these philosophical elements already present in the teaching and whether we intend that they should be taught.

Incorporating philosophical with physical education

The broadest implication has to do with the nature of physical education itself. Embracing philosophical education as a primary purpose of the profession means making physical education very different than it generally has been. However, many diverse movement-awareness disciplines are already being included in physical education. Disciplines such as aikido, karate, t'ai chi chuan, yoga, Alexander work, Laban movement analysis, and the Feldenkrais Method are already bringing philosophical approaches to movement into physical education.

Incorporating philosophical education into physical education would offer a real opportunity to the profession. The area of education dealing with self-awareness and philosophical understanding has been very underdeveloped in our culture's system of education. Our society is long on knowledge and short on wisdom, and philosophical education should be included in the educational system in order to provide students with better abilities to deal with life. Physical education is a perfect place for philosophical education because movement offers the best opportunity to make philosophical issues real to people. The danger in doing substantive philosophy as a merely verbal exercise is that it can get lost in the clouds and turn into mere theory. But when people experience philosophical problems and possible solutions directly in their bodies and their movements, the whole process comes alive for them. Physical education could take its place as one of the primary humanities disciplines if it included philosophical education alongside its other functions, and it would certainly be a service to our students and our society for it to do so.

A comparison of the vernacular dance of two countries: Japanese Kabuki and American jazz

Lisa P. Hofsess
Iowa State University

Dance is an illusive, yet pervasive phenomenon. Although it appears in a myriad of forms across cultures, it is extremely difficult to define. Nearly all definitions of dance, however varied, contain two basic elements: periodicity and nonutility. In other words, pared down to the essentials, any noninstrumental movement performed in a rhythmical fashion is dance (Lange, 1975). Despite this deceptively simple definition, the concept of dance has been transformed by human culture and intellect into a plethora of complex, extensively codified activities. We humans have social dance, religious dance, and even aerobic dance. We dance for health, for courtship; we dance to drive away evil spirits, to appease our multifarious gods, to entertain one another, and sometimes even just to have fun. While some of the activities could be considered indirectly useful, the movements themselves remain essentially symbolic, and therefore fall within the criterion of nonutility.

Each culture in turn develops its own classification system to describe those activities it designates as dance. This chapter presents a brief comparison of the movement patterns classified as popular folk dance in two very different countries: Japan and the United States. Japanese Kabuki and American jazz are as different as two aspects of the same cultural component can be. Virtually the only similarity, aside from the mutual classification as indigenous folk art, is the popular appeal of each dance form in its respective country. Kabuki is considered the least rigorous and sophisticated form of traditional dance in Japan. Likewise in the United States, jazz is dismissed by professional dancers as decadent and quite popular, but, nevertheless, a minor dance style (Giordano, 1975; Terry, 1982). The differences between Kabuki and jazz, on the other hand, are plentiful, each reflecting the unique aspects of its respective culture.

One of the most obvious differences between Kabuki and jazz is the striking dissimilarity in the lengths of their histories—roughly 250 years. The origins of Kabuki can be traced back to a form of women's folk dance in the early 1600s.

Jazz claims as its roots the folk dance forms of the black slaves of the pre-Civil War period. Ironically enough, the developments or innovations in Kabuki and jazz are inversely related to the length of their histories. Kabuki has survived relatively unchanged since its inception. Jazz, however, reflecting the dizzying rate of change in the industrial and now postindustrial society out of which it emerged, changes almost yearly.

The styles of movement themselves represent physical as well as philosophical opposites. Kabuki uses subtle, refined gestures which reflect the contained, inner-directed aspects of the Japanese culture. Jazz, with its volatile, exaggerated, almost vulgar movements, is the epitome of the bold, extraverted American personality.

HISTORY OF THE DANCE FORMS

Japanese Kabuki

According to Japanese mythology, the very first dance was performed to appease the deity of the sun in the days of the gods and goddesses. Amaterasu-Omikami, Goddess of the Sun, had withdrawn in anger into a rock cave, leaving the world in darkness. Another goddess, Ame-no-Uzeme-no-Mikoto, performed an obscene and hilarious dance in front of the rock cave to lure the angry goddess back out-side. Amaterasu-Omikami, her curiosity aroused by the laughter of the deities despite the eternal nighttime, peered out of her hiding place. The trick worked; and hence, dance brought daylight back to Japan (Matida, 1938; Sachs, 1963). The Mikagura ceremonies, which are still performed when a new ruler ascends the Japanese throne, are a reenactment of this myth.

Kabuki itself was originated at the turn of the 17th century by a woman named Okumi of Izumo. She developed formal arrangement of traditional religous and folk dances. Her style became the basis of what was known as Women's Kabuki. Using Okumi of Izumo's movements, groups of women performed dance-dramas in local theaters. The dances always featured three characters: a teahouse girl, her lover, and a comic clownlike person, all played by females. They ended with a mass dance, or finale. However, in 1629, Women's Kabuki was banned by government decree for allegedly promoting immorality and licentiousness. It was replaced by a similar form performed by males, appropriately called Young Men's Kabuki. By 1652, this, too, was banned for its erotic nature. During the next 200 years, Kabuki went through a period in which it stabilized into its current form that is primarily performed by mature men.

In addition, by the early 1900s, women were again allowed to dance in public. They revived the old Kabuki forms and began presenting them outside the theater as pure dance. These forms were incorporated into local festivals which took place at various times during the year. Bon odori, the annual summertime festival honor-ing the memory of the dead, is the most well known. These celebrations include group dancing, following the pattern set by the revived Women's Kabuki.

American Jazz

Since the Europeans who "discovered America" and eventually formed the United States totally rejected the Native Americans and almost extinguished their rich and varied culture, nearly all present American cultural roots are found abroad (Giordano, 1975). Dance is no exception. Although jazz is considered the only truly indigenous dance form, an "urban folk dance" (Giordano, 1975), its origins are found in "primitive" African dance forms which were transferred to the United States through the institution of black slavery. What was later to become known as jazz was originally called "Negro Dance."

Pearl Primus (1951), a contemporary jazz artist, observed, "Africans used their bodies as instruments through which every conceivable emotion or event was projected." White Americans latched on to this expressive quality of movement as they observed their slaves' dancing and modified it to suit their own culture. Throughout their histories both jazz music and dance have consisted of white adaptations of black art forms (Stearns & Stearns, 1968).

In pre-Civil War days, whites imitated black dancing in their buck and wing, and minstrel shows (forms of popular entertainment). From the Civil War through the last 20 years, the history of jazz is the history of social dance in America. The first half of the 20th century saw jazz expressed as the various popular dances from the Charleston of the '20s to the Big Apple of the '30s, and the Lindy and Jitterbug of the '40s. Finally, in the 1950s, a white entertainer, whose rock and roll style still thrives, gave the United States the foundation for its present popular dance forms. The intense, frantic fluidity of Elvis Presley, imitating the sensual, suggestive movements of his black contemporaries, notably Earl "Snake Hips" Tucker, provided the final link between black and white dance (Highwater, 1978).

Variations of these volatile social dance forms were adopted by choreographers for commercial use in musical theater. In some ways the use of dance in Broadway musicals parallels Kabuki dance-dramas. Dance, however, tends to be an embellishment or interlude in American theater and a more integral, central part of Japanese theater.

Broadway choreographer Jack Cole is credited as being the father of Broadway jazz in the 1940s (Philip, 1982). However, jazz was not accepted by professional dancers as a legitimate dance style until the 1960s. Since that time, jazz has gained recognition as a legitimate performing art form. But even so, modern and ballet dance companies today far outnumber touring companies whose primary style is jazz.

ELEMENTS OF MOVEMENT

The term *Kabuki* is made up of three separate words: *ka* (song), *bu* (dance), and *ki* (skill) (Ikema, 1981). The English word *dance* is derived from the Old High German *danson*, meaning "to stretch the body" (Gunji, 1970). These very dissimilar derivations illustrate the philosophical and physical differences between Japanese and American dance. The former is an integral part of a complex performance in which music, dance, and the dancer are inseparable. Kabuki clearly reflects the Zen philosophy that to do something well a person must become one with the activity. One looks within for perfection, which is in great contrast to the Western philosophy of seeking perfection outside oneself. Another way of expressing this is that Japanese religion and dance worship the earth, while American religion (primarily Judeo-Christian) and dance are focused on the sky, that is, "Heaven." Nevertheless, both forms of movement originate in the center of the dancer, physically as well as philosophically. But whereas Kabuki dancers direct their energy inward, producing subtle, refined movements, the jazz dancers move their energy through their bodies, releasing it in explosive, exaggerated movements.

Representing nature, Kabuki is often mimetic in style, emphasizing soft, delicate hand movements: for example, flowers, trees, or grain swaying in the wind. In Buddhist religion these expressive hand movements, called *mudras*, are part of a ritualistic sign language which calls forth the qualities of the Buddha. Mudras, meditation, and recitation form the three mysteries of Buddha (Sachs, 1963). In sharp contrast, jazz concentrates its movements in the torso and legs, relying on abstract shapes or patterns with no intrinsic meaning. This, too, reflects the contrasting ideologies: Western thought relies on abstraction and linear clarity; Eastern philosophy centers on concrete images and circularity (Ito, 1979).

Several other characteristics of each type of dance show similar contrasts. What are considered meaningful units vary from culture to culture (Royce, 1977). Western minds break down everything from language to emotions to dance into the smallest and most distinct units possible. Jazz dance, for example, is made up of a series of minutely defined steps. Isolations (moving one body segment, such as the rib cage, while keeping the other parts either still or moving in entirely different directions), the cornerstone of jazz, is the most extreme form of this "unit reduction." Kabuki, on the other hand, has no set pattern of vocabulary movement. The meaningful units in dance and cognition, in general, are much larger and more ambiguous (L. Kang, personal communication, June 1, 1983).

Meaningful units include time, as well as space. Again, fundamental, culturally determined conceptual differences are found. The basic Kabuki unit of periodicity, *ma*, is roughly translated into English as "the space or time between one movement and the next or between one pose and the next" (Gunji, 1970). It is not simply blank time or space, but rather artisitically transported time-space. To a clock-watching American, this casual interpretation of time is nearly incomprehensible (Kang, 1983). The basic rhythmic pattern of jazz, borrowed from the music from which it gets its name, is *syncopation*. Musically, syncopation is defined as "playing away from the accent, that is, on weak beats or parts of beats, in order that the stress should be more marked on return to it" (Porter, 1938). Jazz dance uses syncopation not only in a particular dance sequence, but within individual dancers. Jazz dancers must learn to isolate each individual body part and be able to move several parts simultaneously in totally distinct rhythms.

TEACHING STYLES

Jazz draws on all other Western, and occasionally Eastern, forms of dance for its technique and is usually taught as a supplement to one of the more recognized styles. Learning jazz can be a rather haphazard endeavor as it is taught in one form or another in a myriad of places, from colleges to dance studios to local discotheques.

Kabuki, as has been mentioned before, is part of a long tradition of movement forms. Japanese dance education is based on the long established headmaster system. Originally, professional dancers came only from hereditary dance families. The system has expanded somewhat to allow those who can afford it to apprentice in a school run by an established expert or headmaster. In recent years, the system has deteriorated to the point where ill-trained dancers are calling themselves headmasters, a situation which may lead to the breakdown or at least alteration of Kabuki traditions.

Students of jazz learn a progression of distinct steps and techniques, which may vary considerably in form from place to place, but which are presented as unique, established units, nonetheless. After mastering the basic movement vocabulary, students are then taught sequences of basic movements and eventually whole dances. In contrast, Japanese students, begin by learning short, but complete dances. They learn expression and mood and imagery-concepts, which are frequently not introduced in jazz until much later.

PERFORMANCE

Popular forms

Mass dance is a rather rare phenomenon in the United States compared to Japan. Popular forms of Kabuki based on the more formalized performing versions are enjoyed by hundreds of participants in various religious festivals throughout the year. Perhaps the only American equivalent mass usage of jazz can be found in the ballrooms and dance halls of the past and their current counterpart, the discotheques. In this sense jazz is easily distinguished from Kabuki because professional jazz dancers draw their movements from the public, rather than the reverse as in Japan.

Professional staging

Contrasts in the staging of formal Kabuki and jazz performances also reflect the described cultural systems of their respective countries. Dance is just one element in the complex productions of Kabuki theater. The dance itself is the last part to be created. First, a playwright writes a dance-drama based on traditional themes; then musicians create the music to augment the story; and finally, the music is played for a choreographer who creates movement to amplify and interpret the spirit and ideas of the play.

Jazz performances, however, are far less elaborate. Choreographers generally work alone or occasionally collaborate with a composer. Props are limited, costumes comparatively simple, and the movement itself supersedes the context.

Costumes

Costuming presents perhaps the most visible difference. Kabuki dancers are encased in layer upon layer of richly embroidered, hand-painted kimonos, the styles and colors reflecting each dancer's real rank, personality, and imagined character. Dancers change costumes several times during a single performance, sometimes simply by pulling off one outfit to reveal the new one underneath. Jazz dancers in their stark leotards and tights are nearly nude by comparison. The very different potential range of movement inherent in the costuming is obvious.

Music

Musical accompaniment affects movement style and is also quite varied. The Japanese flutes, gongs, bells, and drums produce sounds quite distinct from the sounds of American brass and woodwind instruments, piano, and string bass. The high, often aggressive, piercing sounds of the saxophone dominate jazz music, while Japanese music features the *samisen*, a three-stringed instrument that produces more delicate sounds. Finally, Japanese rhythm advances from weak to strong accents, directly opposite to the Western rhythmic pattern.

Onnagata

Japanese *onnagata*, female impersonators, represent the final contrast. After Women's Kabuki was outlawed, men began dancing female roles. Except for the occasional burlesque female impersonator, no such equivalent exists in jazz. Onnagata study exclusively female roles, which are considered the most demanding. Very little, if any, of the vulgar satire associated with American female impersonators is evident.

CULTURAL AND GEOGRAPHIC INFLUENCES

Like any social phenomenon, dance is influenced a great deal by both the ideology and physical environment out of which it emerges. Japan is a small, mountainous, island country which has preserved its traditions and homogeneous population for centuries. The United States is an enormous country, full of open spaces, which prides itself on the heterogeneity of its population. As has been pointed out, these contrasts are replicated in their respective dance styles.

Japan is a country of tradition, one which venerates the wisdom of age. Hence, the Japanese believe that a Kabuki dancer cannot be judged until he is at least 40 years old (Matida, 1938). The United States, on the other hand, is a country of youth and rebellion; thus, Americans regard a dancer of any style as old at age 35 and, therefore, generally ready to retire. This rebellious youth created much of the impetus for jazz by expressing its discontent in its social dance.

The flappers of the 1920s and their outrageous Charleston have been interpreted as a revolt against Victorianism. The rock and roll of the '50s and '60s challenged the conservatism of the so-called establishment. The punks of the current decade, discouraged by the seemingly hopeless unemployment and economic crises, and terrified by the seeming inevitability of nuclear war, express their sense of futility and helpless rage by satirizing the nuclear, high-technology age. Their disheveled appearance and jerky, violent dancing are a physical representation of the frenzy, apathy, and fatalism which was the central theme of the '70s (Highwater, 1978).

Like any fad, the mannerisms and paraphernalia of the latest dance craze are adopted by those who have little understanding of their underlying meaning. Nevertheless, real social discontent and desire for change remain at the root of all social protest, including the latest dance fad.

JAZZ IN JAPAN

In 1980 the first jazz dance school, the American Dance Machine, sponsored by three Japanese theatrical companies, opened its doors in Tokyo, Japan. Under the direction of an American choreographer and dancer, Lee Theodore, the school provides instruction in Broadway musical-type jazz to Japanese students (Como, 1981).

As of yet, The American Dance Machine has had no direct visible impact on traditional Japanese dance. Although a few modern choreographers have experimented with "Eastern motifs," Japanese dance has had almost no influence on jazz. However, American Broadway musicals are gaining popularity in Japan; in fact, almost anything American is immediately and indiscriminately embraced by young Asians enamored of the material wealth of the West (Kang, 1983). Perhaps a cultural exchange is on its way, although it seems to be going only one way.

American entertainment and the arts are much more available in Japan than Japanese arts are in the United States. This may be an indication of cultural disintegration in Japan because jazz is the one dance form most devoted to rebellion and change; more likely, though, it seems to be a manifestation of the ubiquitous American ethnocentrism. The exchange, however, is in its earliest stages, so judgment will have to be postponed until a more timely date.

CONCLUSION

The inward-directed, refined, subtle gestures of Japanese Kabuki provide a marked contrast to the extraverted athleticism of jazz. The Japanese culture, based on simple, conservative veneration of stability, nature, and concrete meanings in life, expresses itself far differently than the aggressive, volatile, expansive American culture. Perhaps the clearest illustration of these differences is given by a Japanese scholar, S. Ito (1979), who says that Japanese dance (and culture) is like the Eastern ideograph, while American dance is like the Western alphabet. They can both be used to represent the same phenomena, but in slightly unalterable, distinct ways for which there is no direct translation.

REFERENCES

Como, W. (1981, February). On board with the American Dance Machine in Tokyo. *Dance-Magazine*, pp. 50-55.

Giordano, G. (Ed.). (1975). *Anthology of American jazz dance*. Evanston, IL: Orion.

Gunji, M. (1970). *Buyo: The classical dance*. (D. Kenny, Trans.). New York & Tokyo: Walker/Weatherhill.

Highwater, J. (1978). *Dance rituals of experience*. New York: A & W.

Ikema, H. (1981). *Folk dance of Japan*. National Recreation Association of Japan.

Ito, S. (1979). Some characteristics of Japanese expression as they appear in dance. *Dance Research Annual*, pp. 267-277.

Lange, R. (1975). *The nature of dance: An anthropological perspective*. London: Macdonald & Evans.

Matida, K. (1938). *Odori (Japanese dance)*. Board of Tourist Industry, Japanese Government Railways.

Philip, R. (1982, August). Wayne Cilento: The saga of a Broadway dancing man. *Dance-Magazine*, pp. 39-44.

Porter, E. (1938). *Music through the dance*. New York: Charles Scribner's Sons.

Primus, P. (1951). Out of Africa. In W. Sorell (Ed.), *The dance has many faces*. New York: World.

Royce, A. (1977). *The anthropology of dance*. Bloomington: Indiana University Press.

Sachs, C. (1963). *World history of the dance*. New York: W.W. Norton.

Stearns, M. & Stearns, J. (1968). *Jazz dance: The story of American vernacular dance*. New York: Macmillan.

Terry, W. (1982). *How to look at dance*. New York: William Morrow.

The East/West dialectic in modern dance

Mark Wheeler
University of Georgia

As the West's awareness of the East has increased in sophistication throughout the 20th century, the appropriation of the Orient by modern dance has grown more authentic. With this development in the influence of the Orient upon modern dance, a philosophical polarity between classical ballet and modern dance had become increasingly defined by the late 1960s. Before the relationship of this modern dance/ballet dichotomy to the larger East/West dichotomy can be discussed, the actual meeting of East and West in modern dance must be observed. A survey of the appropriation of the Orient by dancers Ruth St. Denis, Martha Graham, and Erick Hawkins reveals the "surface to essence" development alluded to above.

RUTH ST. DENIS AND THE ORIENT

An oriental obsession

The repertory, recorded lectures, autobiography, and other writings of Isadora Duncan, who was the philosophical founder of modern dance, reveal no direct inspiration from the East. The modern dance world would rely upon Ruth St. Denis, a contemporary of Isadora Duncan, to begin the trend of direct appropriation of the Orient by modern dance. St. Denis (1877-1968) was a struggling dancer in musical theatre productions when a poster of the goddess Isis advertising Egyptian Deities cigarettes gave her career a direction. The Orient had been an American stage fascination for decades, but St. Denis had a vision of presenting Oriental dance art of more depth than the stylistic parodies of the day. By presenting Oriental dance, costume, and architectural style seriously, and by teaching a generation of American dancers Oriental dance styles, St. Denis ensured that the Orient would figure in the development of modern dance.

The image of exotic, ancient Egypt began the lifelong obsession which led St. Denis to write, "Some strange element within myself never really came alive except when it was identified with the Orient" (1939, p. 48). The highlight of the Chicago Exposition of 1893 (Ruthie Denis was 16) was the belly dancer billed as "Little Egypt" in the midway attraction, The Streets of Cairo.

Augustin Daly had already set the stage for Little Egypt and for the Oriental skirt dancers of the day when he brought a troupe of Indian nautch dancers to

New York in 1881 (Todd, 1950, p. 25). However, St. Denis sought more than what Ted Shawn later referred to as "a hootchy-kootchy, Little Egypt sort of show" (Mazo, 1977, p. 96). A trip to the amusement park at Coney Island removed Egypt from center stage in St. Denis' theatrical vision, and India entered. A midway attraction billed *The Streets of New Delhi* offered an Indian village enlivened by snake charmers and nautch dancers, both of which St. Denis later portrayed.

St. Denis' library research expanded to include the dances and other customs of all oriental cultures. She recruited individuals of Oriental descent and, in her mother's New Jersey apartment, rehearsed them in scenes of the Indian dance which was to become "Radha." In 1906 "Radha" was seen in various settings and created a vaudeville-Broadway sensation. It was the first of 57 St. Denis dance pieces with Eastern themes, some intimate solos, some pageants of Oriental spectacle.

In 1914 St. Denis married her dance partner, Ted Shawn. The following year in Los Angeles, they merged their talents, their interests in the East, and their names to found the Denishawn School and Denishawn Dancers.

Denishawn Dancers

From 1915 until 1931, the Denishawn Dancers represented dance to a generation of Americans, spreading inspired Orientalism in vaudeville and more serious concert engagements. The popularity of Denishawn and of its stars resulted in St. Denis and Shawn appearing as headliner stars of the *Ziegfield Follies of 1927*, with St. Denis' "Dance of the Red and Gold Saree" and Shawn's "Cosmic Dance of Shiva" audience favorites.

From the time of its founding when Miss Ruth regularly led students in evening yoga meditation, the Denishawn School stressed the teaching of East Indian, Japanese, and Balinese styles of dance. With branches all over the country, the Denishawn School provided the mainstream of dance instruction in the United States until the early 1930s. In so doing, Denishawn versed a generation of professional dancers, including Martha Graham, in the movement ways of the East. Denishawn's development of a method of training dancers outside the ballet academy and its development of a large audience for nonballet dance helped to bring about the modern dance movement. With that organizational groundwork, Ruth St. Denis' original imbuing of stage treatment of the Orient with serious purpose is responsible for the appropriation of the Orient recurring in the history of modern dance.

EASTERN INFLUENCE IN THE THEATRE AESTHETIC AND DANCE TECHNIQUE OF MARTHA GRAHAM

By the 1930s the most progressive and fruitful thread of appropriation of the Orient had passed from the surface imitation of St. Denis to the more physically integrated adaptation of the Orient by Martha Graham (1894-   ). In terms of both body techniques and theatre aesthetic, it was for Graham to explore the full potential lying in the Oriental tradition that she inherited from St. Denis. Her technique retains much of the primitive Eastern line which St. Denis popularized in the West. It was Graham, with her breath-inspired movement dynamic of contraction-release, and the rest of her technical warm-up which places the pelvis firmly on the floor, who first objectified the gospel of modern dance which Isadora Duncan had been able to only state subjectively: Dance movement is initiated from the *center*. Conceiving of energy flowing outward from that *center*, Graham opened up new vistas of the East for appropriation by modern dancers.

Graham began studying at the Denishawn School in Los Angeles in 1916;

the school's blend of Oriental styles, ballet *barre*, and Delsarte exercises provided the basis of her training. Eventually, she taught at the school and danced with the Denishawn Dancers until 1923. In the fifth annual *Greenwich Village Follies of 1923*, Graham danced in a number "arranged" by Michio Ito, the Japanese dancer whose talents had been seen since 1916 in New York.

In 1926, at the age of 32, Martha Graham gave her first independent dance recital in New York. In costuming, decor, and particularly in the lyrical movement style of one of her solos, Graham emphasized the Oriental, exotic look which had worked for her in Denishawn and in the *Greenwich Village Follies*. Dancers in kimonos and chiffon shifts, and the shiney lacquer finish of a piece of scenery were "in the shadow of Denishawn" (McDonagh, 1973, p. 50).

Graham's acquaintance with an Eastern worldview is suggested by books on the Orient referred to in *The Notebooks of Martha Graham* (1973):

* *Noh* (1916) by Ernest Fenollosa and Ezra Pound;
* Ananda Coomaraswamy's *The Mirror of Gesture* (1917) with photographs of Indian dance in sculpture, and *The Transformation of Nature in Art* (1935);
* W.Y. Evans-Wentz' translation of *The Tibetan Book of the Dead* (1927), which C.J. Jung claimed as "constant companion" (1960:XXXVI);
* Jung's *Psychology of Consciousness* (1916) with its analysis of Hindu lore, especially pertinent in light of Graham's undergoing Jungian psychoanalysis during the early 1940s;
* Heinrich Zimmer's *Philosophies of India*, published posthumously in 1951;
* E.B. Havell's *The History of Aryan Rule in India* (1918); and
* Santha Rama Rau's *Home to India* (1945).

The awareness of the East which Graham gained through such exposure is exhibited in her theatre aesthetic and her technique. Although the treatment of time, and the use of costumes and scenic props in the Graham dance theatre are among Graham's appropriations of the Orient, Eastern overtones in the Graham technique receive attention here.

In Martha Graham, the concerns of Isadora Duncan and Ruth St. Denis merge in a classical technique of modern dance. To see a Graham class or concert is to see realized the organization of Isadora's naive call for movement from within. As revealed in a comparison of the various body shapes of the Graham technique with those of Indian, Balinese, and Japanese dance, and as *The Notebooks of Martha Graham* testify, Graham carried on American dance's serious treatment of the Orient begun by St. Denis. Compared with St. Denis' appropriation of the East, Graham's was less an imitation, more an informed assimilation and synthesis. In Tokyo during the Graham Company's Far East tour of 1955-56, Graham was asked if she would borrow from the Japanese dance she had been observing.

> She answered that she would not copy Japanese dance forms unless she knew their spirit, that copying only the surface of something would be pointless. In a profound way, Graham's answer articulated the difference between herself and her first teachers, Ruth St. Denis and Ted Shawn, who went all over the world collecting dances and using them in their own brand of eclectic programming. Graham would not borrow anything until she understood the core of the art, and then what she reproduced would reflect the original source only tangentially (McDonagh, 1973, p. 244).

Body shapes

A crucial determinant of the Graham technique was the very nature of Graham's body. It is only natural that a technique whose most readily distinguishable characteristic is the alternating hollowing and extension of the spine would be devised by an individual possessing an elongated torso characteristic of the Oriental. It is not purely coincidental that dozens of Japanese dancers have studied at the Graham School in New York, that several have become members of the Graham Company, and that many of Graham's solo roles were bequeathed to the Japanese dancer Yuriko. Trained by Graham, Anna Sokolow and Bertram Ross have contributed to the Japanese connection with the Graham technique through residencies at the American Cultural Center in Tokyo. The relationship of torso length to hip joint flexibility so crucial in Graham's floor work was observed by Ernestine Stodelle (1969) during a Sokolow class at the Center in 1967: "And there is no doubt that the Japanese dancer's body has a built-in adaptability for the intricacies of modern dance movement, especially of the Graham School" (p. 78).

The presence, within Graham technique exercises and within choreography, of body shapes derived from Eastern dance constitutes Graham's surface appropriation of the Orient. The "Bali attitude" to which Graham frequently refers in *The Notebooks* is a variation of the traditional stance of Shiva on one bent leg with the other leg lifted and bent. In the extension of one leg in the spiral opening on the floor and in the lunge position into which the dancer falls after the standing turns around the back, Graham uses the tonic reflex position prominent in Bharata Natyam and in the related Hindu dance of Java. One of the Graham floor exercises for flexibility and center strength employs a sitting posture like that of the Javanese Wayang Wong. The Graham sitting fourth position from which many exercises develop finds precedent in Indian sculptural representations of the flying position of Hindu dance. Finally, the alternating curved arm, which, with its attendant torso change initiates much of the spiraling action so prominent in the Graham technique, is frequently seen in sculptural representations of the Cosmic Dance of Shiva.

"The breathings"

Numerous aspects of the Graham technique constitute an appropriation of the essence of the East. The standard Graham technique warm-up of the body begins with the pelvis on the floor, moving soon to the cross-legged sitting position of yoga and zazen. "The breathings," or elementary contraction-release exercises, reveal the organic dynamic of breathing as the core inspiration of the entire technique. Graham betrays her association with yoga in the breathings and particularly in the release, criticizing students with "There's no kundalini" (McDonagh, 1973, p. 196). The interplay between the complementary extremes of inhalation and exhalation, introduced in the simple breathings as the release and the contraction, infuse the sustained muscle action of the entire Graham dynamic. In the various elaborations of the contraction-release, the body of the Graham dancer is fully involved in the stylized exhalation of the contraction and inhalation of the release.

Just as the dialectic of the *yin* and *yang* totality communicate a conception of an organic progression of phenomena, there is built into the Graham technique physical representation of inevitable movement between polarities. The two principle movement dynamics within the technique—the contraction-release and the spirals—are the source of this organic quality. The contraction-release infuses the technique with the inevitable play of breathing which serves as the basis of yoga, t'ai chi ch'uan, and Zen meditation. The spiraling action of the torso, taught in the Graham floor exercises and used throughout the class and repertoire, results in trace patterns of the limbs similar to the "circles, curves, arcs, and spirals that move in opposition or concurrently" in t'ai chi (Weng, 1979) and to the immediately identifiable undulating arms of Shiva.

The spiraling torso

When de Mille (1963, p. 157) observes of Graham that "she stressed continuous unfolding movement from a central core...but added spasm and resistance," she observes the organic quality cited above. Most notably in the spiral openings from the cross-legged position and in the spiral turns around the back in the seated fourth position, there is in every torso-initiated movement to one direction the seed of movement to an opposing direction. Observing this sustained opposition in the Graham dynamic, one notes its similarity to t'ai chi in which "every action is followed by a counter action in an 'attack-retreat' fashion" (Weng, 1979).

One cannot profess to know where Graham derived the spiral action so fundamental to the technique; however, her study of Oriental culture ensures Graham's acquaintance with the image of Shiva, head of the Hindu diadem. The balanced and yet dynamic gestures of the four arms of Shiva express the unity of the universe despite the constant flux within it. De Mille (1980) contributes to this discussion of the pull of opposing forces in the Graham spiral dynamic: "Ballet has striven always to conceal effort; she on the contrary thought that effort was important since, in fact, effort was life" (p. 95).

Floor work

"The floor work is probably one of the most innovative aspects of Graham technique" (Dudley, 1977, p. 160). In contrast to ballet's defiance or denial of gravity, Graham's use of gravity and of its province, the floor, would seem to be in line with Isadora's quest for nature. The falls and recoveries which Graham invented to permit the dancer interplay between standing work and floor work are as innovative as the floor work itself. Again, the contraction-release and the spiral initiate and sustain the falls to the floor and the recoveries from them. In general, in the Graham technique, "all movement into space is the result of the subtle off-balancing of the dancer's weight" (Dudley, 1977, p. 159). This characteristic of the Graham movement dynamic, particularly in light of the off-balancing that takes the dancer to the floor and up again, allies Graham's work with the sophisticated studies of weight and momentum which propel the practitioner of judo, karate, and aikido.

The Orient influenced Graham's development of the essential characteristics of her technique: the contraction-release based in breathing, angularity or jointedness, use of the floor, use of a spiraling torso, and attention to weight through use of off-balancing. The vital dynamics within the Graham technique have rendered modern dancers susceptible to further influence by an increasingly accessible Orient.

ERICK HAWKINS AND THE ZEN PERSPECTIVE

When Erick Hawkins (1909-   ) left the Graham company in 1950, Zen was highly "accessible." He had spent 1935-38 studying and performing ballet with George Balanchine, and since 1938 had been a principal dancer with Graham. His break with ballet and Graham related to both technique and theatre aesthetic. Reading R.H. Blyth's translations of haiku poetry and Suzuki's (1949) *Essays on Zen Buddhism* when he left Graham, Hawkins was guided in his search for alternatives by a Zen perspective.

Hawkins' search for a less stressful technique, provoked by his experience with injury, was aided by M. Todd's (1949) *The Thinking Body* and Sweigard's (1974) "ideokinetic" research, observing that involuntary execution of body action through mental imaging is a better facilitator than voluntary execution. Todd and Sweigard constituted for Hawkins scientific validation of Zen truth. Words of the master in Herrigel's (1971) *Zen and the Art of Archery* could have been Sweigard's: "What stands in your way is that you have a much too willfull will. You think that what you do not do yourself will not happen" (p. 51). Zen presented to Hawkins the possibility of "learning to dance without forcing the movement to happen, but rather by letting the movement happen, by letting 'it' dance in the dancer's body" (Brown, 1971/72, p. 10). Hawkins emphasizes kinesthetic awareness, merging "intellectual knowing with sensuous experiencing" in his term *think-feel* (Brown, 1971/72, p. 11-12), and stresses the give-and-take of weight in movement from the pelvis.

Hawkins' concern with awareness in technique led him to a "here and now" momentness in his dance theatre. Titles like "Openings of the Eye" (1953), "Here and Now With Watchers" (1957), and "8 Clear Places" (1960) suggest the stark immediacy of much of Hawkins' repertory.

Hawkins studied Isadora Duncan (1878-1927) through the eyes of Zen. He saw her indictment of ballet in terms of Northrop's (1946) distinction between East and West. Isadora and Hawkins are repelled by the toe shoe which enables the ballerina, representing the spirit, to escape the clutches of gravity and the corporeal world of her male dance partner.

> Ballet did not satisfy me because it was too much like a diagram and, for me, too much of the indescribable pure poetry of movement had to be left out. It moved like a diagram because it had developed at a period in Western culture that emphasized theoretical knowledge and—if not puricanical—at least extremely unsensuous attitudes toward the body (Hawkins, 1965, p. 39).

Isadora Duncan initiated a modern dance/ballet dichotomy which, in retrospect, relates to that between an integrated, experiential East and a dualistic, theoretical West. The genius of Isadora, while not directly influenced by the East, is non-Western. Modern dancers' awareness of the East, increasing throughout the century, has permitted them a full recognition of her "triumph of self-awareness, wholeness, integration" (Harris, 1982, p. 16).

REFERENCES

Brown, B. (1971/72, fall/winter). Training to dance with Erick Hawkins. *Dance Scope*, pp. 6-30.
de Mille, A. (1963). *The book of the dance*. New York: Golden Press.
de Mille, A. (1980). Martha Graham. In C. Steinberg (Ed.), *The dance anthology* (pp. 91-104). New York: New American Library.
Dudley, J. (1977). Graham technique. In M. Clarke & D. Vaughn (Eds.), *The encyclopedia of dance and ballet* (pp. 159-160). New York: G.P. Putnam's Sons.
Graham, M. (1973). *The notebooks of Martha Graham*. New York: Harcourt Brace Jovanovich.
Harris, D. (1982, February). Isadora. *Ballet News*, pp. 12-16, 45.
Hawkins, E. (1965). Pure poetry. In S.J. Cohen (Ed.), *The modern dance: Seven statements of belief* (pp. 39-51). Middletown, CT: Wesleyan University Press.
Herrigel, E. (1971). *Zen in the art of archery*. New York: Vintage.
Jung, C.G. (1960). Psychological commentary. In W.Y. Evans-Wentz, *The Tibetan book of the dead*. Oxford: Oxford University Press.
Mazo, J. (1977). *Prime movers*. New York: William Morrow.
McDonagh, D. (1973). *Martha Graham*. New York: Praeger.
Northrop, F.S.C. (1946). *The meeting of East and West*. New York: Macmillan.

St. Denis, R. (1939). *Ruth St. Denis: An unfinished life*. New York: Harper and Brothers.

Stodelle, E. (1969, January). Anna Sokolow in Japan. *DanceMagazine, 43*(1), 40-42, 78-80.

Suzuki, D.T. (1949). *Essays on Zen Buddhism*. New York: Harper.

Sweigard, L. (1974). *Human movement potential: Its ideokinetic facilitation*. New York: Harper and Row.

Todd, M. (1950, December). The rise of musical comedy in America. *DanceMagazine, 14*(12), 23-25, 38, 39.

Todd, M. (1949). *The thinking body*. Boston: G.T. Banford.

Weng, D. (1979). *What is t'ai chi ch'uan?* Paper presented in graduate forum, The Ohio State University.

SECTION IV

Attempts at resolution

In the previous section, Förster and Hsu point out that the appropriation of and the development of technical proficiency in an Eastern movement form is not sufficient for full understanding. In part 4, Scott Watson and Robert Sparks extend this argument. Watson argues that although the archery master in Herrigel's *Zen in the Art of Archery* and Tim Gallwey in *The Inner Game of Tennis* appear to be using the same methodological principles, they do not have the same ontological commitment. The lesson to be learned is that intention and commitment are just as important as (perhaps even more important than) pedagogy. The adoption of Eastern methods alone will not lead necessarily to the same commitment.

Robert Sparks calls our attention to the futility of attempting to explain the Zen master's skill in the traditional Western way, "in terms of lower brain functions and automaticity." Zen skill is a spiritual one and mystical expression cannot be understood "in terms of material or physical embodiment. There is only one avenue for apprehending spirit and that is through the real practice of meditation, the spiritual equivalent of the scientific method."

With these caveats in mind, the reader is encouraged to look carefully at Chic Johnson's attempt to develop a "revisionist philosophy of coaching." Here, a Western coach looks to the East and attempts to utilize techniques which challenge traditional approaches to sport. Can Johnson's prescription withstand the scrutiny of critics like Watson? Is there more here than Gallwey's utilization of Eastern ideas for Western purposes? The concluding section of Johnson's essay implies there may be.

Split-brain research, of late, has been the subject of a great deal of attention. In fact, some have contended that in Eastern culture, the right hemisphere plays the dominant role while the reverse is true in the West. Richard Garner in "Hemispheric Imperialism" cautions against placing too much emphasis on one mode of thought as opposed to another. The search for "reality" beyond the experiential cannot be achieved either by left- or right-brained thinking. "Both hemispheres must be allowed to carry on work that has more bearing on our actual needs and projects...silent meditation (is) the way to harmonious integration and (is) the middle way between all extremes."

Ann Brunner offers her attempt at resolution by witnessing for the value and importance of educating the self. Her experientially descriptive essay gives us another glimpse of the emerging paradigm which will result in the formation of a new culture "beyond East and West."

Is there more to practice than the pursuit of perfection?

Scott B. Watson
Ithaca College

In this paper, the problem of ontological commitment, or commitment concerning the ultimate or fundamental nature or constitution of reality will be considered. This kind of commitment is problematical for several reasons. First, we are often unknowingly guilty of ontological commitments, a way of putting our plight that a lover of ontological deserts such as Quine (1948) might find particularly apt or congenial. To put this differently, it might not be too bold to claim that we rarely realize the ontological commitments which we make in our daily lives. Second, to what our ontological commitments are is often unclear, even when we are certain that ontological commitments are involved. Often, close analysis does not clarify such commitments, at least not apparently if agreement is an indication of clarity. To add to these difficulties is the question (a burning one in some circles), To what should our ontological commitments be? Thus, to consider the topic of ontological commitment a problem may well be appropriate and not just another instance of trying to make something out of nothing.

ONTOLOGICAL COMMITMENT IN SPORTLIKE PHYSICAL ACTIVITIES

The topic of ontological commitment in the context of sportlike physical activities is fraught with at least the three difficulties already mentioned. Consideration of ontological commitment in such a context has yet another difficulty, namely that of venturing into even more alien territories than usual by most discussions of ontological commitment. This observation might be made in spite of several good discussions of sport and ontology, particularly if ontology is understood to include a concern with existence or being as such, or in the world in general, in addition to a focus on the nature of human existence or being. Such concern with existence leads to most perplexing reflections on what there is as well as to considerations of how reality is to be divided in a logical sense.

The observation gains additional credence if it is noted that while considerations of ontological commitment are probably universally absent in sportlike physical activity (something which need not be said about all physical activity even in the Western world—dance is a possible counterexample), it is not quite so alien a consideration in language usage. One might even wonder whether ontological commitments are involved in sportlike physical activity at all, and whether participation in such activity involves commitment of any kind concerning the nature of reality. Elaboration of the comparison of language and sportlike physical activity may clarify the idea of ontological commitment as well as address the issue of such commitment in sportlike physical activity.

Comparison of language and sportlike physical activity

In our use of language we refer to and implicitly posit the existence of certain things, consequently making ontological commitments to what there is in the world. Just for examples, commitments are often to such things as individual objects, classes and kinds of objects, properties, attributes, and sometimes other abstract entities. Without trying to push too far Austin's (1963) and Searle's (1969) points about talking as performatives and speech acts, it seems reasonable to suggest that not only does the way one talks about the world involve ontological commitments, but also the way one acts in the world in a variety of other ways involves ontological commitments. Thus, how one plays a game, if I may be allowed the conceptual license of viewing that as a kind of unitary act, may involve ontological commitments. Also, and more pertinent to the subsequent dialectic, how one learns or practices some physical activity, again if viewed as a unitary act, may involve some ontological commitments.

Serious reservation concerning the path just taken to the conclusion that practice may involve some ontological commitments should be felt. That reservation should stem from concern over a too facile interchange of individuals from a single class. A more explicit tracing of the argument might reveal that troublesome facility as

Assumption 1:   The way one talks about the world involves ontological commitments.

Assumption 2:   Following Austin and Searle, talking is one way of acting in the world.

Assumption 3:   Learning and practicing a physical activity is another way of acting in the world.

Conclusion: Practicings involve ontological commitments. The argument slips from one particular way of acting in the world, namely talking, to a second particular way of acting in the world, namely practicing, and while doing so, retains the claim for ontological commitment. This move hides some assumption about acts in the world such as

Assumption 4:   All ways of acting in the world involve ontological commitments.

The argument is now at least completely explicit if still not quite acceptable. The premises may be just too much to swallow. This might be the case if the premises are considered independently for their individual merit, but would definitely be the case if Assumptions 2, 3, and 4 are related in the following way:

If the act of talking, as a member of the class called "ways of acting in the world," involves ontological commitment, then all members of the class, "ways of acting in the world," involve ontological commitment; therefore, because practicing a physical activity is a member of the class, "ways of acting in the world," then practicings also involve ontological commitment.

This is clearly an incorrect treatment of class membership and the relations which hold between class members.

The argument, then, concerning the practice of physical activities involving ontological commitments as originating in the comparison of language and sportlike physical activity is unacceptable as constructed. This, however, is not yet reason to abandon the conclusion as false. Just as a true conclusion can follow correctly and ineluctably from utterly false premises, the failure of a particular group of premises to lead to a conclusion does not render that conclusion untrue. Although the ontological commitments involved in what one says or how one talks about the world are surely more refined and apparently more conscious than any such commitments which might be involved in how one practices a physical activity, there still may be sense in pursuing the possibility that some such commitments may be involved in practicing.

The relationship of methodology with ontology

Another approach to the problem of ontological commitment in the context of sportlike physical activities might be through the following roughly sketched argument. If practicing is understood or viewed as a methodology in the sense of general principles which ought to guide an inquiry or activity, and if methodology cannot be separated from ontology, then ontological commitments may be involved in how one practices. Here, the claim that methodology cannot be separated from ontology requires some explanation. Just how is this claim concerning a relationship between ontology and methodology to be understood?

One understanding might be the claim that ontology, in general, cannot be separated from methodology, in general. Thus, on one side of the relationship any methodology involves some ontology, and on the other side, any ontology involves some methodology. This might be to say, then, that one simply does not think on how to go about doing something in the world without thinking on what kind of world one is doing it in; one does not attempt to deal with objects or things in themselves without reference to the ways in which such things come to be known. This understanding of the relationship between methodology and ontology is adequate (if one also accepts practicing as a kind of methodology) to lead to the conclusion that ontological commitments may be involved in how one practices a physical activity. It is adequate provided one does not insist that specific methodologies involve specific ontological commitments.

A second understanding of the claim that methodology and ontology cannot be separated is one which makes the relationship considerably more specific and determinant. Whereas the first interpretation was general in the same way as the claim that anything which goes up must come down is general, the second interpretation is more specific. An example is the claim that anything of a specific weight which goes up at a specific angle and at a specific velocity from place X will come down at place Y. Thus, one might interpret the relationship as if anytime and anywhere a particular methodology occurs, then particular, distinct, and specific ontological commitments are involved, and not just some ontological commitment.

Thus, how one decides to go about doing something in the world involves commitment to a very specific belief about the nature of reality. However, one might ask, Is it not possible that a single, particular methodology might involve or at least permit different, that is, contrasting, ontological commitments? Consideration of two examples might answer this question: One example is the way of practicing archery as discussed by Herrigel (1971); the other is the way of practicing tennis as discussed by Gallwey (1974).

Similarities in methodologies of practicing: Two examples

Zen in the art of archery. In *Zen in the Art of Archery*, Eugen Herrigel (1971) describes the course of study a student of the art of archery must complete. The foremost objective of Herrigel's practice was to detach himself from all care and concern, even from concern with hitting the target or shooting correctly. Herrigel was instructed to practice technique to the point of repletion, as it is the mastery of form that the Japanese method of instruction of the traditional arts seeks to inculcate (pp. 61-62). This is in order to achieve what might be called the "everyday mind," which is without reflection, deliberation, or conceptualization. Such practice, through methodical immersion in oneself or immersion in the form and technique of what one is doing leads to self-detachment (p. 72). The student is directed toward this purposelessness, self-detachment, immersion, everyday mind through the suggestion of concentrating on breathing (p. 40) and through numerous natural examples: the release of a baby's grasp (p. 49), snow falling from a bending bamboo leaf (p. 48), an unstirring centipede (p. 48), and the bursting open of the skin of a ripe fruit (p. 50). The way of practicing archery as discussed by Herrigel, the methodology of the art of archery, if you will, involves virtually a single concern to the point that students are admonished at times not to practice "anything except self-detaching immersion" (p. 72).

Herrigel's discussion of the art of archery does not only include this methodological point concerning the kind of singular objective of the practice of archery. Indeed, this methodological point about archery leads directly to the ontological point of archery. Herrigel writes that "the right frame of mind for the artist is only reached when the preparing and the creating, the technical and the artistic, the material and the spiritual, the project and the object, flow together without a break" (p. 66). The bow and arrow are only a pretext for what, as D.T. Suzuki (1971) writes in the introduction to *Zen in the Art of Archery*, is a most significant feature of the practice of all the arts as studied in Japan: "They are not intended for utilitarian purposes only or for purely aesthetic enjoyments, but are meant to train the mind; indeed, to bring it into contact with the ultimate reality" (p. 9).

Herrigel further emphasizes this by pointing toward the variously expressed goal of a soul sunk within itself, standing in the "plenitude of its nameless origin" (p. 56), of the immediate experience of the "bottomless ground of being" (p. 21), and "of one's becoming aware, in the deepest ground of the soul, of the unnameable Groundlessness and Qualitylessness—nay more, to one's becoming one with it" (p. 22). It is very clear in Herrigel's discussion that this ontological point, this ontological commitment, is explicit and central in the art of archery as practiced in Japan. This is so to the point of absolutely excluding other, and in some contexts more common, objectives such as hitting the target, which at best might be viewed as outward confirmation of an inner goal or event (p. 82). Herrigel's discussion of the art of archery is a strong statement concerning the relationship between methodology and ontological commitment. It apparently draws a rather specific line between the practice of archery and a very particular ontological commitment.

The inner game of tennis. To some extent, W. Timothy Gallwey's (1974) discussion of practicing tennis in *The Inner Game of Tennis* includes principles similar to those discussed by Herrigel. Gallwey observed that the origin of the problems of many tennis players is mental, such as thinking too much about shots, trying too hard to control movements, and being too concerned with results (p. 129). These tendencies undermine concentration which is a key to spontaneous, high-level tennis. Gallwey insists that these tendencies must be countered by "letting go of our attachments to the idea of controlling our own development" (p. 139), by adopting an attitude of abandon in which the player "stops caring about the outcome and plays all out" (p. 138), which is, according to Gallwey, the true meaning of detachment, and by practicing the master art of concentration. One of the techniques proposed in the practice of tennis is to attend to breathing (p. 103). The spontaneous performance sought in Gallwey's tennis is described as occurring "only when the mind is calm" (p. 13). Finally, the objective of the tennis player is to reach a state such that

> his mind is so concentrated, so focused, that it is *still*. It becomes one with what the body is doing, and the unconscious or automatic functions are working without interference from thoughts. The concentrated mind has no room for thinking how well the body is doing, much less of the how-to's of the doing (p. 21).

This method of practicing tennis, this goal of at least the "inner game" of tennis, is remarkably similar to the way of practicing archery as described by Herrigel with its foremost objective of detachment from all care and concern.

Dissimilarity in ontological commitment

If the methodologies of the two examples are strikingly similar, then how do the examples compare in terms of ontology? Following the more specific and deter-minant second interpretation of the claim concerning the relationship between methodology and ontology, because the methodologies of the two examples appear similar, the ontological commitments of the two examples might be expected to be similar, as well. This is apparently not the case, however. In spite of the claim "that the true goal of the Inner Game is to be found within" (p. 141) and the claim that a change in orientation from learning concentration in order to improve tennis to practicing tennis in order to improve concentration is a crucial shift in values from the outer to the inner, two claims which are similar to points concerning ontological commitment in the art of archery, the methodological points discussed by Gallwey concerning how to practice tennis do not lead in a very clear or distinct fashion to points concerning ontology.

To further muddle the relationship, there are simply too many different claims concerning apparently conflicting goals and objectives with which the method-ology or practice of tennis is concerned. One remains unconvinced about "the true goal" of the inner game when reading claims that it is the game played "to overcome all habits of mind which inhibit excellence in performance" (p. 13), and that the subject of the book is "how to develop the mental skills, without which high performance is impossible" (p. 17).

Effort to salvage at least the possibility of some similarity in terms of ontological commitment between the two examples might be pursued by suggesting that Gallwey simply failed to disclaim any real importance for performance by not more explicitly acknowledging that mysterious relationship referred to by Her-rigel of results as merely outward confirmation of inner goals or events. Maybe so, but Gallwey's particular discussion of the importation or adoption of a methodology or a way of practicing is not all that is at issue here, after all. There are certainly other examples of the adoption of practice principles which are similar to those discussed by Herrigel, even if they have often been distorted in the pro-cess of importation. Most such examples would undoubtedly have no semblance whatsoever of similarity to Herrigel's art of archery in terms of ontological com-mitment. I suspect that improved performance is the unabashedly admitted reason and hope behind most adoptions of Herrigel-like ways of practice.

The more specific and determinant second interpretation of the claim that methodology cannot be separated from ontology would lead one to expect that whenever two examples were substantially similar in terms of methodology, they would also be substantially similar in terms of ontological commitment. Com-parison of the two examples discussed in this chapter casts doubt on this inter-pretation of the claim. That doubt leaves in its wake only what can be salvaged from the following five disjunctions: a) The principles behind the ways of practicing in the two examples are not properly considered methodologies; *or* b) they are not substantially similar, *or* c) there are no instances in either of the two examples of a relationship between the methodology and an ontological commitment; *or* d) both examples involved substantially the same ontological commitments; *or* e) it is not the case that methodology cannot even in a specific and determinant sense be separated from ontology.

CONCLUSION

What then is to be salvaged? There are three points with which I wish to conclude. First, maybe it is simply mistaken to construe the two examples as involving instances of the methodology and ontological commitment relationship. Maybe this has been an example of an argument gone wrong in its premises because the analogies or instances employed were faulty. Of this I am not convinced. The ways of practicing discussed do seem like methodologies of a kind and similar methodologies at that. Nevertheless, it is worth acknowledging that a way of practicing involves a complexity and multifacetedness that may render the license I begged for considering practicing as a unitary act a tremendous burden to bear.

Second, the methodology discussed in the art of archery led directly to an ontological commitment. In light of this rather clear example of such an activity involving ontological commitment, or commitment concerning the ultimate nature of reality, if one is going to bother at all about ontological commitment, then one probably ought to bother about it even in the context of sportlike physical activity.

Third, the very specific and determinant ontological commitment involved in the methodology or way of practicing archery is apparently not involved in other instances in which the same way of practicing is employed. This dissimilarity in the examples in terms of ontological commitment, while undermining the more specific and determinant second interpretation of the claim that methodology cannot be separated from ontology, still does not undermine the more general first interpretation of the relationship. The dissimilarity in the examples may only point to the possibility that the world's complexity is such that it can embrace inconsistency in human action, at least when it has to do with the relationship between a way of practicing as a methodology and ontological commitments. That, however, is not a call or even a justification for us, as humans, to embrace or court such inconsistency ourselves. Indeed, we might do well to think again about such inconsistency.

REFERENCES

Austin, J.L. (1963). *How to do things with words*. Cambridge, MA: Harvard University Press.

Gallwey, T. (1974). *The inner game of tennis*. New York: Random House.

Herrigel, E. (1971). *Zen in the art of archery*. New York: Vintage. (Original work published 1953)

Quine, W.V.O. (1948). On what there is. *Review of Metaphysics*, **2**, 21-28.

Searle, J.R. (1969). *Speech acts*. London: Cambridge University Press.

Suzuki, D.T. (1971). Introduction. In E. Herrigel, *Zen in the art of archery*. New York: Vintage. (Original work published 1953)

Mystical and material embodiment: A comparative analysis

Robert E.C. Sparks
The University of British Columbia

Over the past several decades, there has been a growing interest in the West to explain some of the so-called ''paranormal'' abilities of adepts in Eastern mystical traditions in the idiom of Western science. In the '60s and '70s, for example, there was a great deal of interest in the explanatory potential of brain waves in their application with biofeedback. More recently, new work in cybernetics, cognitive psychology, and neurophysiology has increased our scientific understanding of the human brain, and further efforts can be expected to expand this knowledge to include mystical experience.

Recently, a colleague suggested at a thesis defense that a Zen master's skill, in this case, archery, might better be explained in terms of lower brain functions and automaticity than in the traditional terms of spiritual attainment and enlightenment. That is, instead of presenting Zen Skill as a spiritual skill, he preferred to represent it as a motor skill and to explain it in terms of subsconscious motor control by the brain, rendering a skill automatic through overlearning. Anyone with a modicum of sensitivity for the traditional view should realize that this is a travesty and should be concerned that something vital is being lost in this kind of translation of tradition into the new idiom. Out of this concern, I have devoted this chapter to the task of demonstrating the misunderstanding inherent in all attempts such as this to explain mystical expression in terms of material or physical embodiment.

To accomplish this task, I offer a comparison of Western and Eastern conceptions of embodiment, situating each relative to the other and outlining their respective claims to knowledge and truth. In conclusion, I hope to make clear that neither view is necessarily mutually exclusive; instead each has its own dimension of truth in the presence of the other. In the overall scheme of things, however, mysticism is seen to have a more encompassing world-view than science; thus, ultimately, it is able to incorporate the materialism of science into its own broader sphere, whereas science offers little hope of providing any real explanation or support for the edifice of mystical experience.

BASIS FOR COMPARATIVE ANALYSIS

In the history of ideas, fewer views are probably less disposed for effective comparison than are Eastern mysticism and the materialist empiricism of Western science. Not only are these two positions generally accepted as philosophically opposed, but their very enterprises in most circles are considered antithetical. The hallmark of mysticism is meditative subjectivity and that of science is empirically based objectivity. If mysticism as an idealist philosophical tradition may be understood as oppositional to the materialist tenets of modern science, as a transcendental meditative practice, it is seen to be steadfastly the negation of things rational and theoretical and thus as antithetical to the whole scientific enterprise. Despite these overwhelming differences, however, when elevated to the level of distinctive worldviews and examined carefully for their respective positions on embodiment, Eastern mysticism and Western materialist science are seen to have adequate theoretical terrain in common to suggest a basis for their comparative analysis.[1]

Areas of concordance

Thus, for example, both views in some measure support the related beliefs that human beings have a physical aspect called a body and that the body grounds or anchors them in the physical universe. The account of the five Skandhas or five aggregates of attachment in Buddhism is explicit in including physical being in its ontology and takes pains to show how sense organs link the body to the objects of the external world (Rahula, 1964, pp. 20-26). This concurs with other mystical accounts.[2] The view of science is equally as explicit. Physiologically, humans are understood to be physical beings who participate in the physical universe via their motile and perceptual capacities. The latter, in fact, is a prerequisite for science, because as an empirically validated theoretical system, science requires objective validity of human sense perception of the world.

A second area of agreement between the two views, integrating embodiment and human agency, is in the shared acknowledgement that humans are not the

---

[1]The step of treating mysticism as a worldview is itself not unproblematic, as it takes mysticism several steps away from its unmediated, intuitive roots and pushes it toward identification as a "system of thought" having some sort of "theoretical basis," a view to which mysticism itself is vehemently opposed. Nevertheless, it is felt that the step is worth taking, as the results of the exercise yield a point of view which, while constrained to intellectual understanding, does underscore the differences between these two basic positions on life.

[2]Traditional mystical ontology situates the human agent in the world via the body and the senses. Although some accounts are not as exhaustive as that of the five Skandhas in Buddhism, they do share this element in common. For example, in the *Tao-Te-Ching* (Feng & English, 1972), repeated reference is made to the "ten thousand things" (of the physical world) which are understood to arise with the Tao—they "depend upon it"; it "nourishes" them; they "return to it" (chapter 34)—and to be apprehended in some manner by the senses: "the five colors blind the eye; "the five flavors dull the taste" (chapter 12). One important distinction to make here, however, is that physical existence is phenomenal existence in mysticism, not actual or ultimate existence, and herein it departs from science. In Taoism, for example, the ten thousand things, while dependent on the Tao, are equally the result of our apprehending and cataloguing the world. What is important in context, however, is not the divergence of mysticism and science (already demonstrated) but their sharing of the notion that people do in some measure participate in a physical universe. This convergence yields joint theoretical terrain between the views on which a more detailed comparison of their central tenets can be mapped out.

sole agents of their actions. Both views hold in some measure that humans and the selves they perceive themselves to be are determined by universal forces which shape their thought patterns, their existences, and their destinies. Here again, the five Skandhas are instructive, because like other mystical accounts, they both specify the nature of being of the individual self and link the individual to universal laws and principles, in this case the laws of karma.[3] Similarly, materialist science sees individual human life as shaped by heredity and forces in the environment, and with the mystics, concurs that human thought and existence are to some extent defined and determined by these forces.

Finally, both views conversely agree that humans are in some measure free agents, at least more so than other living things, and that they are able to freely express themselves and exert their will within the limits of their own lived existential boundaries. Both science and mysticism see humankind as at the apex of the evolutionary ladder, and thus as the most free of living creatures. Even within the confines of fairly rigid notions of universal causality, whether Eastern or Western, both see the individual as essentially free to exercise his or her will and be self-expressive.

The story of Arjuna's dilemma in the Hindu text, the *Bhagavad Gita* (Edgerton, 1965) is a perfect case in point. Poised on a field of battle and seeing friends and relatives on both sides, Arjuna is divided about whether he should fight, concerned about whom he might kill. His charioteer, actually an incarnate form of the god Vishnu, tries a variety of arguments to convince him he should. Finally, he reveals his godhood to Arjuna and stipulates that the fates of the men he would kill are already determined, saying, ''Therefore arise thou, win glory, Conquer thine enemies and enjoy prospered kingship; By me myself they have already been slain long ago; Be thou the mere instrument, left-handed archer!'' (p. 58).

This would appear to be a strict case of predetermination, but on a larger scale it is not, because the whole direction of the account to that point is Vishnu's attempt to persuade Arjuna to fight. Thus, even within the constraints of a predetermined event, the human agent is seen as having freedom as well as a moral obligation to choose a course of action. In this regard, both science and mysticism share a comfortable margin of agreement. The human may very well be constrained by history, biology, and universal events, but within this framework, he or she remains yet a free agent. On all these matters and actually, on many more, science and mysticism agree.

Philosophical distinctions

The primary difference between the two views is that Western materialist science claims it can explain human life in physical terms alone, whereas mysticism appeals to other dimensions of reality. This is, in fact, their most significant philosophical distinction. One can argue that this, coupled with the high level of sophistication of contemporary scientific theory and research, rather than weakening the scientific position, actually makes it reasonably compelling. Recent work in computer science, artificial intelligence, neurochemistry, and neurophysiology has made great strides toward explaining the more subtle arrangements and workings of the organ that behaviorists only recently called the "black box." Brain researchers are now able to plot out many of the brain's major neurological events, and more information becomes available all the time.

---

[3]Other mystical accounts of universal laws and principles are the "natural way" of the Tao and the anthropomorphized sense of universal determinism in the Judeo-Christian understanding of "God's will" and "God's grace." Essentially, all mystical traditions in some measure provide such accounts.

Of course, if brain maps are becoming clearer and better developed, it does not mean that the theory behind how that which is being mapped functions necessarily follows suit. Theorists still divide into two camps, the so-called wets and dries (the neurochemists and artificial intelligence [computer model] specialists). The chemists seek explanation in the organic chemistry of the nervous system, the artificial intelligence specialists in its electric impulses and potentialities. Despite their differences, however, some researchers still speculate that in the near future, we will be able to account for all human cognitive activity, even including human consciousness.

Linear theories versus the experience of the infinite

The claims are intriguing and the theoretical edifices supporting them impressive, but as we move these structures away from their own context and toward that of mysticism, a variety of difficulties evolve. For one, it is apparent that materialist theories of embodiment are, for the most part, all linear information, or timeline theories; the systems these theories describe have information that can be processed in and out or to higher levels. For example, if I put my hand on a hot stove, that signal gets linearly processed as information to the brain or to a subsystem that in turn responds with information (a command) for my hand to be raised.

Although mysticism certainly would not deny this, the nature of mystical experience is such that the stock concepts of stimulus and information in cognitive psychology simply will not do. The experience of the infinite, for example, a well-known phenomenon in higher levels of mystical attainment, simply cannot be the result of an infinite stimulus, delivering infinite information to the sensory system. The solution here for the materialist, of course, is to redefine the conditions of the event and to specify that the experience of the infinite is only that— an experience; it requires neither an infinite stimulus nor infinite information, only an activation of neurons in the "infinite experience area" of the brain.[4] A more trenchant difficulty for the materialist, however, lies in the linearity of the system, especially in those theories that rely on artificial intelligence/computer models. The cosmology of mysticism is specific about this: The universe is whole unto itself, and each of its parts contains the whole. This notion of the interpenetration of all things is at the heart of the *I Ching* and the *Tao-te-Ching* as well as other notable texts in the mystical tradition.

Theories that rely on linearity simply cannot have all things at the same place at the same time, namely all things timelessly interpenetrated, as mysticism requires. Therefore, this tenet which itself is necessary in mystical cosmology to explain the timeless, spaceless nature of enlightened awareness, summarily

---

[4]While compelling, this sort of escape from the difficulty of explaining the experience of the infinite in material terms is itself flawed in two ways. On the one hand, it implies a simple identity between brain states and our mental experiences, a connection which is viewed as problematic in current work in philosophy of mind and which, therefore, cannot simply be assumed without rigorous supportive argument (Rosenthal, 1971). Second, even if this difficulty is surmounted by softening the connection and making the experience of the infinite a result of functional capacities of the brain (thus sidestepping the problems of the identity thesis), the difficulty still remains of why there should be an experience of the infinite at all, as well as in what its actual ontological status might consist. Having the brain capacity to "experience the infinite" seems to be counter to the notion of parsimony, as there is no good reason to be able to have the experience other than if it is really an experience of the infinite. Of course, if it is an experience of something real (the infinite), then the ontological status of the experience must be put in doubt for the reasons already given in context. Either way, the experience of the infinite remains a problem for materialist explanations.

dismisses all modern theories of the brain, cognition, and motor control that rely upon linear, information-processing models. If we allow that the mystic's experience of the infinite is of something more real than a brain state, and that the timeless, spaceless quality of enlightenment as described by mystics is actual, then all but one modern materialist explanation of embodiment must be discarded: The explanation retained is based on the holographic paradigm presently being debated by the new-age thinkers. As this is the strongest of the new materialist theories, it merits further discussion.[5]

The holographic paradigm

A *hologram* is the record that is made on a photographic plate when light from a laser is split by a mirror and allowed to bounce off a subject, then merge back with its own beam at the surface of the plate. The resultant interference pattern gets recorded and can subsequently be used to create a three-dimensional image in space by reversing the procedure and sending the light back across the plate (see Figure 1). The fascination of the new-age thinkers with the hologram, and the reason they have chosen it as representative of a new paradigm, is because the image recorded, unlike a lens-focused image in a camera, is stored in its entirety throughout the hologram. Thus, like the mystical notion of interpenetration, the holographic image is timelessly interspersed across its film surface. The cause of this is the manner in which the laser light generates the interference pattern on the plate, but the result is such that if you break off one small piece of the hologram, you still have the entire image that was illuminated recorded on that piece. David Bohm and Karl Pribram, two notable scientists among the new-age thinkers, have made use of this property of holograms in theory construction in their respective fields.

David Bohm, a theoretical physicist who studied under Einstein, demonstrated that in order to balance the ledger of forces in the universe, one must assume that the universe itself is holographic. Essentially, Bohm showed that within the void of space between subatomic particles there must be quantum amounts of energy in order for the universe to function as it does. This energy and the particles it supports enfold upon themselves in a way that Bohm describes as holographic, or in the dynamic sense, as holomovement (Bohm, 1982).

In a slightly different vein, well-known cognitive psychologist Karl Pribram concluded that the human brain itself must be holographic to perform the sorts of operations of which it is capable. Studies in visual and auditory perception bear out this conclusion and show that the brain essentially perceives in a dimension of frequency interferences and stores these perceptions three-dimensionally within and throughout itself. This helps to explain, for example, why patients who have sustained severe brain damage as a result of a stroke do not lose memory as would be the case if memory were only associated with specific locales (Coleman, 1979; Wilber, 1982; Pribram, 1969, 1982).

Bohm's and Pribram's work, though not yet officially endorsed by the scientific community at large, is the subject of ongoing debate in theoretical physics

---

[5]The "new-age thinkers" comprise a group of researchers who for the past several years have been actively proposing and debating a paradigm shift in the sciences based upon a fused spiritualist-materialist global view of reality that has come to be known as the holographic paradigm. These thinkers include David Bohm, Fritjon Capra, Marilyn Ferguson, Karl Pribram, Renee Weber, and Ken Wilber. A major portion of their debate has occurred in *ReVision Journal*. Ken Wilber has extracted essential papers from the journal and assembled them in book form in a work entitled *The Holographic Paradigm and Other Paradoxes: Exploring the Leading Edge of Science*. This book and *Eye to Eye: The Quest for the New Paradigm*, also by Ken Wilber, are primary source books for information on the debate surrounding the holographic paradigm.

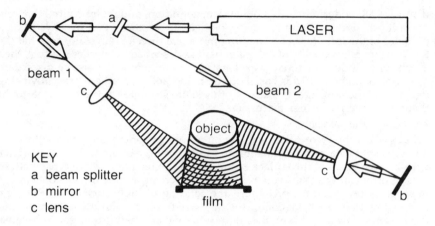

KEY
a beam splitter
b mirror
c lens

Figure 1. How a hologram works. (*Psychology Today*, February, 1979)

and cognitive psychology. Part of the difficulty in having their views accepted is that they are using a new paradigm that does not mesh with some of the major tenets of the existing paradigm, among them the law of parsimony. For the time being, however, I think it is safe to accept their views as scholarly and as representative of a type of theory which will be certain to receive more attention in materialist science. Thus, given the support of their arguments that the brain itself may function as a hologram to holographically interrogate and interpret a holographic universe, it seems that a main objection of mysticism to materialist conceptions of embodiment—the inability to account for the mutual interpenetration of all things—can be met.

Shortcomings of materialist embodiment theories

Again, however, the conceptual edifice is more impressive than its reality. Materialist theories of embodiment, even sophisticated ones like the holographic paradigm, fall short in accounting for mysticism and mystical experience in three general ways. As theories they perforce are destined to always be external, objectified renderings of what is inherently an internal, subjective reality in mysticism. Second, their explanations, by the nature of the very idiom in which they are expressed, are incapable of apprehending the content of mystical events. As Wilber has stated, attempting to explain mystical experience in material terms is like trying to describe the Mona Lisa by the chemistry of its paint, or Hamlet by the kind of paper on which it is printed (Wilber, 1982, pp. 184, 272). Finally, materialist theories of embodiment are inherently reductionist, and in their reductionism lose the phenomenon they attempt to explain. I shall examine each of these objections in turn.

Externality

The concepts of internality and externality, subjectivity and objectivity help to point out essential differences in the focus and direction of the positions as well as in what they are capable of describing. This not only aids in clarifying the two views but also in underscoring some of their relative strengths and weaknesses. As has been shown, mysticism has no difficulty in accepting physical (albeit phenomenal) reality into its cosmology. Traditions like Buddhism and Taoism do not deny physical existence; they simply deny this aspect of reality as the correct one on which to focus if higher awareness and sage wisdom, or enlightenment is desired. Thus, if these are the goals for which one is striving, then one must look to the internal, subjective side of reality accessed through meditation.

Even in making this distinction, however, mysticism acknowledges existence of at least two realities—one internal and subjective, the other external and objective—of which materialism by its own rigorous design can admit only one: the external, phenomenal reality objectively experienced by the senses. While this is not a penetrating criticism of materialism, it does demonstrate that whereas mysticism can and does assimilate science into its worldview, science (at least of a materialist bent) can only assimilate half of the account of mysticism—the externalized, measurable, quantifiable half.

The degree of the externality of materialist science, however, is not limited to its cosmology or the criteria by which it decides validity. In materialist science, we not only restrict focus to substance which is objectively measurable and quantifiable, we render our measurements and quantifications into rational, objectified terms, symbols, that are externalized versions of our original empirical observations. Thus, not only are the observations restricted to sense experience of the material, external world, the very terms in which we apprehend and record them are external to the immediacy and subjectivity of the experience itself. This externalizes scientific theory from its own subjective origins and negates any possibility of ever rendering the internality and subjectivity of mystical experience in these terms.

In the scientific scheme, sense perceptions beget objectified data; objectified data validate hypotheses; hypotheses support theorems; theorems articulate with theories; and an entire hierarchy of externalized conceptual structure is created based upon what was initially a subjective experience. Viewed in this manner, the process of science is thus the objectification and externalization of personal knowledge. By contrast, that of mysticism is inherently the reverse, or the subjectification and internalization of knowledge via the focusing of attention on the root and elemental basis of all knowing, intuition. In mystical tradition, while objectivity and rational thought are in no way denied, they are understood to already be an externalization of the intuitive knowledge of the subjective self. Because the latter is considered to be the sole access to the subjective internality of the universe, and thus to real universal truth, the former is disclaimed and disregarded as not warranting attention. In both respects, that is, being limited to externality and objectively observable substance, and being limited to rational, objective explanation, materialist science falls short of the mark of being able to account for mystical experience and for the resultant cosmology mystics have developed. By contrast, it is apparent that mysticism allows for the materialist orientation of science but negates its ultimate explanatory power and significance. The latter is neither an arbitrary nor a trivial assertion, however.

Inaccountability of mystical experience

As much as this evidence already reveals shortcomings in the scientific account of mysticism, the second criticism is more telling. As already pointed out, the idiom of materialist science is unable to in any way account for the lived reality of mystical experience. A hierarchical conceptual scheme developed by Wilber clarifies this (Wilber, 1982, pp. 267–269). If we accept the traditional view of embodiment in our culture—that of spirit, mind, and body—as grounds for a mystical cosmology, we end up with a hierarchical scheme of reality in which not only substance is vertically organized, but knowledge along with it. Corresponding to each of the three levels of spirit, mind and body may be posited three modes of knowing: intuitive, symbolic, and sensory (see Figure 2).

Substance	*Knowledge*
Spirit	Intuitive
Mind	Symbolic
Body	Sensory

Figure 2. Traditional view of embodiment. (Wilber, 1982, p. 267)

According to Wilber, these forms of knowing correspondent to the three traditional levels of being are not new. Aristotle referred to them as theoria, praxs (or phronesis), and techne. Christian mystics refer to them as the eye of contemplation, the eye of reason, and the eye of the flesh (Wilber, 1982, p. 267). Simple at the outset, the three-level scheme is complicated by the fact that the mind as the reflective seat of awareness can look not only at its own level, but at the other two levels as well. That is, the mind can symbolically represent and interpret sensory and intuitive knowledge in addition to its own symbolic knowledge, resulting with a fundamentally different kind of knowledge generated in each case.

Wilber argues that when mind confines itself to sensory knowledge, the new mode of knowledge (or reason) generated is empirical-analytic, and its interest is technical (Figure 3). This, in Wilber's scheme, is the level of scientific inquiry. The symbolic reason of mind is applied to sensory knowledge to achieve technical ends, as for example, when an educational psychologist monitors behavior to validate a hypothesis about learning. According to Wilber, when mind works with other minds (or with itself), the mode is hermeneutic, phenomenological, historic, or rational, and its interest may be practical or moral. This is the level at which we interpret and explain the meanings of things or engage in logic or moral discourse: For example, we debate the value of self-expressive forms of play or attempt to decide whether something should or should not be done. The mind employs symbolic reason to interpret its own (or others) symbolic knowledge.

Finally, at the top of his scheme, Wilber contends that when the mind attempts to cognize the spiritual realm, what results is a series of impenetrable paradoxes; therefore, he characterizes this mode as paradoxical or radically dialectic. Essentially, the wholeness of intuitive knowledge becomes dialectic and paradoxical when interpreted through symbolic reason. Examples include classic mystical tenets such as the universe being one and separate unto itself, and the human agent being both God and not-God. The following two examples from *Zen Koans* (Miura & Sasaki, 1965) also reflect the paradoxical nature of intuitive knowledge:

> Thinking neither of good nor of evil, at this very moment what was your original aspect before your father and mother were born? (p. 44)

> Empty-handed, yet holding a hoe;
> Walking, yet riding a water buffalo. (p. 45)

```
                    ┌→ Spirit — Paradoxical — Mandalic/Soteriological
        Mind ───────┼→ Mind — Hermeneutic — Phenomenological/Moral
                    └→ Matter — Empirical — Analytical/Technical
```

Figure 3. Interface of mind with other levels of being (traditional view) (Wilber, 1982, p. 268)

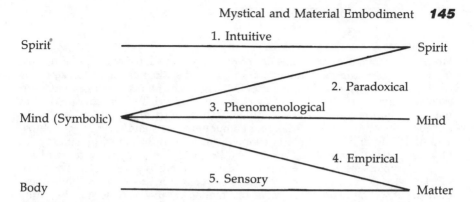

Figure 4. Elaborated hierarchy of knowledge in traditional view of embodiment (Wilber, 1982, p. 269)

A third term Wilber sometimes uses for this kind of knowledge is *mandalic reason*, by which I take him to mean the same notion of paradox, but here allied with mandalic symbolism. Because in attempting to cognize the spiritual realm, the mind is in effect trying to gain access to it, Wilber defined the interest of this kind of reason as *soteriological*, that is, as seeking salvation from divine agency.

When combined, Wilber's two hierarchical schemes yield three levels of reality and five levels of knowledge which, taken in total, constitute an elementary form of the mystical Great Chain of Being (see Figures 4 & 5). This scheme enables us to situate materialism and materialist science within the framework of mysticism. Within this context, the futility of science (see Figure 4, Level 4) attempting to account for the phenomenological meaning of an idea (Level 3), let alone the meaning of mystical intuition (Level 1), should be apparent. As a knowledge system, science is restricted to phenomenal explanations cast in the terms or symbols of the objectifiable world; the meanings of these terms will never have equivalency with the meaning of the terms we use to debate meaning (Level 3) nor with the intuitive events that surpass the meaning of all terms (Level 1). Mystical intuition and the cosmology it supports cannot be apprehended in the terms of science any more than the symbolic meaning of a painting can be apprehended in terms of the chemistry of its paint. Intuition, symbolic meaning, and chemistry are different layers (levels) of reality, as perennially presented in the mystical Great Chain of Being (see Figure 5). Thus, mystical experience and agency (i.e., mystical skill) simply cannot be rendered in the terms of materialist science.

Ultimate   — consciousness as such, the source and true nature of all lower levels
Causal   — formless radiance, perfect transcendence
Subtle   — archetypal, trans-individual, intuitive
Mental   — ego, logic, thinking
Biological — living, pranic, sentient matter/energy
Physical   — nonliving matter/energy

Figure 5. Hierarchy of being in perennial philosophy—Great Chain of Being (Wilber, 1982, p. 159)

Reductionism

Finally, in keeping with this same line of reasoning, we should take caution against the reductionism inherent in modern science and against its impact on accounts of mysticism and mystical experience. One of the chief tenets in force in modern science is the principle of the unity of nature. Essentially this tenet holds that nature is uniform throughout such that the study of nature can ultimately be reduced to the study of its underlying component parts and their relationships. The unity of nature principle is coupled with the principle of parsimony (or Ockham's razor): gratuitous ideas in explanation should be cut away and the simplest hypothesis that can explain the data accepted. The result is that as scientific knowledge becomes more sophisticated, increased attempts are made to explain what was previously the focus of "higher" branches of science in reductionist terms of more fundamental branches: for example, sociology explained in terms of sociobiology, heredity in terms of cellular chemistry, and the mind in terms of brain physiology and neurochemistry. Presently, even these explanations (we are told) are reducible to universal, physical explanations stated in terms of the fundamental forces and building blocks of the universe (that is, physics).

This general theoretical orientation accounts in part for the fascination of scientists such as Bohm and Pribram with the potential for physical explanations of mystical cosmology and experience. However, there are two insurmountable difficulties here. First, in reducing macrophenomena to microphenomena, one inherently risks losing the significance of forces and events in the macrosphere: For example, one misses the dynamics of ecological forces in the environment if one only focuses on the molecular structures or quantum mass of the constituents of the environment. Essentially one cannot reduce biological events of an ecosystem to physics without losing the impact of those events biologically in the system. The same is certainly true of mystical experience and the cosmology it supports. If one reduces mutual interpenetration to holomovement of subatomic particles, for example, the impact of mutual interpenetration on human experience, human agency, and moral conduct is completely lost as well (Wilber, 1982, pp. 166).

Second, and more important, however, is the fact that in attempting to reduce all phenomena to simplified material terms, the terms themselves only attain meaning to the extent that they are manifested and communicated within an intersubjective reality, which cannot itself be reduced to simplified material terms. No amount of explanation of electrons, neurons, or brain waves, for example, could help to explain the symbolic logic of $2 + 2 = 4$, or account for our understanding the differentiation between atoms and molecules. The logic and intersubjective meaning of the material explanations of science simply escape the material limitations scientists like to impose upon the world. If this is the case with the materialist explanations of scientists, it is even more the case with the pure subjectivity of mystical intuition.

Reducing mysticism to physical terms, accordingly, may be understood as a misapplication of science. It neither explains mysticism nor captures it nor approximates it. A scientist cannot prove or disprove mystical cosmology. For a scientist to begin to appreciate this problem, he or she needs to focus upon the basis on which scientific information about the universe itself attains meaning and in precisely what form such meaning is constituted. If the answer is "symbolically" (which it must be), then there can be no question that the symbolism of the scientist transcends and cannot be reduced to his or her own materialism, in the same way as the intuition of the mystic transcends and cannot be reduced to our own dialectical reason.

THE DOMAIN OF SCIENTIFIC APPLICABILITY AND TRUTH

Thus, it can be concluded that although science can offer explanations of mystical internality in terms of externality and physical substance, it cannot ultimately account for mysticism or mystical experience. Scientific explanations of mysticism inherently reduce the internal to the external, the subjective to the objective, and the spiritual to the material. Further, science itself is ultimately a rational, symbolic medium limited to empirical-analytical knowledge. At best, therefore, science may be able to one day explain the physical substrate of mystical experience, but certainly not its content and meaning, and never its true (absolute) subjectivity. As it is the latter, which in the end constitutes mystical experience, or if you will, which is mysticism, I hope it is clear that attempts to account for mysticism and mystical agency in physical, material terms are misled. Perhaps science may one day fully account for physical reality, but it is simply the wrong tool to engage and to plumb spiritual reality even as much as symbolic reality. There is only one avenue for apprehending spirit and that is through the real practice of meditation, the spiritual equivalent of the scientific method. This does not dismiss the scientific view, but rather qualifies its domain of applicability and truth, which I hope discourages simple-minded translation of mysticism into science.

REFERENCES

Bohm, D. (1982). *Wholeness and the implicate order*. London: Routledge & Kegan Paul.

Coleman, D. (1979, February). Holographic memory. *Psychology Today*, **12**(9).

Edgerton, F. (Trans.). (1965). *The Bhagavad Gita*. New York: Harper & Row.

Feng, G.-F., & English, J. (Trans.). (1972). *Lao Tsu: Tao Te Ching*. New York: Random House.

Miura, I., & Sasaki, R. (1965). *The Zen Koan*. New York: Harcourt, Brace & World.

Pribram, K. (1969). The neurophysiology of remembering. *Scientific American*, **220**(1).

Pribram, K. (1982). *Languages of the brain: Experimental paradoxes and principles in neuropsychology*. New York: Brandon House.

Rahula, W. (1964). *What the Buddha taught*. New York: Random House.

Rosenthal, D. (1971). *Materialism and the mind-body problem*. Englewood Cliffs, NJ: Prentice Hall.

Wilber, K. (Ed.). (1982). *The Holographic paradigm and other paradoxes: Exploring the leading edge of science*. Boulder, CO: Shambhala.

Wilber, K. (1983). *Eye to eye: The quest for the new paradigm*. Garden City, NY: Anchor Books.

Toward a revisionist philosophy of coaching

Chic Johnson
Southwest Missouri State University

We are all products of our heritage and environment, captives of our culture, prisoners to our perspectives. As we move through the various stages of our lives, we assimilate and regurgitate the popular trends, maxims, and aphorisms that reflect our present stages of evolution. Largely to our detriment, we tend to parent the way we have been parented, teach the way we have been taught, and coach the way we have been coached. This forebodes a retarded evolutionary process as evidenced by the 350 years it has taken for Cartesian dualism to self-destruct. In nurturing a fundamental division into two separate and independent realms, that of mind and that of matter, a mechanistic worldview was contrived and perpetuated by the Western world. Newton, who constructed his mechanics on this basis, made it the foundation of Western scientific thought, and ever since, the West has functioned within a well-defined, easily measured set of dimensions of space, time, energy, mass, and cause-and-effect relationships.

Opposed to the mechanistic conception of the world is the view of Eastern masters which is characterized by words like *organic, holistic,* and *ecological.* The view is one of simplicity and naturalism and regards all phenomena in the universe as integral parts of an inseparable, harmonious whole. For the Eastern master, all things and events perceived by the senses are interrelated and connected and are different aspects and manifestations of the same ultimate reality. Eastern masters see objects as having a fluid and ever-changing character. The Eastern worldview, thus, is intrinsically dynamic, with time and change as essential features. The entire cosmos is seen as one inseparable reality—forever in motion, alive, organic, spiritual, and material at the same time.

The Western tendency to divide the perceived world into individual and separate things and to experience ourselves as isolated egos in this world is depicted as an illusion springing from our mentality of measuring, standardizing, and categorizing.

It is against this apparent contradiction that Eastern and Western views are juxtaposed in an attempt to bring a semblance of balance and jurisprudence to the area of coaching, which is the art and science of interacting with individuals who aspire to gain experience in sport/athletic endeavors.

BALANCING EAST WITH WEST

Startling gains in athletic prowess have been attributed to improved technological training methods, equipment, environmental control, facilities construction, and nutrition. In concert with significant technological advances, however, lies human intentionality, the purpose of which is evolution, transcendence, and transformation (Kapleau, 1980b, p. 285). Who are we? What are we? For what purpose do we exist? More specifically, why do we engage in sport? These questions are intrinsically oriented and humanistically inspired, directed toward people rather than machines. Third-force psychology, given impetus by Carl Rogers and Abraham Maslow, is seen as a welcome antidote to the mechanistic character of behaviorism and the gloomy, despairing character of psychoanalysis (Schultz, 1977, p. 60). We are in the midst of a new revolution, a revolution that has as its genesis the quality of self-determinism, which is people making choices about the determination of their own destinies. Recognized as an essential ingredient of this revolutionary attitude is the formulation of a positive and meaningful self-concept, the foundation upon which all other aspects of the revolution adhere.

The Integrated Individual

The characteristics that epitomize the integrated individual are being reborn and transformed. An entirely new model is emerging. Powerful movements are taking root that have as their basis the integration of mind, body, will, and spirit, which is the transpersonal nature of the human being. These movements touch every sector of the population from sports psychologists to holistic medical practitioners, and from nuclear physicists to housewives. Additionally, adherents to the philosophical tenets of existentialism, phenomenology, Zen Buddhism, and humanism play a key role in revising our views on the nature of men and women with respect to human potential and the quality of existence.

In a contraindicated fashion, philosophical techniques have developed over the years including categorizing, characterizing, classifying, identifying, judging, and selecting. These techniques provide a means to understanding, clarifying, and learning, but serve also as a form of dichotomizing things as separate and independently identifiable. It appears that an inordinate amount of time and effort has been spent noting distinctions rather than similarities. Dwelling on differences spawns separatism, fortifies nationalism, nurtures religious pride and self-righteousness, fosters racism, and encourages chauvinistic attitudes and behavior. Emphasizing similarities, on the other hand, promotes harmony, singleness of purpose, mutual respect, camaraderie, cohesiveness, cooperation, and balance. As we evolve to higher levels of awareness of the interdependency and unity of all living forms, we become more perfectly balanced until ultimately we reach a point of emotional, spiritual, and mental androgyny.

It is in this light that this chapter explores the potential of the world of the athlete: the athlete in motion, the athlete in thought, and the athlete in control.

Concentration (ego-consciousness) versus "no-mind" (un-self-consciousness)

Ego-consciousness

The ego is that aspect of one's consciousness which is preoccupied with expectations, assumptions, limitations, judgments, guilt, and fear. These learned behaviors have led us into a sense of separation and alienation that distorts our self-concept, perverts our value constructs, and usurps our self-determination and prospects for freedom. There is no constraint so repressive and restrictive as that which is self-imposed and no reprieve so genuinely appreciated when we become liberated from it. Timothy Gallwey (Gallwey & Kriegel, 1977) wonderfully characterizes the ego in his depiction of Self One.

Most minds are active with a flow of instructions about how to do this and how to avoid doing that—self-criticism, self-analysis, worries, doubts and fears. In many cases the chatter is less than friendly. In the inner game approach, the voice that is doing all the talking, judging, worrying and doubting is Self One, and it is instructing Self Two, the body that performs the actions. Self One is the ego mind that has to be in control, so it tells you how or how not to perform, that you are hopeless or great, that you are better than some, but worse than others. In most minds, these two selves don't get along well, a condition that makes performing to one's optimum impossible. ... Through experience we soon discover that we perform best when we are thinking least. When Self One is in a quiet state our awareness increases and we discover Self Two, that part of us that can respond to any situation instantaneously, with its fullest capacities. The main objective of the inner game is to free ourselves of whatever inner obstacles prevent Self Two's fullest development and expression (p. 27).

No-mindedness

For centuries, Far Eastern masters have proposed the integration of mental and physical functioning, speaking of such characteristics as harmony, centeredness, and consciousness of the "oneness." Actually, it is more than integration:

It is a state of wholeness in which the mind functions freely and easily, without the sensation of a second mind or ego standing over it with a club. ... This unconsciousness is not coma, but what the exponents of Zen signify as "no-mind" (Watts, 1957, p. 23).

No-mindedness employs the whole mind; it means the totality of psychic functioning rather than an exclusive intellectual or thinking mind, or even surface consciousness. The important point is that the center of the mind's activity is not in the conscious thinking process; it is not in the ego. George Leonard (1977), in *The Ultimate Athlete*, states that "Western thought, unlike that of the East, has by and large rejected direct experience as a path to the highest knowledge" (p. 55). Westerners' approach to knowledge remains largely dialectical and cognitive.

Galileo, Kepler, Descartes, and Newton lived in a dreamworld of forces and motion and manipulation without touch or taste or color or smell. Later, Locke and Hume and the Positivists might have been expected to bring us back to our senses, but they only reinforced the scientific mentality that has moved us to control the world and lose ourselves. ... And we are taught from earliest childhood to trust instruments more than our own deepest feelings. We are encouraged to view as true that which is most removed from our own persons. (Leonard, 1977, p. 56)

In speaking of his own aikido teacher, Leonard (1977) reports:

The physical education experts continue their work of breaking down every skill into smaller and smaller fragments, analyzing every movement and submovement with the help of film, computers, advanced mechanics, and math. This may help well-coached athletes achieve step-by-step improvements, but it can't bring forth the quantum leaps in human functioning that are possible. What is more, the principles learned in aikido should influence the way you play golf, drive, talk to your children, work at your job, make love—the way you live. (p. 58)

Robert Nideffer (1976) has fashioned a Western definition for this concept:

Functioning is integrated within a particular competitive situation when both mental and physical processes are working together to accomplish a particular goal. ... Your feelings and thoughts have to be totally oriented toward, and concentrated on, aiding your actual physical performance. This doesn't mean being hung up on winning (ego) but rather playing as well as you can for yourself and your team. It means playing for the joy of the sport. (p. 10)

Gallwey & Kriegel (1977) express similar views:

When we participate in a sport in which the object is winning or reaching a destination point, we tend to think more about the score, the goal, the end of the journey. Our efforts are concentrated on what we must do to beat our opponents, and if we aren't winning, we aren't enjoying. But the pleasures of participating lie in being totally involved; in the way we feel when the body is in motion—the delight in a skill well executed; the sense of our own natural rhythm and flow. The goal then is a feeling of harmony both with ourselves and with our environment. The prize is in the process itself. We learn that without appreciating the path, reaching the goal is often meaningless. Moreover, we discover that games of all kinds are more often won when first they are enjoyed. (p. 16)

Everything fits. That which opposes is only the other end of the continuum; one cannot be known without the other. Learning to create harmony may be why we exist.

Typical of the West, at the conclusion of athletic events one frequently hears such postmortems as, "I couldn't concentrate," "I became distracted," "I just wasn't with it today," "I couldn't relax," and "My mind kept drifting." Substantially, what occurs is that outside problems creep into one's consciousness concerning family, friends, finances, sexual concerns, and other frustrations. Influences surrounding the activity itself, such as unfamiliar conditions and equipment, spectators, actions of teammates and opponents, and the behavior of coaches, may prove extremely distracting to the performer.

When attempting to concentrate on one's performance, it is essential to eliminate extraneous thoughts from the ego-mind. Internalization and dissociation are skills demanded of the high achiever. Athletes must have the ability to broaden or narrow their focus to the internal as well as the external circumstances and conditions that confront them. Dissociation, on the other hand, allows a blocking out of distractions and irritations, and permits a high level of concentration on the tasks to be performed.

In exploring the martial arts, popular in the Far East, considerable emphasis is placed on the ability to control the mental-emotional processes that lead to becoming "one with the universe."

Training in aikido calls for no theoretical study. From the beginning, we realize the multiplicity of perception and being through direct experience. The secret of aikido is to harmonize ourselves with the movement of the universe and bring ourselves into accord with the universe itself. This is not mere theory, you practice it. Then you will accept the great power of oneness with nature. Just as the perfect movement exists, each perceived event, even one in which we "do" something, is already happening. There is a flow to the universe and our task is to join it. The Way abides in non-action, yet nothing is left undone. (Leonard, 1977, pp. 59–60)

To expect nothing, but be ready for everything, is the essence of the message. When this skill is mastered, the athlete is sensitive to even the most subtle changes in the environment and hence can react accordingly. The inner athlete learns to respond "intuitively," calling upon that sixth sense that only now are we beginning to comprehend. "All cultivation of concentration is wrong-minded from the start. For how, by cultivating concentration, could one obtain concentration?" (Watts, 1957, p. 96).

Cultivating changed consciousness levels and motivation

Athletes today, maturing in a different sociocultural environment, are perhaps more aware and less fearful of authority figures. They are less intimidated, more assertive, and do not respond well to the authoritarian, command-oriented coaching styles. The insightful and perceptive contemporary coaches are becoming cognizant of the necessity to challenge the athlete mentally and psychologically. They recognize the change in consciousness levels that this departure from dualism has nurtured. Some positive attributes these coaches cultivate include:

- Harmony of mind, body and spirit, and an ability to unite the internal with the external. This is synonymous with Tibetan Buddhist position. "The external world and the inner world are only two sides of the same fabric in which the threads of all forces and all events, of all forms of consciousness and of their objects, are woven into an inseparable net of endless, mutually conditioned relations" (Capra, 1977, p. 50).
- A deeply marked sense of responsibility for one's own life and the desire to design alternative futures. Knowing what is in one's best interests involves quieting the mind while gently assessing the here and now. The most valuable experiences of our lives are those in which we are called upon to take a risk, to act on a decision, to make a choice.
- Willingness to reevaluate belief systems and traditions, to choose intuitively, not only rationally. Being open to new systems and alternate values requires an ability to continually "let go" and select new forms. The only thing that we can speak of with any degree of certainty is that things will change.
- A compelling drive to grow, to discover, to evolve in contrast to conquering, controlling, and coercing. The difference between growing and conquering lies primarily in the quality and feeling of the action.

A significant challenge to coaches today is maintaining the athlete's motivation and enthusiasm in an event when he or she reaches an inevitable performance plateau. Physical performance plateaus are encountered following the spontaneity and accelerated learning that occurs with one's initiation to sport. Diminishing performance results quickly sap one's enthusiasm for hard work and self-sacrifice. The athlete wants more positive feedback and needs to be able to recognize growth, improvement, and progress. Focusing only on the physical aspects of performance at this time may not achieve these results. To avoid this problem, the coach should encourage incorporating the "whole" athlete by integrating physical, mental, and emotional functioning and establishing relevant contributions to the athlete's performance, ultimately improving the athlete's lifestyle.

Greg Marsden (1983), a phenomenally successful gymnastics coach at the University of Utah, comments,

Mental abilities and psychological development are the key areas which determine how successful an athlete can become. Many individuals are blessed with physical talents and attributes, but only a few competitors develop the necessary psychological skills to reach or remain at the top. These are learned skills. Psychological training must be a part of every day's work-out. It is important when an athlete finishes his or her career that they feel good about themselves. This too must be by design. (pp. 38–39)

Ken Ravizza (1983), a sports psychologist at the University of California, Fullerton, echoes similar sentiments.

The primary goal of the mental training program is to equip the gymnast with skills that enhance the likelihood that peak performance states will be experienced. Peak performance research makes it clear that athletes gain inherent satisfaction and a greater depth of motivation from peak experiences. The mental training program seeks to use concentration skills both as a method of improving performance while encouraging the gymnasts to take a more active role in assessing and developing their gymnastics potential. (p. 114)

WESTERN "GOALS," EASTERN "EXPERIENCE," AND THE "IN-BETWEEN"

Innumerable avenues are accessible to the coach and athlete for the acquisition of mental-emotional development, which, due to the fact of the integrated nature of the individual, nurtures the physiological development as well. Philosophic-psychological techniques and interventions typically include: relaxation procedures, breathing techniques, mental imagery, visualization, meditation, hypnosis, biofeedback, systematic desensitization, assertiveness training, and time management. Each of these interventions is conspicuous in its attempt to bring the individual into a sense of "oneness," "harmony," "balance," and "centeredness." However, despite the use of apparently similar techniques between the Western and Far East sociocultural climates, it is essential to go to the source, the *raison d'etre*, for the purpose relative to the selection and utilization of these procedures.

The Western attitude is primarily goal-oriented, pragmatic, and reductionist, leading to the consideration of a product rather than a process, ends rather than means, and goals rather than experiences for their own merit. In contrast, Easterners see opposites as relational and fundamentally harmonious. They recognize no division of products and process, ends or means, or goals and experience.

This is a first principle in the study of Zen and Far Eastern art: hurry, and all that involves, is fatal. There is no goal to be attained. The moment a goal is conceived it becomes impossible to practice the discipline of the art, to master the very rigor of its technique. It is only when there is no goal and no rush that the human senses are fully open to receive the world. (Watts, 1957, p. 176)

Anthropomaximology means the scientific study of the upper limits of human capability. It has been extensively developed, and the results of the research are being applied in a variety of countries, particularly in athletics and the performing arts. The techniques of anthropomaximology include psychic self-regulation (PSR), deep relaxation, mental imagery, and mental rehearsal. PSR theory has a neurophysiological base. When a person is in a state of profound relaxation, the brain and central nervous system cannot distinguish between a deeply imprinted image and the physical event. For example, if an athlete preparing for a particular feat can achieve a sufficient depth of relaxation and clarity of image and can imagine him or herself successfully completing the feat, the brain and central nervous system imprint the event as though the body has actually experienced it with concomitant changes even in pulse and blood pressure. The achievement of the actual feat can then be accomplished with an ease and effortlessness generally unmatched by physical training alone. Although this kind of mental rehearsal technique is difficult to accomplish, it is not only a learned phenomenon, but also may be transferred from one arena to another. The technique is as applicable to the novice as it is to the professional (Benz, 1982, p. 39).

SUMMARY

Along with the contention that these skills and characteristics are learnable, emphasis is directed to the fact that effective application of such skills in high-level performance can occur only in conjunction with the introspection and examination of one's own life and assessment of counterproductive and self-limiting beliefs and attitudes. Failure to address one's personal evolution as an ongoing concern in any attempt at high-level performance is to evade the issue of why we are doing it. We're talking about basic changes in attitudes and our perceptions of who we are, what we are, and why we are engaging in sport.

Coaches in the Western hemisphere will be hard-pressed to maintain their present level of efficiency and achievement if they do not become grounded in the techniques and conceptualizations of "quieting the ego-mind" and getting to the "source," and employ these distinctions to a significant degree in their training regimen.

To concentrate does not mean to think more. On the contrary, it implies less mental activity. It does not signify trying harder; it means to relax more, to move into the flow of energy that is already transpiring. The game, the routine, the course, is already fixed. What the athlete has to do is simply join it!

REFERENCES

Benz, J. (1982, December). Peak performance [Interview with Charles Garfield]. *New Realities* , 5(2), 38-40.

Capra, F. (1977). Ancient Buddhism in modern physics. *New Realities*, 1(1).

Gallwey, T.W., & Kriegel, B. (1977). *Inner skiing*. New York: Random House.

Kapleau, R.P. (1980b). *Zen: Dawn in the West*. Garden City, NY: Anchor Press/Doubleday.

Leonard, G. (1977). *The ultimate athlete*. New York: Avon. (Original work published 1974)

Marsden, G. (1983). A coach's perspective of the psychological aspects of gymnastics. In L.-E Unestahl (Ed.), *The mental aspects of gymnastics*. Orebro, Sweden: Veje.

Nideffer, R. (1976). *The inner athlete*. New York: Thomas Crowell.

Ravizza, K. (1983). Developing concentration skills for gymnastics performance. In L.-E. Unestahl (Ed.), *The mental aspects of gymnastics*. Orebro, Sweden: Veje.

Schultz, D. (1977). *Growth psychology*. New York: D. Van Nostrand.

Watts, A.W. (1957). *The way of Zen*. New York: Random House.

Hemispheric imperialism

Richard T. Garner
The Ohio State University

Many of the papers in this conference refer to the two-fold nature of the brain and to the related dualisms we use to make sense of experience, consciousness, thought, action, and human nature. Dualisms have often fallen into justifiable disrepute but *this* one is different. The brain itself is divided into two hemispheres which are now known to have different functions. Yin and yang, positive and negative, reason and intuition, conscious and unconscious, active and passive—all exemplify an underlying dualism that may have both its origin and its explanation in the dual nature of the human brain.

The hypothesis of *hemispheric specialization* assigns different tasks to the hemispheres of the brain. The left hemisphere is logical, linear, and linguistic; it is the home of verbalized thought. The right hemisphere is intuitive, holistic, and good at solving spatial and relational problems; linguistically, it is stunted. The hypothesis of hemispheric specialization means that while there is a place for language, logic, concepts, and verbalized thought, enough is enough. Compulsive talkers, planners, and debaters have a left hemisphere that has imperialistically appropriated projects that are literally none of its business. When there should be silence, it talks; when there should be spontaneity, it produces a plan; and when there should be a search for agreement, it argues. Because the left hemisphere controls the right side of the body, a physical manifestation of left hemisphere *dominance* (found in 90% of us) is right-handedness. Left hemisphere dominance may be the price we have to pay for our linguistic and logical abilities, and as a strategy for coping, it has not fared so badly. But when dominance by the left hemisphere is carried too far, it becomes left hemisphere *imperialism*, which, as a strategy for coping, is a disaster. We can live with the physical manifestations of left hemisphere dominance, but those associated with left hemisphere imperialism may literally bend us out of shape.

In the first half of the 20th century, brain researchers habitually underestimated the role and the importance of the right hemisphere of the brain. They called the right side the "minor" hemisphere and thought of it as an inactive, automatic, and dormant "back-up sytem." This is hemispheric imperialism in theory rather than in practice, but it is equally dangerous because theory can be used to promote and perpetuate useless and obsolete practices. *Philosophical* theories suffer from left hemisphere imperialism when they pay too much attention to language and logic, and from right hemisphere imperialism when they wallow in irrationality. Spinoza and Descartes, who thought that all the truths about the world can be set out in a deductive logical system, offer theories of the first sort.

We can say, then, that hemispheric imperialism occurs when the operations of one hemisphere displace legitimate work of the other, or when a theory is proposed according to which the work of one hemisphere is (or ought to be) less extensive and less important than the work of the other. I accept the hypothesis of hemispheric specialization, and am willing to live with hemispheric dominance, but I believe that hemispheric imperialism is no better than imperialism of the political and economic variety.

Examined in the first part of this chapter is the theory of hemispheric specialization that grew out of research with surgically divided human brains and led to the idea that different kinds of "thought" take place in the two hemispheres. In the second part, we see that the division between the modes of thought of the two hemispheres does not match a difference between the "Eastern mind" and the "Western mind" because almost everyone who speaks a language is located somewhere between left hemisphere dominance and left hemisphere imperialism. In the third part some of the methods devised for overcoming imperialism by either hemisphere and achieving a balance are discussed. Then, the final section concludes with a warning against a way we have of tricking ourselves into spending the lion's share of our effort and energy on the projects of the left hemisphere, even after we have seen through and tried to contain its imperialism.

THE HEMISPHERES OF THE BRAIN

The brain is dual, and the thesis of hemispheric specialization says that the different hemispheres make different contributions to the task of processing information and formulating responses to events. Roger Sperry won a share in the 1981 Nobel Prize in medicine for his work with surgically divided brains. By cutting the *corpus callosum* (a cable of nerves connecting the two hemispheres), Sperry was able to halt seizure-producing "electrical storms" in the brains of some epileptics. Michael S. Gazzaniga (1973) summarizes his work with Sperry and concludes (as did Sperry) that "in a split brain situation we are really dealing with two brains, each separately capable of mental functions of a high order" (p. 98). By testing their split-brain patients, Sperry and his associates confirmed the belief that most linguistic and logical abilities are concentrated in the left hemisphere, but they also observed that the *right* hemisphere was able to perform a variety of non-verbal tasks, and that it even "excels the left in some specialized functions" (Gazzaniga, 1973, p. 97). Recent research is reported by Norman Geschwind (1979), who mentions music and the recognition of complex visual patterns as talents for which the right hemisphere is dominant, and both Gazzaniga and Geschwind observe that the right hemisphere has much to do with generating and interpreting emotional responses. According to Geschwind (1979),

> A patient with damage on the left side may not be able to comprehend a statement, but in many cases he can still recognize the emotional tone with which it is spoken. A patient with a disorder of the right hemisphere usually understands the meaning of what is said, but he often fails to recognize that it is spoken in an angry or a humorous way. (p. 192)

By now it is difficult to deny the thesis of hemispheric specialization, and many researchers are willing to go so far as to say that there are two types of thought that roughly correspond to left and right hemispheric activity. This opinion is expressed by Robert E. Ornstein (1973) in his introduction to a collection of papers on the topic of human consciousness. He speaks of two modes of thinking which together "form the basis of complete human consciousness....One mode, the articulate or verbal intellectual, involves reason, language, analysis, and sequence. The 'other' mode is tacit, 'sensuous,' and spatial, and operates in a holistic, relational manner'' (p. 63).

Joseph E. Bogen (1973), whose article is also in Ornstein's collection, thinks that it is too simple to say that the left hemisphere is verbal and the right hemisphere is spatial. He points out that the right hemisphere uses words, though not in the way the left hemisphere uses them. Thought in the left hemisphere is propositional, logical, and often grammatical. About "thought" (or perhaps we need a more neutral term like "processing") in the right hemisphere, we know much less, and Bogen introduces the word *appositional* (in contrast to *propositional*) to characterize it:

> We can say that the right hemisphere has a highly developed "appositional" capacity. This term implies a capacity for apposing or comparing of percep- tions, schemas, engrams, etc., but has in addition the virtue that it implies little else. If it is correct that the right hemisphere excels in capacities as yet unknown to us, the full meaning of "appositional" will emerge as these capacities are further studied and understood. (p. 111)

In another article in Ornstein's collection, Arthur J. Deikman (1973) distin- guishes two quite different approaches to reality: He says that we may find ourselves either in the *action mode* or in the *receptive mode*. The action mode is a "state organized to manipulate the environment." It involves "focal attention, object-based logic, heightened boundary perception, and the dominance of for- mal characteristics over the sensory." It is a "state of striving, oriented toward achieving personal goals that range from nutrition to defense to obtaining social rewards" (p. 68). The receptive mode, on the other hand, is "organized around intake of the environment rather than manipulation" (p. 69). Deikman says that language is "the very essence of the action mode; through it we discriminate, analyze, and divide up the world into pieces or objects which can then be grasped (psychologically and biologically) and acted upon" (p. 70).

Although Deikman does not relate the difference between his two modes to two parts of the brain, given what we already know about the left and the right hemispheres, we can see that control by the right hemisphere would be correlated with the receptive mode, and left hemisphere control would be correlated with the action mode.

Figure 1 provides a summary of right and left brain hemispheric functions described by researchers Ornstein, Deikman, and Bogen.

	Left brain	Right brain
Ornstein	reason language analysis sequence	tacit operation sensuous spatial holistic
Deikman	action mode manipulate environment object-based logic heightened boundary perception linguistic	reception mode intake
Bogen	propositional thought logical, analytic thought	appositional thought comparing perceptions, schemas, and engrams

Figure 1. Left and right brain hemisphere functions described by three researchers.

EAST AND WEST AND RIGHT AND LEFT

When he wanted to illustrate some differences between the East and the West, the Zen teacher D.T. Suzuki (1960) compared a poem by the 17th century Japanese poet Basho with one written by the 19th century British poet Tennyson. Basho's poem is a 17-syllable *haiku*:

> When I look carefully
> I see the nazuna blooming
> By the hedge!

Tennyson's verse also deals with a flower:

> Flower in the crannied wall,
> I pluck you out of the crannies;—
> Hold you here, root and all, in my hand,
> Little flower—but if I could understand
> What you are, root and all, and all in all,
> I should know what God and man is. (p. 3)

Basho looks, Tennyson plucks. Tennyson tries to understand, Basho experiences. Suzuki says that Basho "lets an exclamation point say everything he wishes to say" (p. 3). Tennyson not only wants to understand the flower, he wants to use it as a means to satisfy his epistemological lust to understand everything else, even God and man.

Suzuki says that Tennyson exemplifies the Western mind, which is analytical, discriminating, objective, scientific, conceptual, organizing, individualistic, power-wielding, and disposed to impose its will on others. Basho, on the other hand, represents the Eastern mind which, according to Suzuki, is synthetic, nondiscriminative, subjective, nonsystematic, intuitive, nondiscursive, and interested in harmonious solutions to problems.

Although Suzuki's generalizations are accurate about some Westerners and some Easterners, and certainly well illustrated by the two poems, they may mislead us. One is not saved from left hemisphere imperialism by living in the East or from right hemisphere imperialism by living in the West. Both forms of imperialism, in both theory and practice, are found wherever people form theories and live lives. Yet right hemisphere imperialism, which shows up in thoughtless and self-damaging spontaneity and a repudiation of clarity, consistency, and verbal communication, is not nearly as common a phenomenon as left hemisphere imperialism. The very fact that we find the first and the best efforts to control excessive verbalization and conceptualization in India and in China counts against the claim that Indians and Chinese are more "right-brained" and, hence, less dependent on words and concepts than Westerners. If they had not developed monkey-minds, filled with noise, random thoughts, and needless verbalizations, there would have been no need for them to have developed yoga and meditation and to have attacked conceptualization and verbalization.

Hinduism and Buddhism

Hundreds of years before Buddha's enlightenment, Indians explored and developed techniques of concentration and mind-control. They did this in a world in which the majority of people lived selfish, social, word-filled lives. Hindu scriptures encourage males to spend their first 25 years learning and their second 25 years working, seeking wealth, and raising a family. Only after completing these two stages were they supposed to withdraw from the world to seek mental tranquility, peace, and silence—what they called "release" (*mokṣa*)—through contemplation and ascetic discipline.

Buddha tried to offer enlightenment to a wider, a younger, and more mixed audience, and to do so independently of the religion, metaphysics, ritual, and superstition he found in Hinduism. Originally, Buddhism was little more than a nonreligious way to end suffering, a spiritual therapy drawing on a centuries long tradition of concentration and meditation. Taken as such, it surely includes (but is not limited to) an effort to diminish our left brain activity, to silence our thoughts, to "pacify our minds."

But time passed, and as Buddhism traveled to new places, it took on new characteristics, developed gods, heavens and hells, and accommodated itself to the needs and to the beliefs of the people it hoped to liberate from suffering. Buddhism evolved. Some Buddhists indulged in metaphysics, logic, or dialectical reasoning, while others promoted trance, devotion, ritual and prayer. Many forms of Buddhism insisted on withdrawal from society, but others were tailored to people who were unwilling to leave their families and their work.

In both China and Japan, Buddhism dropped its moral requirement of non-injury (*ahimsā*) and became involved with the martial arts. Some forms of Buddhism promised rewards and punishments after death; others promised simple extinction, which at least was guaranteed to put an end to suffering. Quite a few offered, believe it or not, omniscience. Although Buddhism began as a tried and tested secular method to eliminate suffering by finding a "middle way" through the imperialistic tendencies of both hemispheres, it developed in so many different directions that its relatively simple psychological remedy for suffering occasionally got lost in the shuffle.

Confucianism and Daoism

When we look at the situation in China before the introduction of Buddhism, it is easy to see the contrast between the Confucians and the Daoists in terms of our left/right dichotomy. The Confucians were interested in language and learning. They urged everyone to call things by their proper names and to study and learn for their entire lives. The Daoists reversed these recommendations: They were careless about names and even insisted that what was real and important was nameless; they urged people to abandon learning. Furthermore, the Confucians promoted conformity and devised elaborate conventions of behavior, speech, and dress. In contrast, the Daoists thought that these straightjackets of conduct interfered with spontaneity and with naturally harmonious interactions among humans and stood as a sign that we have lost sight of the Way (Dao).

The Confucians were exhibiting all the symptoms of left-hemisphere imperialism: devotion to verbal categorizations, mistrust of intuition, of spontaneity, and of meditation, and a Tennyson-like desire to understand what everything is. The Daoists who refused to talk to others, who reveled in their flights of creative imagination and poetic fantasy, who drank wine to dull their rational faculties, and who interpreted nonaction with slothful literalness, were probably suffering from the opposite disease. It is a common thought among Chinese that a person needs something of both the Confucian and the Daoist in his makeup.

The Han Dynasty (206 B.C. - 220 A.D.) was a time of war and commerce. The official philosophy and religion was a peculiar form of Confucianism that squandered its energy categorizing things into groups of five (five flavors, metals, directions, colors, etc.) and devising elaborate metaphysical rationalizations to support the political aspirations of the rulers. There was, of course, nothing particularly receptive, appositional, or right-brained about any of this.

When the Han Dynasty and the Confucianism it promoted collapsed, many of the exotic forms of Buddhism that had developed in India made their way to

China. Madhyamika Buddhists were subtle dialecticians, trying to reason reasoning out of existence. By an elaborate logical process, they negated opposites and denied denials in an effort to stun the rational mind into silence. Another Indian form of Buddhism that found success in China taught that reality is purely mental and promoted trance-like states of consciousness to verify this metaphysical claim. A third form, very popular with the common people, emphasized devotion to a Savior and transformed meditation into prayer and supplication. These dialectical, metaphysical, and religious forms of Buddhism mirror similar movements in the West, and, except for a persistent attachment to meditation, they do not seem any more free of left brain, rational, conceptual trappings than do their Western counterparts.

SMASHING HEMISPHERIC IMPERIALISM

It is only when we turn to Zen Buddhism (and perhaps Daoism) that we meet the relatively pure receptive approach Suzuki finds in Basho's poem. Zen Buddhism does not tie itself to any scripture, or to any religious or metaphysical belief. It mistrusts arguments and puts language in its place. It promotes balance, and the long hours of meditation it requires are designed to quiet the nervous activity of both our hemispheres. In Zen one learns to restrain one's responses, to sit still, to listen, to wait, and to act with spontaneous and natural efficiency.

When we take Zen to be a paradigm of Eastern thought, we are leaving out all the other forms of Buddhism, all the other forms of yoga, Hinduism with its gods and its schools of philosophers, Confucianism with its rituals and conventions, the Westernization of Japan, and the Marxification of China. There is far more to Eastern thought than Zen Buddhism. In fact, Zen, which rejects religion, scriptures, metaphysics, conventions, rationality, and worldliness, is no more typical of Eastern thought than it is of Western thought. It is not even typical of Buddhism, though it is the closest Buddhism has come to the original message of the Buddha, which was a doctrineless technique for smashing hemispheric imperialism. If Zen seems more interested in smashing left hemisphere imperialism, this is because there is so much of it around.

Not only is the left hemisphere dominant in the majority of humans everywhere, speaking beings all over the world have a natural tendency to allow rational, sequential, verbalized thought to override and displace less linear and more intuitive approaches to problems. It is common practice among imperialists to see those they oppress as low, ignorant, or evil, and hemispheric imperialism is no exception. William Domhoff (1973) presents evidence that there is a near universal tendency among humans to associate the right (which is the domain of the left hemisphere) with the good and the left with the bad. Australian aborigines, American Indians, Bedouin Arabs, African Bantus, and "well-educated Americans" all exhibit many symptoms of left hemisphere imperialism. The Maori of New Zealand "associate the Left with the bad, the dark, the profane, the feminine, the night, homosexuality, and death, while the polar opposites of these concepts are associated with the Right" (Domhoff, 1973, p. 145).

Left hemisphere imperialism can obviously get out of hand. Not only can it distort our physical posture, it can wreck our social structure and make a shambles out of our personal lives. It has led to the slaughter of people who happened to favor the wrong hemisphere, the subjugation and mistreatment of women, and an unending chain of inappropriate solutions. If we do not want to smash it, it will not be smashed; but when we decide that some halt should be called, some balance restored, there are techniques available to help us. Yoga, meditation, the martial arts, concentration, even the chanting in which devotees of Krishna indulge, all have the effect of quieting the rational consciousness and allowing other parts of the system to participate in decisions and actions.

But it is also true that these techniques can (and should) be used to oppose imperialistic expeditions by the right hemisphere. The right hemisphere generates emotional responses and makes connections on a holistic and intuitive basis. This means that it will from time to time generate and thrust into consciousness feelings and hunches that the left hemisphere can only dismiss as irrational. When our lives and choices are guided by these irrational fears, illogical leaps, and unconscious programs from our past, we are suffering from right hemisphere imperialism. Although this can be as unhealthy as left hemisphere imperialism, we do need to acknowledge that there are times we need to listen to our emotions and our instincts, and forget what seems logical and rational. The strength we acquire through yoga and meditation steadies us in the wake of the sudden and often unanticipated onslaughts of emotion and intuition from the right side of the brain. Only if we are strong and stable enough to attend to them without leaping to a response can we begin to distinguish between those that deserve our attention and those that do not.

When we smash imperialism of either hemisphere, not only do we give the other hemisphere its proper work back, we free the perpetrator of the imperialism from the burden of many of its self-designated responsibilities. We are after balance: We want our hemispheres to work together harmoniously. When it is time for logic, we want logic, and when it is time for intuition, we want intuition. If a fear is irrational and groundless, we want that to matter, but if it is the result of some brilliant right hemisphere intuition, we want to be open enough to realize it. The techniques of mind-control developed in the East were designed to help us achieve a balance between our two sides by teaching us how to restrain both the noisy verbal chatter from the left hemisphere and the relating and emoting from the right.

LEFT BRAIN TRAPS

Many of these Eastern forms of mind-control are accompanied by deep metaphysical assumptions and extravagant epistemological claims. According to Franklin Edgerton (1944, p. 126), it is the unanimous doctrine of the *Upaniṣads* that knowledge gives power and leads to salvation. This knowledge is knowledge of Brahman, which the authors of the *Upaniṣads* understood to have two "aspects." There is a higher Brahman, which is formless, motionless, eternal, and imperishable, and a lower one, which is formed, moving, temporal, and perishable. This distinction is similar to the familiar Western distinction between "appearance" and "reality," between things as they appear and things as they are "in themselves," between phenomena and noumena. Because our physical faculties were only designed to process appearances, reality cannot be appreciated through the ordinary channels, nor can it be described or characterized in language, for language was invented to operate in the world of appearance.

The Hindus never doubted that behind the picture-show of our phenomenal world there was a reality that we can apprehend if we make the right effort. Heinrich Zimmer (1951) said that the ultimate goal of the Brahmans was to know the "basic reality which underlies the phenomenal realm" (p. 41). John M. Koller (1982) identified the respect for this reality behind our experience as one of the basic ideas of Indian thought:

The world of distinct and separate things and processes is seen to be a manifestation of a more fundamental level of reality that is undivided and unconditioned. Sometimes referred to as the unconditioned or nondual reality, this undivided wholeness constituting the ultimate level of reality is called by various names: Brahman, Ātman, Buddha nature, Thusness, Purusa, Jīva, Lord, and so on. (p. 6)

This distinction between appearance and reality is usually accompanied by a denigration of "mere" appearance. We are thereby soured on the world of our ordinary experience and sent off on a hopeless quest for Being in Itself. Scientists, mystics, and metaphysicians, Tennyson, the Upanishadic thinkers, and scores of philosophers from all over the globe have been unwilling to give up the impossible dream of looking behind the veil of appearance to see what is really there. Caught up by the lure of the noumenon, they aim to apprehend the Imperishable.

It is natural to want to know what is going on around us and what things are like. Appearances can be deceptive, and it makes sense to wonder sometimes whether things are the way they appear to be. These are perfectly normal questions and when we answer them, we can only hope that our stories and descriptions are as accurate as conditions permit. But the metaphysician in us pushes further. We may say that we know what is happening, but we tell ourselves that we want to know what is *really* happening. We know who we are for all practical purposes—our names, our history, our connections—but we want something more: We want to know who we *really* are, and *what* we are, and, while we are at it, what God is. Some of these questions are extensions or analogs of questions that do make sense and can be answered, but they are all out of our range, beyond our comprehension. Try as we might, our words will never express, our thoughts will never encompass, things as they are in themselves—Reality.

Because our nagging metaphysical questions can not be given a decent answer by our rational, linguistic, language-bound conceptual thinking, sooner or later the left hemisphere has to throw in the towel. But then (and this is when we fall into the trap) we imagine that we will be able to accomplish with the right hemisphere the task its partner had to abandon: that is, the task of apprehending the Imperishable. The mistake is to suppose that discipline, yoga, meditation, austerity, or concentration will help us mobilize our right hemisphere to perform what is essentially a left hemisphere task. If we can not know Reality (Brahman, God, the Absolute, etc.) with our rational, word and concept-bound left hemisphere, why should we think that we can do any better with our right hemisphere? It is true that the right hemisphere makes connections, sees things holistically, and looks at the big picture, but these are facts about the way it functions, not about what it knows. There is no reason to suppose that the right hemisphere has any conception of or interest in the totality of all that is. Just because the right brain makes connections and sees the larger picture, we must not conclude that it has connected everything with everything else or that it has seen an infinite picture.

The Zen Buddhist is the one who sees that this entire transcendental, metaphysical, epistemological quest can be tossed out the window, that knowledge is not the issue, and that both hemispheres must be allowed to carry on work that has more bearing on our actual needs and projects. It is at precisely this point that Zen Buddhism makes contact with the Buddha, who refused to discuss metaphysical questions, who condemned scholastic debates and excess verbalization, and who identified silent meditation as the way to harmonious integration and as the middle way between all the extremes.

REFERENCES

Bogen, J.E. (1973). The other side of the brain: An appositional mind. In R.E. Ornstein (Ed.), *The nature of human consciousness* (pp. 101-105). San Francisco: W.E. Freeman.

Deikman, A.J. (1973). Bimodal consciousness. In R.E. Ornstein (Ed.), *The nature of human consciousness* (pp. 67-86). San Francisco: W.E. Freeman.

Domhoff, G.W. (1973). But why did they sit on the king's right in the first place? In R.E. Ornstein (Ed.), *The nature of human consciousness* (pp. 143-147). San Francisco: W.E. Freeman.

Edgerton, F. (Trans.). (1944). *The Bhagavad Gita.* Cambridge, MA: Harvard University Press.

Gazzaniga, M.S. (1973). The split brain in man. In R.E. Ornstein (Ed.), *The nature of human consciousness* (pp. 87-100). San Francisco: W.E. Freeman.

Geschwind, N. (1979, September). Specializations of the human brain. *Scientific American,* **241**, 180-199.

Koller, J.M. (1982). *The Indian way.* New York: Macmillan.

Ornstein, R.E. (Ed.). (1973). The nature of human consciousness. San Francisco: W.H. Freeman.

Suzuki, D.T. (1960). Lectures on Zen Buddhism. In E. Fromm, D.T. Suzuki, & R. De Martino, *Zen Buddhism and psychoanalysis* (p. 1-76). New York: Harper & Row.

Zimmer, H. (1951). *Philosophies of India.* Princeton, NJ: Princeton University Press.

Beyond East and West: From influence to confluence

Ann Brunner
The Ohio State University

In the Fall 1982 issue of the Institute of Noetic Sciences *Newsletter*, Willis Harman presented the lead article entitled "Hope for the Earth: Connecting Our Social, Spiritual, and Ecological Visions." A major thrust of his essay is that scientific research regarding the nature of human consciousness has dissolved traditional dualistic interpretations of existence. Harman (1982) quotes Roger Sperry:

> Current concepts of the mind-brain relation involve a direct break with the long-established materialist and behaviorist doctrine that has dominated neuroscience for many decades....The new interpretation gives full recognition to the primacy of inner conscious awareness as a causal reality....The seeming irreconcilable dichotomies and paradoxes that formerly prevailed with respect to mind vs. matter, determinism vs. free will, and objective fact vs. subjective value become reconciled in a single comprehensive and unifying view of mind, brain and man in nature. (p. 24)

Harman points out that what Western science is finally coming to know through research, Eastern mystics have known for centuries. The pragmatic value of this "new" knowledge lies in the realization that because our cultural beliefs shape our experience and that because we live within the limitations we impose on ourselves, it has become necessary to open our minds and change the values which have led us to the edge of nuclear destruction before we fulfill this negative potential.

In the face of such an enormous task, I am reminded of Lao-tzu's observation that the journey of a thousand miles begins right under one's feet. With this in mind, I am able to bring the global effort down to a personal level and approach the challenge in the way I am most likely to be effective: as a die-hard teacher who believes in the potential of education to enlighten the society it serves, one individual at a time, with the confidence that each individual makes a difference to the whole.

The title of this chapter, "Beyond East and West: From Influence to Confluence," is an image I chose to convey my conviction that it is imperative for us to eradicate our separatist ways of describing ourselves and our dualistic ways of interpreting our experience. If you look at a map of the world designed in this country, you notice that the United States is placed in the center with Asia to the west and Europe to the east. Right away you see that the convention of what is East and what is West is a European notion. When a globe is consulted, it becomes more evident that east and west are directions of travel on earth, and that either way you go eventually brings you home. Returning to the two-dimensional map for the usefulness of its image, North America may appear as a great resting place in the midst of a vast ocean separating Europe from Asia. If one could see the flow of ideas, the United States might appear to be the place of confluence, the forming of a new culture which is neither traditionally Western nor Eastern. I believe that we are at least waist-deep in this new river and that the confluent worldview evolving here indicates the emergence of human values which are organically wholistic.

EMERGENCE OF A NEW CULTURE

Desire for wholeness

The rapid advance of technology, in an attempt to make our lives here somehow more convenient, tends to remove us from our organic nature. The experience of this distancing of the moving-breathing-sensing organism from our earthly source is leading us back to the fundamental, innate desire to feel whole through the full cultivation of our human capacities. People are not willing to abandon the global dimension of sentient being in favor of the linear dimension of rational thought or the flatness of mechanical precision. Because we obviously cannot scrap the tools of technology altogether, we are having to rediscover and learn new ways of being fully human and spiritually alive. Teachers must be prepared to accept the responsibility to educate within the new context of our culture.

Although the philosophical foundations of our present educational system pay lip service to wholistic ideals, the actual practices within the system do not foster experiences of wholeness. The delineation of physical education as separate from mindful education is a prime example of a well-intended scheme which in reality promotes an unhealthy schism in the organic wholeness of being. In light of this, a soft voice among educationists today implores teachers to make education a meaningful experience. An existential point of view recognizes subjective reality as primordial and places the responsibility for meaningful existence in the hands of each of us. As "meaning hunters," human beings must redefine themselves as "meaning givers" and learn to derive meaning from their own experiences. Applying this point of view to the educational setting, one hopes that teachers who find meaning in their own lives are able to share living knowledge with their students and help those students find their own meanings.

In my personal development toward becoming a teacher, I am indebted to Seymour Kleinman whose work in the field of physical education has been a struggle to keep us in touch with our sensing-breathing-moving selves. Kleinman has long recognized the significance of human movement and has encouraged the search for personal meaning in the sport and dance experience. Through a process Kleinman refers to as "experiential description," he challenges many of his students to explore new dimensions of their involvement in movement arts and discover aspects of themselves and existence in general that may otherwise remain outside their awareness. The following reflections relate my personal process of coming to understand myself and the universe through movement. I offer this narrative to you in good faith, fully aware that it is an adult interpretation of a childhood experience; it is true, nevertheless.

Reflections on personal understanding through movement

I can remember learning how to body surf in the Pacific Ocean when I was a little girl. I already knew how to swim, and water was a comfortable environment for me. Meeting the ocean, however, was a very different kind of experience than swimming in the blue transparency of a controlled, chlorinated, well-guarded, over-sized bath tub. At the ocean, water moved toward me out of a vastness that went on forever. As far as I could see was nothing but water and sky.

I could stand on the wet sand and just wait, knowing that soon I would be ankle deep in a dizzying rush of movement toward me, past me, all around me, then reverse, until the water was gone again and I ended up ankle-deep in sand, teetering with flapping arms as I struggled to keep my balance. Or, I could run after the retreating water only to find it suddenly chasing me as fast as I could run back to the dry sand. Hurray! I got away. I could go farther than the water, I could stay dry. Back and forth, rushing toward and pulling away, again and again—the waves never stopped. But I, with pounding heart, had to rest. These trips to the beach became very important to me and were very frequent. I was making a new friend—the waves were always there, coming in and going out in a reliable way.

As I ventured farther away from safety, I began to notice more and more things about the ocean and myself. The waves broke with a force strong enough to knock me down. The water was salty and pushed its way into my nose and mouth. I could crash like a wall against the tumbling foam sending huge blobs of water sky-high; I could dive over the wave so that it never touched me; or I could meet the wave head-on, propelling myself with all my strength into the froth. I will never forget the day I discovered that underneath the wave there is a calm and quiet place, that I could dive deep and lie still in the darkness against the sand while the wave rumbled over me as if nothing was happening. When I surfaced, the wave was behind me, and I was already waiting for the next one.

At first, I thought that each wave was just another wave like the one before it. After a while, however, each wave revealed its own identity and seemed to invite me to experience it in its own way. As I was learning to read the waves and to decipher the messages before me, I began to look more closely, more carefully at each individual wave. Thus, my wave-reading skills improved; looking became seeing the wave as a swell in the distance. I was drawn farther away from shore trying to see the wave before it formed. Where was it coming from? How did it start? What made it happen? I could not find the origin, but I could feel the surging depths of the sea and I knew its power and darkness. Anything could happen out there, and it was up to me to get home again.

Not long after I realized that each wave had its own shape, its own size and force, I began to experience a rhythm of groups of waves. Each group had its own expression, its own timing between waves, and its own number of waves. To me it was a little dance. I took to the deeper area in the swell after I mastered the foamy broken waves, and I liked riding the swells up on one side, over the top, and down the other side as if dancing with them. I could go shooting up with the rising motion and fall deep beneath the surface on the other side; or I could lie flat on the surface and feel the wave travel underneath me: First my feet would rise, followed by knees, butt, back, shoulders, head. If I made myself soft and noodle-like, my whole body would wave; if I became hard and stick-like, the wave surrounded me and passed over my face.

But no matter what I did, it did not affect the wave at all; I could not stop it or change it in any way. I felt invited to play with the waves, and they were, I thought, very playful, but they were waves coming from who-knows-where and I was just me from across the street. They were kind, they were fun, and I knew the waves would be there even while I was home sleeping.

Through their transformations the waves also taught me about change: the weather, the tides, the seasons, myself. I accepted the fact that I could not affect the waves and began to enjoy being able to adjust myself in relation to their moods. Whatever they asked for, I could give: Gentle waves made me calm; thunderous waves demanded my full strength and kept me alert; windblown waves were agitated with flashes of white jumping up everywhere, slapping me in the face; and on these days, I learned to keep my mouth closed above the surface and to be ready for anything.

Just as each of my earlier experiences had their own lessons, learning to ride waves drew me into another dimension. To go with the wave toward its destination seemed very simple at first—it pushed me toward the shore, anyway. But soon I was challenged to ride the wave longer distances and wanted to improve my skills. In search of the best technique, I figured out what to do with my legs, my arms, my energy. I learned what "streamlined" meant and why. Reading waves became increasingly more important. A swell taking shape before breaking carries much valuable information: where, how much, what direction, when. I learned to position myself to catch just the right part of the wave: How must I swim—to the right or left? When should I take off? Good timing was essential and inseparable from being in the right place and choosing the appropriate direction. Many, many waves participated in my education.

To ride a wave just right is to ride the motion of the universe. Nothing compares with the view of the inside of the tube of a wave: In the center of all the external commotion is a glistening, curving wall of stillness. There is no more natural and raw experience of being connected with the flow of the cosmos. It is momentary, yet timeless, and brings a felt understanding of how all things work together in harmony: The water is riding the wave, too, and the wave is riding me.

Board surfing added a new dimension to my ocean understanding: Blending and harmonizing while balancing vertically on a moving platform requires a technique I have since learned to call dynamic centering. There is nothing to hold on to; nobody else can keep you up; and it all happens very fast.

Learning to surf tandem brought in another human element: coordinating, cooperating with, and trusting another person. Feeling a responsibility to more than just myself, sharing the joy of success and the frustration of falling are other invaluable experiences which live in the timeless dimension of universal truth: the making of one out of two. Words can merely suggest the deeper meanings of human relatedness.

THE FUNDAMENTAL EXPERIENCES OF MOVEMENT

Childhood experiences provide a foundation for who we are as adults. Those are the days when our senses are most alive and the whole organism is living fully, exploring the ways of the universe and ourselves within it. Movement is fundamental to the discoveries we make and essential to learning about ourselves. I am still involved in ocean sports and often experience life as waves. Sometimes I hover at the top of a swell in that moment of weightless suspension, staying with it and trusting myself to ride through even the bumpiest wave. Sometimes I know I have to "kick-out" and wait patiently for the next wave. Sometimes I "wipe-out," and am thankful for surviving and for the opportunity to examine the fall, always looking for more clues. The waves continue. What could be more assuring than the constancy of motion?

The discovery of principles of movement through experience is fundamental to teaching in the field of physical education and requires multidimensional thinking, or as I prefer to call it, organic thinking, which both precedes and transcends a verbal mode. Teachers of the movement arts must prepare themselves to share their meanings and the significance of being in motion as well as their skills. Communicating this knowledge then becomes the challenge that can only be met through reaching out to new perspectives, searching for new modes of awareness, and developing a language which captures the essence of the felt experience of movement.

Eastern concepts and attitudes toward the moving self shape an experience of wholeness that Westerners are beginning to value and to incorporate into their lives. For many of us who shared the Eastern approach of moving with its natural flow of energy and in harmony with the universe, meeting the East meant waking up as we recognized ourselves in their ideas and their ideas in us. Herein lies the confluence. A wholistic paradigm for physical education must embrace Eastern movement forms which give us new images and new ways of describing our experience as well as new techniques which reveal universal principles of movement.

The felt experience of harmony may encourage humankind to reshape beliefs and to live beyond antiquated limitations. Global understanding begins with our organic connection to one earth, suspended in a delicate balance with the rest of the universe.

SECTION V

Possibilities and beginnings

In recent years a number of "outsiders" to the field of physical education and sport have contributed enormously to increasing our understanding of the nature of physical activity and human movement. George Leonard and George Sheehan have proved to be two of our best champions as well as our severist critics. However, no one presents us with a greater challenge as to our possibilities than Thomas Hanna.

In 1970 Hanna pointed to the inevitableness of the emergence of a somatic culture. In the years that have followed, it has become increasingly evident that not only are we looking at our bodies in a new way, but we are living them in a new way. While we continue to argue the "mind-body" problem in scholarly fashion, the somatic revolution continues to affect us in its inevitable way. The ultimate test for us as teachers, coaches, performers, and human beings is one which we can no longer avoid. How shall we meet this test? What must we do? Hanna provides us with his vision of a somatic education for the future. It is one of "somatic self-responsibility." It remains for those of us who care deeply about this field to develop these alternatives, explore these possibilities and, in so doing, seize the initiative by regaining and maintaining the ability to shape our own destiny.

Physical education as somatic education: A scenario of the future

Thomas Hanna
Novato Institute for
Somatic Research and Training

During the 1960s a profound cultural change began in the United States. Two decades have now elapsed since the explosive events of that era, and from the perspective of 20 years, it is clear that the era of the '60s is not dead: Its tides have washed through the '70s and into the '80s, radically changing the ways in which we traditionally have thought about ourselves and about how our lives should be lived.

It requires 30 years for a full generation to elapse. We are now two thirds of the way through a generational transition that has reoriented the lives of American citizens along very different pathways, and the effects of this reorientation are gradually radiating outward to the rest of the world.

The changes to which I refer are many-sided: They are changes in lifestyle and in our conception of "the good life"; they are changes in the way we think about courtship, sexuality, marriage, child raising, education, interpersonal relationships, and political responsibility.

But the profoundest of these cultural changes is a reorientation in how we think of ourselves: namely, who we are as human beings, what our capacities are, and what we as individuals believe we can experience and accomplish in our lives. It is on this level—the individual's conception of self—that two crucial developments have converged during the last two decades. These developments come from two very different sources—one moral and one scientific—but in their convergence, they are having an impact upon our society that is nothing short of revolutionary.

This revolution, however, is neither violent nor unpleasant. It is, instead, like a gradual awakening to who we really are and what each of us can come to experience and accomplish during the course of our individual lifetime. The moral and scientific events motivating this gentle revolution are becoming increasingly prominent during what is now the concluding third of this generational change. These two convergent events are a) the ethic of self-responsibility, and b) the science of self-responsibility.

THE ETHIC OF SELF-RESPONSIBILITY

A dramatic discovery of the '60s was that individuals have other options than to follow traditional roles, lifestyles, and vocations from generation to generation. A new generation of Americans discovered that they did not need to be told what to be, what to think, and what to do. Instead, they could do these things by themselves and for themselves.

Even though on the surface this seemed to be an abrupt departure from what was called "the American way of life," it was, in fact, a dramatic rediscovery of the 18th century wellsprings of American life in the spirit of Tom Paine, Patrick Henry, and Thomas Jefferson. During the mid-18th century, a youthful America did not choose to be told what to be, think, and do by a traditional monarchy, and in the mid-20th century, a youthful America reaffirmed the same independence.

However, independence is the abrasive side of a coin whose opposite side is self-responsibility. Americans of the mid-20th century brazenly asserted their independence on the same grounds as did Jefferson, namely, that it was an in-born, inalienable right of all human individuals. It was one of the bitter ironies of the '60s that the not very "silent majority" felt strongly that these Jeffersonian sentiments were "un-American."

The morality of self-responsibility held that individuals not only should determine their destiny but *could* do so: An inborn right implies an inborn capability. But the insistence on deciding one's own role, lifestyle, and vocation overlay a more personal insistence: the insistence to determine one's own experience, one's own individual consciousness.

Altered states of consciousness

Probably no single event disturbed the conservative mentality so much as this demand to experience whatever one wished to experience. Psychoanalysts could have a field day exploring why conservative American parents shuddered at the thought of their children having experiences they themselves had never had—and also why these children did just that with a vengeance. Altering one's state of consciousness was a characteristic practice of the counter-culture. But no one at that time realized that experiencing altered states of consciousness and recognizing the altered realities this entails is also the necessary first step in controlling one's state of consciousness.

Two decades ago, the preferred ways of altering one's consciousness were drugs, sex, and rock music. Two decades later, the use of drugs has sharply declined, promiscuity is a health threat, and rock music has mellowed into a sound that is nonthreatening to the eardrums. But the right to alter one's state of consciousness continues to be an accepted prerogative. The drugs are being replaced by meditation, the promiscuity is being replaced by sensual coupling, and the pounding of rock music by the pounding of Adidas and Nikes on the jogging paths. In two decades everything has changed and yet the cultural discoveries of the '60s have not changed at all but have become profoundly rooted in our ways of living.

To deliberately change one's state of consciousness is no longer considered dangerous or radical. Instead, it is seen to make good sense. If one is highly stressed, meditation "gets one down"; if one is depressed, music "gets one up"; if one seeks excitement, a 3-mile run "gets one high." Rather than holding to the rigid Victorian belief that we should cling at all costs to a stabilized single state of consciousness, the morality of self-responsibility sees consciousness as a many-splendored thing that should be fluidly adaptable.

Beneath this practice of adaptable consciousness is a presumption that is truly revolutionary: It is the recognition that one's bodily states and one's mental states are inseparably connected. Without anyone realizing it, the past 20 years have witnessed the solution of the mind-body problem, not by philosophical debate but by cultural transformation.

Somatic conception of human nature

The theoretical separation of mind and body molted into an existential recognition of their somatic unity. Individuals no longer separate themselves into mental, bodily, and emotional compartments; instead they live with a practical recognition of their living somatic unity. Without arguing the matter, the first person reality of consciousness and the third person reality of body have come to be seen as a somatic whole: The blissful consciousness of meditation and the quietude of the body are indissoluble; the ecstasy of love and the organic drives of sex are as one; the transcendent consciousness of a marathon run and the rhythmicity of the body are of the same thread.

The cultural legacy of the 1980s is the practical knowledge that a greater richness of conscious experience goes hand in hand with a greater diversity of bodily activities.

The lives that we now live show us that the culture of the new generation is explicitly somatic. This means that we frankly recognize responsibility for our psychological and physiological states. Two decades ago, the nutritional life of the average American citizen was radically different than it is now. Two decades ago, health food stores were virtually nonexistent and the American way of life and the American consciousness were identical with caffeine-laden Coca Cola, sugar-laden Twinkies, offal-laden hot dogs, and gooey apple pie. Sugar, red food dyes, and junk food were at that time virtually synonymous with patriotism.

This is no longer the case because of the universal recognition that what we put into our bodies is not separate from our minds, emotions, and performance, but is powerfully and directly connected. Extensive literature is now available on just this topic, dealing with "experiential nutrition" and detailing the ways in which certain foods create certain states of consciousness. Formerly, this was a concern only of the religious ascetic whose dietetic concerns were in support of his spiritual aspirations. Presently, this is a concern of George and Irma who live next door.

The ethic of self-responsibility is a somatic ethic and arises from a conception of ourselves that is higher and deeper and broader than our former conception of human nature. We should make no mistake about it: This is a crucially different conception of human nature—a revision of our understanding of the human race and the capacities of the human being. I would like to insist that a somatic conception of human nature has the most profound effect on cultural evolution: Such a revised conception of who we are leads directly to a revised conception of where we, as a race, are going and how we can get there. It means a revision in the direction the human species is going, a revision which, in the light of our increasingly desperate contemporary history, is sorely needed.

THE SCIENCE OF SELF-RESPONSIBILITY

By itself, the morality of self-responsibility has brought into the cultural mainstream a somatic conception of the human individual, a conception that has already powerfully affected our current history and will continue to do so. Simultaneous with this cultural event has been a parallel development that is equally portentous: It is the emergence of somatic science.

Somatic science

About two decades ago, a University of Chicago psychologist, Joe Kamiya, made an astonishing discovery. In the course of research with an electroencephalogram, he discovered that humans could consciously control their own brain waves. This was clearly impossible because the orthodox viewpoint in neurophysiology held just the opposite view. The prevailing scientific belief at that time was that human consciousness was purely the effect of brain functions and had no independent status whatsoever. As recently as 20 years ago, it was popular for neurophysiologists and philosophers of science to refer to human awareness as a mere "epiphenomenon" of the nervous system.

However, Kamiya clearly showed that consciousness was not at all simply the illusory effect of neural causes but could itself be the cause of neural effects. The idea that presumed involuntary physiological states, such as our brain waves, could be controlled voluntarily was as revolutionary as the idea that we can and should be fully responsible for ourselves. Indeed, from the scientific point of view, it was the same idea.

Kamiya's discovery opened a floodgate of research on voluntary control of internal bodily states. It soon became apparent that humans could also voluntarily control their heart beat, rate of gastric secretion, blood pressure, skin temperature, and even the dominance of the sympathetic and parasympathetic nervous system. Obviously, human awareness was no mere "epiphenomenon" of the body, but had a superintending function over the bodily process.

The clinical science of biofeedback technology was spawned by this research and, after an initial response of shock and disbelief, biofeedback techniques became assimilated into hospitals and medical clinics. But it did not stop there. Suddenly, there was an acute interest in the age-old claims of oriental ascetics being able to control various aspects of their bodily functions. Zen monks were taped with EEG monitors, and it was found that when they chose to go into meditation, their brain waves dropped down to an easy-going alpha rhythm of about 10 cycles a second.

The Menninger Clinic did research with yogis, discovering that infinitely subtle controls could be maintained over the central nervous system. In one instance, Dr. Elmer Green made startling films of a man who could so control bleeding that when a large knitting needle punctured his upper arm and then was removed, the hole made by the needle simply closed up like a sphincter.

Then a man from Israel named Moshe Feldenkrais appeared and demonstrated that one could directly teach extraordinary muscular control to human beings, even those who had presumably been paralyzed permanently by stroke, cerebral palsy, or brain damage.

It has now become an open question as to the degree that humans can control and modify their own physiological states. No one knows what the limit is or even whether there is a clear limit. Within 20 years, a somatic science has taken shape which has absolutely exploded what we had thought to be the limits of what human beings can learn consciously to do with their own bodies and central nervous systems.

The rapidity of this scientific development is simply stunning. Hardly two decades after the once firm belief in the epiphenomenal nature of inner consciousness, the great American psychologist Roger Sperry (1982) accepted the 1981 Nobel Prize with these words:

The events of inner experience, as emergent properties of brain processes, become themselves explanatory causal constructs in their own right, interacting at their own level with their own laws and dynamics. The whole world of inner experience (the world of the humanities) long rejected by 20th century scientific materialism thus becomes recognized and included with the domain of science (p. 1226).

In these remarks Sperry lays the foundation for an authentic science of self-responsibility, which, as he says, involves a "revised concept of the nature of consciousness and its fundamental relation to brain processing."

We must look more closely at the way in which consciousness learns to control the body. It is important to recognize that in all instances—from biofeedback, to yoga, to Feldenkrais—a learning takes place. Gaining voluntary control of otherwise involuntary functions is a learning process. This process of self-education can take place only if we focus our consciousness inward upon our bodily functions. We must pay attention to the internal, proprioceptive sensations which our nervous system liberally supplies to our brain.

Learning internal somatic sensations

What we learn is to recognize patterns of sensations which formerly went unrecognized: The sensory feedback was there, but to our consciousness, it was as unintelligible as a scrambled code message. Learning to recognize an internal proprioceptive pattern is not essentially different from learning to recognize the visual outlines of a map or the aural structure of a melody. Proprioceptive sensations of the body's inner movements are different from the external sensations of the eye or ear, even though the brain's task of pattern recognition is the same.

At first, it is devilishly difficult to recognize the different "feelings" that accompany brain wave states of 15 cycles a second, 10 cycles a second, and 5 cycles a second. But with the aid of an electronic signal informing us when we are in any of these three states, we can gradually distinguish each pattern and do so consistently. That is what biofeedback has shown to be possible.

In the same way, it is at first impossible for a paralytic to feel the difference between, for example, the movement of his leg and of his back; initially, no differentiation is felt—for the leg and back are indistinguishable. But when a practitioner of the Feldenkrais system of Functional Integration takes his hands and moves the hip and back in different directions, creating two different sets of sensations, the paralyzed person's consciousness picks up that difference. Suddenly the person is aware of the leg as different from the back, and that proprioceptive awareness is the first step toward voluntary control of his or her leg and back in relearning to walk.

So then, consciousness must first learn to recognize the incoming patterns of sensory information before it is able to send outcoming commands which will control involuntary processes. In brief, new sensory input is necessary to create new motor output. Today, we refer to the sensorimotor system as a feedback loop and describe its informational functions very much in the way we talk about computers.

Expressed in simple language, somatic science is a science of self-awareness, a self-knowledge that surprisingly leads directly to self-control. This is a very different kind of knowledge from visual knowledge or auditory knowledge. To recognize a visual or auditory pattern *outside* of ourselves does not, in itself, lead to control of what is seen or heard; but self-knowledge through the *internal* proprioceptive senses leads directly to internal control of ourselves.

The ascetic disciplines and martial arts of Asia are exemplary in showing the extraordinary degree of internal control that humans can attain. Yogic control of autonomic bodily processes was a demonstrable fact thousands of years before biofeedback proved to occidental science that humans were not mindless bodies. The incredible prowess of Asian martial artists has demonstrated that the upward limits of athletic performance are dramatically expanded when external performance is wedded with internal awareness.

Unitary conception of human nature

The rapid growth of somatic consciousness in the West has opened the eyes of Westerners to an Eastern way of thinking that has always been somatic. Rather than being held down by the crippling strictures of an either/or, black and white, mind/body schism, the Asians have always seen shades of gray between mind and body. This is to say that the Asian viewpoint wisely and correctly sees the human being as a single unity with many gradations, whereas the Western viewpoint has seen the human as a phantasmagoria of matter and spirit with no real connection. The Asians have been blessed with a unitary, holistic conception of human nature; the occidentals have been cursed with a Hellenic-Christian conception of human nature. The former sees the human as an integrated unity; the latter as a disintegrated duality.

The Asian religious and martial art traditions are a special gift to Western culture because they restore to human beings their *depth*. Viewed merely as a schism, the human body is without meaning and the human spirit is without potency. Viewed as a unity of many processes, the human body is one of many interconnected layers that descend toward the spiritual centrum in which the body is rooted.

From this point of view, the human is a being of layered depths, the body gaining its meaning and rootage in the spirit, the spirit gaining its expressiveness and potency in the body. To recognize that our bodies are inspirited is to ennoble the body. To recognize that our spirits are embodied is to empower the spirit. To recognize both is to ennoble and empower the human being and see ourselves as far more capable, far more potent, far more sensitive than we had heretofore believed.

The Asian somatic tradition is a resounding confirmation of the contemporary Western ethic of self-responsibility and the Western science of self-responsibility. Together, these powerful confluents move us into the position of taking greater control of ourselves, of taking greater possession of our bodily, emotional, cognitive, and spiritual lives than we have ever before imagined.

NEWLY ENVISIONED SOMATIC EDUCATION

By weaving together the disparate strands of our bodies and minds, the emerging somatic tradition has sketched out a new vision of human possibility. We, as humans, are seen as capable of immensely more than we had believed, and, therefore, we are responsible for immensely more. There is an unwritten law here: Human self-responsibility expands in direct proportion to human capability.

These newly envisioned capabilities are as much physiological as they are psychological. The range of our self-responsibility is, thus, far greater than we thought it to be. This is another way of saying that our freedom and independence, physiologically and psychologically, from technical experts is increased. The ethics and science of self-responsibility combine with the religious and martial disciplines of Asia to teach us that our physical well-being and our emotional and intellectual well-being are far more in our own hands than our medical and therapeutic and academic traditions might wish us believe.

If capability means reponsibility, then responsibility means we are to do something for ourselves. "Doing" is neither more nor less than a learning—a process of educating ourselves to do more with ourselves, by ourselves, and for ourselves. This learning is somatic and holistic, involving the development of both gross and subtle bodily faculties as well as our mental faculties.

Such a new vision of human self-responsibility places a large emphasis on learning to do for ourselves. Such a learning deals as much with the bodily arts and sciences as it does with the mental arts and sciences. The Western tradition of education has split and impoverished both bodily and mental education by demeaning the former and disembodying the latter. An educational system of self-responsibility would find that physical education was exactly of equal importance to mental education: The success of attaining new mental skills was utterly dependent upon attaining new bodily skills, and vice versa, even if these skills were as subtle as controlling one's brain waves for enhancing intellectual performance or controlling one's emotional tone for enhancing athletic performance.

Given the evidence we now have, a unitary system of somatic education is both already possible and already past due. An opening of educational programs to the fullness of human possibility would have an immense impact on the public health picture of the future. To educate a generation in greater somatic self-awareness and control is to create a population that can monitor and control the physiological bases of its own health. I would predict that a universal system of somatically envisioned education could, in the course of one generation, see the virtual disappearance of the major public health problems of coronary, respiratory, and carcinogenous ailments.

The elimination of such negative problems is of far less significance than the emergence of a population of far more capable and independent individuals. That somatic self-responsibility leads to greater health maintenance is merely one of the ways in which it leads to greater self-improvement.

To envision a future that is somatically oriented is, as these remarks have suggested, not a new or unexpected possibility. It is not in the least a pipe dream for the simple reason that it is already taking place. Such being the case, it is necessary that we be reminded of the immense importance of the movement toward greater self-responsibility that is now occurring, so that we may, ourselves, consciously enhance this movement in practical, organizational, ongoing ways.

The learning of greater somatic self-responsibility is vitally important, not only because it is a giant step forward in reducing the wasteful indignity of human dependence, but more significantly, because it suddenly moves us nearer to achieving the profoundest of all human needs: individual freedom.

REFERENCE

Sperry, R. (1982, September 24). Some effects of disconnecting the cerebral hemispheres. *Science, 217*, 1226.

Big Ten Physical Education Body of Knowledge Series

Mind and Body: East Meets West is the 15th volume in the Physical Education Body of Knowledge Series sponsored by the Committee on Institutional Cooperation (CIC) Big Ten Physical Education Directors Steering Committee. The series was initiated in 1968 to encourage the development and dissemination of knowledge considered basic to the discipline of physical education. Each volume in the series represents the exploration of new concepts and ideas within the various subdisciplines of physical education and provides direction for future development within the field.

Other volumes in the series available from Human Kinetics Publishers

Teaching in Physical Education
Volume 14, Big Ten Physical Education Body of Knowledge Series
Edited by Thomas J. Templin, PhD, and Janice K. Olson, PhD

Based on the 1982 conference held at Purdue University, this volume contains contributions from 40 noted professionals in the field of pedagogy. Teacher decision-making, social psychological perspectives of teaching physical education, student teaching, pre-service and in-service professional preparation, academic learning time in physical education, teaching styles, and research on teaching in physical education settings are among the topics examined.

1983 • ISBN 0-931250-48-X • Hardcover • 384 pp • $26.95

Frontiers of Exercise Biology
Volume 13, Big Ten Physical Education Body of Knowledge Series
Edited by Katarina T. Borer, PhD, D.W. Edington, PhD, and Timothy P. White, PhD

The 18 papers presented in 1981 at the University of Michigan represent the work of selected scientists actively researching the body's cellular adaptations to exercise. The contributions examine muscle physiology, microvasculature, endocrine physiology, neural function, and the interactions between these disciplines.

1983 • ISBN 0-931250-49-8 • Hardcover • 304 pp • $31.95